THE
DEPORTER

THE
DEPORTER

*One Agent's Struggle Against the
U.S. Government's Refusal
to Expel Criminal Aliens*

AMES HOLBROOK

Sentinel

SENTINEL
Published by the Penguin Group
Penguin Group (USA) Inc., 375 Hudson Street, New York, New York 10014, U.S.A.
Penguin Group (Canada), 90 Eglinton Avenue East, Suite 700, Toronto, Ontario, Canada M4P 2Y3
(a division of Pearson Penguin Canada Inc.)
Penguin Books Ltd, 80 Strand, London WC2R 0RL, England
Penguin Ireland, 25 St. Stephen's Green, Dublin 2, Ireland (a division of Penguin Books Ltd)
Penguin Books Australia Ltd, 250 Camberwell Road, Camberwell, Victoria 3124, Australia
(a division of Pearson Australia Group Pty Ltd)
Penguin Books India Pvt Ltd, 11 Community Centre, Panchsheel Park, New Delhi – 110 017, India
Penguin Group (NZ), 67 Apollo Drive, Rosedale, North Shore 0632, New Zealand
(a division of Pearson New Zealand Ltd)
Penguin Books (South Africa) (Pty) Ltd, 24 Sturdee Avenue, Rosebank, Johannesburg 2196, South Africa

Penguin Books Ltd, Registered Offices:
80 Strand, London WC2R 0RL, England

First published in 2007 by Sentinel,
a member of Penguin Group (USA) Inc.

1 3 5 7 9 10 8 6 4 2

Copyright © Ames Holbrook, 2007
All rights reserved

LIBRARY OF CONGRESS CATALOGING IN PUBLICATION DATA
Holbrook, Ames.
The deporter : one agent's struggle against the U.S. government's refusal to expel criminal aliens / Ames
Holbrook.
    p. cm.
Includes index.
ISBN 978-1-59523-041-6
1. United States—Emigration and immigration.   2. Alien criminals—United States.   3. Deportation—
United States.   4. Holbrook, Ames.   I. Title.
JV6483.H64 2007
325.73092—dc22
[B]   2007004458

Printed in the United States of America

Set in Adobe Garamond
Designed by Spring Hoteling

To the DOs in New Orleans

Author's Note

Immigration issues boil over as I write. There is dissension within communities, within political parties, within the United States as a whole. From coast to coast there are boycotts, protests and counterprotests, marches, economic activism, vigilantism, human chains, mock trials, and every other form of turbulent public expression. It is nothing new. Immigration arguments always rattle our country because immigration is in the very foundation of our country. Those who believe immigration is and always has been bad for America can be divided safely into two groups, the insane and the Native American. For the rest of us, it is a matter of how much we love immigration. Do we love it indiscriminately, so that we see no need for controls, borders, or rules? Or do we love it in a tough love way, with a yearning to whip it into perfect shape?

Today's most charged debates run along the illegal immigration and amnesty line. My perspective on that topic will come out incidentally during this story, as will my perspectives on other politically hot immigration topics, because nearly all our immigration problems feed the crisis I am about to expose. But this is not a partisan book, and I am not a political person. I am of the firm conviction that when it comes to the most alarming immigration emergency, no party is getting it right. If on rare occasion

I come down hard on President George W. Bush, it is only because he is the president during the time of my story. And he is our president now. And he has said, "The most solemn duty of the American President is to protect the American people."

We have an immigration crisis in our country all right, and it is a good deal more demonstrably wrong than the millions of illegal aliens in the shadows. It is far costlier to the fabric of American life than the September 11 attacks were. Illogical, deadly, ruinous. Yet none of our leaders is raising a finger to stop it. On the contrary, it is our leaders who drive the destruction.

When we finally end this madness, let us resume discussion of the other immigration issues. It will be healthy, and if it leads to some positive change, all the better.

But first, this. Please.

—A. H.
May 4, 2006

FOREWORD

"The mission of the United States Deportation Officer: 1. Apprehend criminal aliens in America. 2. Effect the removal of criminal aliens from America. 3. Everything in between."

An instructor at the academy defined my job that way. Her words branded into my brain as I awaited my first street-level assignment to one of the most notorious deportation districts in the country. It was then an apt summary of the job that remains equally apt today. All the roughly six hundred standing Deportation Officers (known as DOs in enforcement circles) were incorporated into the Department of Homeland Security in the spring of 2003, at the same time the Immigration & Naturalization Service was abolished. While Homeland Security's dramatic birth meant upheaval for other federal organizations, no aspect of the DO job—responsibilities, game rules, dangers, frustrations, conflicts, and enemies—changed at all. If their appointment to Homeland's glittering new Bureau of Immigration and Customs Enforcement (ICE) was the government's belated recognition of the critical role Deportation Officers play in safeguarding America, the DOs themselves barely took notice. They were too busy trying to do what they'd always been trying to do.

1. "Apprehend criminal aliens in America." Anyone who's seen movies or television series in which police track fugitives and arrest them has some idea of where the Deportation Officer's job begins. Deportation Officers are not unlike other warrant-serving police agencies in this role. They are stretched thinner than most, more compelled to choose nasty targets from an unquantifiable flood, but the obvious distinction is that Deportation Officers don't go after U.S. citizens.

2. "Effect the removal of criminal aliens from America." This is the deportation itself, buckling aliens into foreign-bound aircraft (or buses when it comes to numerous Canadians and Mexicans) and personally escorting the most dangerous thugs into their motherlands.

My academy instructor's points one and two are the A and Z of the Deportation Officer's existence. They are the time when the clock starts and stops on any given case, when a DO meets the threat and when he says good-bye, till next time. They are the first and last responsibility DOs have with criminal aliens, and they are the easiest two responsibilities to explain.

After the academy, I returned to the Federal Law Enforcement Training Center (FLETC, pronounced "fletsy" by most) in Glynco, Georgia, two more times for advanced Deportation Officer tactics. My formal DO training on the Georgia coast lasted more than twenty-two weeks. With regard to the three-point job summary provided by that academy instructor, my twenty-two weeks focused almost exclusively on points one and two. I came out of FLETC fluent in immigration law. I knew whom I could sack up on the street, for what, and why. I knew how to find underground fugitives using computer tools and invisible surveillance. When I did locate them, I knew how to subdue the berserkers with a collapsible baton, pepper spray, and my bare hands. I would have no problem with the big bad aliens. I was trained to come out on top even if they were cutting me to ribbons with ten-inch cleavers. In a gunfight I could fight past a wounding of my shooting arm and fell my adversary from fifteen yards with my left hand. And when I finally had the savages under control, I was well practiced in the art of shipping them home. I came out of Glynco with a swagger. I had the world by the tail, and I was sure I knew it all.

I knew nothing.

What my instructor failed to tell me was point three is a bastard. "Everything in between" is an unteachable, maybe even unknowable box of shadows. It's an ineluctable baptism by fire that scorches good DOs to the soul every day they have the nerve to show up for work.

That "everything in between" is the subject of this book.

The Gratitude List

While writing this nonfiction manuscript, I avoided accepting help (though it was generously offered) from my former coworkers, so as to insulate them from professional repercussions. What I got wrong or right is on me. While I acknowledge the others below for their help on this book, I thank those coworkers for what they did when I ran with them, when this book wasn't even a thought, when matters of far greater consequence pressed us to the grill, and we knew in each moment who had our backs. This book does not adequately portray their heroic service, nor does it—with its single-issue fixation—come close to capturing their universe. Just the same, much love:

Enforcers

Phil Miller, more than anyone else, for anything good I did, and for La Paz and Mumbai. John Seright for all the bars, and Pretoria, Bridgetown, Tallinn, and Reykjavik. Tyrone Bowman for 70119 (plus Port-of-Spain, St. John's, Dubrovnik, and the Zagreb bonus). Fenwick Johnson for the Bogotá miracle and Skopje and Shanghai. Bobby Smith for life's lessons and the B&Bs. Craig Robinson for the brilliant leadership under constant fire. David Boyd for the roof and Hong Kong. Patrick Pullet (Beijing and Bequia). Sal Gonzalez (San Pedro Sula and Carnival in Roseau).

Charles Cameron. John Thomas. Frank DaRosa (Luanda). Norm Willette (Petra and especially the Dubai rescue).
Sam Edwards. Adam Minze. Steve Igyarto. Toni Thaggard (Moscow).
Andy Guevarra. Lynne Underdown. Doug Henkel. Dan Bell.
Eddy Wang. Sam Chung. Chris Siouris. Patrick Hudgens. Pablo Campos, in advance for your book, whenever you decide to write it.

Abettors

Vicki Lemon, Lynn Pope, Pierre St. John, Trenia Lewis, Cynthia O'Connor, Mardi-Gras Dave, and my Guatemala City cabby in the 1953 Plymouth Belvedere.

Chargés d'Affaires

The diplomats I won't name, whose commitment to do right made the world a better place. You did your countries proud.

Mujer de Negocios

My ace literary agent Mollie Glick.

Dream Editor

Bernadette Malone Serton. I am an optimist, but one dismal fate I foresee is that I will never work with another like you.

Blood

Sisira. Soraya.
My mother Susan Holbrook who always wished she could give me financial support for my writing, but gave me plenty of the support that really mattered.
Willard Ames Holbrook III.
Stephanie. Sumalaya.

Outcasts

All the aliens I deported. Sorry things didn't work out.

Contents

Contents

Contents

Contents

America will never seek a permission slip
to defend the security of our people.

—President George W. Bush

ONE

Rodolfo and the Problem

At the first stoplight off the freeway, I looked over my shoulder at the alien. By *alien* I mean other than a U.S. citizen. He avoided my stare. I'd already seen he was high, saw that when I picked him up at the jail. His eyes were red; he was zoning. He couldn't even play it straight for his last day.

"So, you ready for this, Mr. Rodolfo?" I asked him.

"*Sí,*" he said unconvincingly.

"Great." This guy wasn't ready to tie his shoes. That I mean literally. At the jail I'd let him exchange his jumpsuit for travel duds. After shuffling out of his shower flip-flops, he'd taken five minutes to construct something resembling bows in his shoelaces, both of which had blown out before we'd made it to the sally port. The deputy had looked at me before he'd buzzed us through. He knew the Deportation rule that said we couldn't let our aliens walk around with their shoelaces dragging. It was an alien safety issue. But considering how long it had taken this screwup to put those self-destructing bows together the first time, I couldn't imagine stopping to let him try again with the handcuffs on. And I wasn't about to tie Rodolfo's shoes for him. There were elements of babysitting in the DO job, but I wasn't going to take it that far.

The deputy had finally read that in me. "Is he like them other ones?" he'd asked through the glass.

"Yeah," I'd said. "Rough week."

I'd marched my charge out to my government Chevrolet Lumina in the double-gated prisoner loading area and buckled him in behind the cage. Driving in the rain across the swamp, I'd checked Rodolfo in the rearview and reflected on what had brought us here.

From the day we'd hauled him in till now, no other Deportation Officer had touched Rodolfo. A Deportation Officer feels a special pride of ownership when he gets to hold on to a case from beginning to end. *Beginning to end,* in a DO's mind, means "apprehension to removal." Scrap with the alien in the street, escort him home on the plane. Professionally, there's nothing more rewarding.

Rodolfo was a bail-skipping fugitive, one of countless outlaws from abroad who'd decided to make New Orleans home. There was the school that believed New Orleans effected a supernatural pull on deviants and that bad apples from all over the globe ended up there because they couldn't help themselves. More scientific judges pointed to the police department's famed reputation for failing to connect criminals with outside warrants. I didn't disbelieve either. Foreign ruffians kept coming to New Orleans, and we did all we could to grab the most threatening of them, the way we'd managed to sack up Rodolfo.

The light turned green. I cruised the few remaining blocks to the downtown Deportation office and parked the Chevrolet along the LAW ENFORCEMENT ONLY curb. I pulled Rodolfo from the back of the sedan, carefully using my palm as a buffer so he wouldn't bang his head on the door frame and knock himself unconscious the rest of the way. I brought him through the automatic doors to the lobby and walked him around the metal detectors. The security guards nodded to me. Security had long ago stopped asking us about the exotic characters we marched through their checkpoint. It was routine to them now. The guards didn't even seem to see the tattooed gangsters bypassing their metal detectors at all hours as long as the gangsters were attached to one of us DOs.

Deportation was headquartered on the ninth floor of 701 Loyola Avenue, the street address better known as the home of New Orleans's main post office. The building housed various federal entities, including the Veterans Administration and postal police, and as soon as I stepped inside, I saw that the lobby was active. Several people scooted past me to join their colleagues waiting for the elevators. I let one car go, and then I turned around and badged off the crowd. One of the flaws of our office was that we didn't have our own elevator. Whenever we took a criminal up from the street to the ninth floor, we had to wave the public off and instruct them to wait for another car. It was for their protection, but they didn't like it. This time I heard a few curses lobbed my way from the annoyed mob.

I marched Rodolfo to the rear of the elevator and released my escort hold. I left him facing the back panel, his nose almost touching it, and I stood at the door as we rode up. Rodolfo appeared at home in the back of the elevator, where it was easy to avoid my stare.

The bell dinged when the elevator stopped at eight, and I said "sorry" to another crop of waiting bystanders as soon as the doors opened between us.

The eighth floor housed Immigration Benefits. Sometimes when I found my frame of reference slipping and I was grimy from my brand of aliens, I came down here to see the proper side of the American Dream. I watched the hopeful, honest immigrants turning in their paperwork to become Americans, and I felt better about the world.

Of course from time to time we got SOS calls from the eighth-floor window personnel when a fingerprint check exposed an applicant as a terrorist or when some off-his-rocker fugitive came in and *demanded* a green card, but the minute we arrested those exceptions and moved them up to the ninth floor—their rightful floor—I found my angelic vision of eighth-floor aliens reestablished.

The elevator clicked into place on nine. When the doors opened, I squeezed Rodolfo's arm and steered him outside. I swiped my passkey at the tinted glass doors and hooked a right in the hallway to the processing area. Pushing through the heavy wooden door there, I was greeted instantly by aliens rapping wildly on the Plexiglas skin of the holding cells. The closest tank was loaded with Nigerians. "Officer Holbrook! Officer Holbrook!" they shouted, beckoning me over to the vent.

I stopped and lifted my head in inquiry.

"Where's our property?" The big men were huddled up there, suspended, blocking the light out of the door.

"You'll get your property. That's why I had you brought in here."

"Good! Good!" They clapped in relief. Then a somber question: "When are we going to Nigeria?"

"You know I won't tell you that." That rule was rock solid: Never tell an alien when he's flying, unless you want his people lying in wait at the airport. There are two ways that can go, and neither is good. The first is his family is there, screaming at you, spitting on you, the ladies in tears, calling you an animal for taking away their father, son, brother, whoever. That's better than the second option, which is a well-planned ambush, a swarm of his criminal associates on you and the getaway set in motion. It all had happened. From the beginning of any DO's career, he heard stories of previous officers' mistakes, and even if he was bold enough to proclaim he would not have made the same mistakes, inside he thanked those DOs for having gone before.

"We need to tell our family," said one Nigerian, "so they can meet us in Lagos."

"You'll be home by the end of the month."

As I moved on with Rodolfo still in my grip, a final question came at me from the Nigerians: "Will you be flying all the way with us, Officer Holbrook?"

I shook my head no. I didn't volunteer that they would be split up and put on their last connections by themselves, with no escorting officers. These large African men had been convicted of white-collar crimes, of bank fraud, wire fraud, colossal swindles, and confidence games involving millions of dollars of gullible people's money. Despite their larcenous hearts, the Nigerians in that cell were not violent or escape-prone, sick, or insane.

Officer escorts all the way to the aliens' destinations were reserved for full-on menaces who were likely to cause harm on the airplane, menaces like the one I was squeezing now.

I pushed Rodolfo forward another three feet, and the next cell erupted. Inside was a mixed bag of fresh catches and long-term detainees who'd just been run in from local jails. "Officer Holbrook!" Two Chinese men were trying especially hard to get my attention. They hadn't been told why they'd been brought here, and the uncertainty was killing them.

"Consul general wants to talk to you," I said, and moved on. That probably sent their minds into even more of a spin. I didn't have time to make it any clearer. There was very important business to be conducted involving those two but not now.

I mentally cataloged those other concerns while I steered Rodolfo onward. Every serviceable DO had to be able to keep a lot of balls in the air for months or even years on end. It was an existence in a constant state of overload. To cope, I tried to keep all my cases in the back of my mind but to focus on only one detainee at a time.

At the farthest recess of the open bay I handed my pistol off to another agent and rolled a couple of fingerprint cards on Rodolfo. If you didn't hand off your weapon before you took prints, a certain type of criminal would seize that opportunity to grab your gun and use it. It was a combination of the alien's side-by-side position with the officer, the fact that his hands were uncuffed for a moment, and the hard reality of seeing his prints entered into eternal record that set a criminal off. The empty holster fingerprinting policy was yet another lesson that unlucky enforcers before us taught from their graves.

As the ink rolled onto his finger grooves from the ink pad and rolled off onto the hard paper stock, Rodolfo yelped as if I were twisting his fingers off. He was probably high enough that he believed I was. I took some more four-plate Polaroids for his A-file. I updated IDENT and all the lookouts. That went without saying. My fellow agent returned my pistol. Finally I claimed a vacant interview room and read through the paperwork.

"Look at me, Mr. Rodolfo. *¿Lo quieres oír en español?*" Every DO gets five weeks of straight Spanish during basic training, enough to survive. In my first couple of years on the job I'd cursed the faculty for not having taught me Vietnamese instead, but lately I'd been grateful for the Spanish.

"*No, oficial.* I understan' English. I understan' everything."

I autographed two copies of the last sheet and slid one his way. "Sign it."

He scripted his name meticulously, the way he'd tied his bows. I took my pen back. Rodolfo was a career criminal with eight felony convictions, burglary to battery, and a sex assault thrown in. I'd seen a thousand like him. I'd been part of the aggravated felon program since my second year on the job. I was now approaching year four.

"Put that in your pocket. Let's go." Rodolfo stood up with me, stooping to pick up his small sack of belongings as we moved. We made our way out of the processing area, up the central hallway, through the swinging tinted doors, and onto the elevator. I hit *L.*

From the lobby we stepped to the automatic exit doors. They popped open, and we walked together into the humid air. My government sedan sat in front of us at the curb.

I'd been waiting to deport Rodolfo since I'd met him. I'd shepherded his case through the system, watched him exhaust his appeals. When the immigration judge's order had at last become final, I had typed up Rodolfo's warrant of deportation myself. The immaculate WD now stood on top of Rodolfo's file, ready to be executed.

I glimpsed through the sedan windshield and saw my airport badge on the dash, where I kept it for convenience. It gave me access to all the airport security doors and even the flight line, so I could drive the deportee right up to the gate and walk him up the external staircase to our airplane, my bird to mission completion, his bird to the life he tried to leave behind.

Outside the lobby Rodolfo crept out a bit in front of me, stepping awkwardly down off the curb. I looked at him stutter-stepping in the parking lot, his hands swinging loosely at his sides, shoelaces dragging like ballast lines. He appeared antsy.

"I'm watching you, Rodolfo," I said.

For the first time today he looked me in the eye. He smiled, one of those smiles that was really more like a laugh.

My brain fired wildly, reacting as the scene went wrong.

Rodolfo put a little more space between us. He moved across the parking lot, and I watched him from where I stood on the curb. Dangerous aliens like Rodolfo were the reason I'd become a Deportation Officer. The welfare of the people of New Orleans—and the American public—depended on his removal from the United States.

He was beyond the parking lot now, set to jaywalk across the busy avenue and mix into the city. My brain kept firing distress signals as I stood frozen. A sickness rose in my stomach to choke me. There was a stream of victims out there waiting to fall prey to Rodolfo.

I had been ordered to set him free.

Two

Ji and an Unapproved Solution

M y watch read five till nine in the morning. I tried to ignore the sick feeling in my stomach and to focus on something else. That something was the call I had set up with the vice-consul of the People's Republic of China. I headed into the lobby for the elevator ride back up.

This is the pace at which a DO operates. It is a process of gearing and regearing that becomes as natural as a weekend drive on a popular mountain road. Lest you, the reader, think that I'm glossing too fast, already skipping ahead to the PRC vice-consul before adequately explaining why I unleashed a deportable criminal like Rodolfo on the United States of America, I'll confide in you that the deportation program is currently facing a bit of a catch-22. It's a paradox of great consequence, and it's at the root of most of a DO's problems, but mine in particular because I am running the aggravated felon docket.

I am responsible for several hundred aggravated felons detained locally, in contract facilities across southeastern Louisiana. All these men (actually I have about a dozen women too) have been ordered removed from the United States by an immigration judge, and those orders are final. If the law were our guide, these foreign criminals would be on the next flight out of Louis Armstrong International Airport. The reason they are not is simple: We cannot deport these criminals because their countries don't want them.

Not all countries refuse to take back their criminals. Many governments act just as America's government does when our citizens wear out their welcomes in foreign lands, which is to say those governments take full responsibility for their criminals and even help facilitate the repatriations. I can name almost a hundred nations that take back their criminals with no hassle. So of the approximately two hundred countries in the world, that leaves the other hundred that stick America with their criminals as often as they can.

If at this point you wonder why we need to get other countries' permission in order to return their rightful citizens, you are asking the magic political question. The question is magic because no one can answer it. The question is magic because every day the fact that we have to ask it becomes less logical. In the time that our story unfolds, and indeed through today, our government increasingly asserts its commitment to protect the American people. It creates new agencies, overhauls our laws, abridges civil liberties, defies other nations, and goes to war on grounds that can be fairly described as less than ironclad, all in the name of making us safe. So when other countries measurably and provably maintain platoons of assassins on our soil to kill America from the inside, we would expect our government to expel these foreign assassins, no second wasted and some reprisals thrown in. Instead our government seeks permission. And when foreign administrations say no, that they will keep their dangerous agents in place to cause death and grave injury to Americans, our government concedes.

This is not easy for a DO to circumvent. As our leaders have relegated us to seeking permission, if the foreign government doesn't grant us a passport or one-way entry pass to bring these felons on the plane with, we're helpless. Receiving airports kick anyone without a travel document (TD) right back into America. Now, we have modern governmental policies, some already in effect at the start of my story, others implemented during the story, that have stripped my agency of its previously held right to detain foreign nationals. This may seem confusing, but right now there is only one thing you need to understand: If a Deportation Officer does not quickly acquire TDs for aliens in his custody, those aliens are bound to be released to the American streets. This applies to all aliens, *including,* as is said, *but not limited to* murderers, rapists, terrorists, kidnappers, armed robbers, arsonists, and child molesters. Pick any stripe of criminal alien; that kind is being set free.

As of that morning, the morning I set Rodolfo free, the same morning I was headed back up to the ninth floor to call the PRC consulate at the appointed time, there were four countries that had formally told the United States to go to hell. As a matter of point-blank national policy, Cuba, Vietnam, Laos, and Cambodia refused to accept their criminals. (In 2002 the Cambodian government signed a financially rewarding repatriation deal with the United States. By then there were perhaps two hundred Cambodians detained, but we are not counting the thousands we had already let loose in our communities.)

For decades, before Cambodia broke ranks, those defiant countries were known as the Big Four. Many DOs I knew respected that quartet for its honesty. There were scores of other nations that publicly presented a U.S.-friendly criminal return policy while privately making the process an obstacle course that more often than not couldn't be negotiated before we had to liberate their criminals here. When a DO arrested a fugitive alien on the street or otherwise drew a new case, the officer could only hope the criminal wasn't out of the Big Four or from one of the other infamous nations (like Guyana, India, Egypt, St. Vincent, Turkey, Gabon, France, Iraq, or any of the former Soviet republics: "Oh, Vadim is not from our country. He was born in 1987, in *Soviet Union,* and that does not now exist, so sorry.") whose governments stalled as long as it took for us to set their criminals free on our own soil.

Even among all these famously irresponsible countries, when it came to resisting the repatriation of their bad apples, few attained the notoriety of the People's Republic of China. Most of the Eastern Region (the Immigration territory encompassing roughly the eastern third of the United States, including the New Orleans district) considered China a write-off. China's slow-motion verification system, in which a government official purportedly traveled to the prospective deportee's home province to interrogate the townspeople for confirmation that he once lived there, was well known. It took a year and usually confirmed only that our detainee had provided false information. Many DOs believed that the verification system was a trick and that the Chinese government was throwing away our TD request packets and simply waiting till a year had gone by to tell us to start over.

After releasing Rodolfo, I traveled upstairs, stepped out of the elevator, and readied myself for the hardest part of my job. On an annoyance level, nothing compared with trying to get the motherland to take its wayward son back. As I started to pull my passkey, Phil threw open the glass door from the inside. "Mr. Ji awaits," he said. "Let's go, quick like a bunny."

Phil and I walked through the processing area together, barely acknowledging the importunate aliens in the cells as we cruised by them to the interview room. A-files for the two Chinese in the near cell sat on the desk. I switched the order, put the fat file on top. I wanted to start with my guy.

Every alien registered in the United States had an alien file, or A-file, in his name. Most A-files stayed with Benefits and wound up in the National Records Center, a two-hundred-thousand-square-foot warehouse in the Missouri backwoods, to stand on the rack forever when immigrants became U.S. citizens. If the A-files instead wound up in Deportation, that was bad news. I flipped open the cover. Two-hole-punched and fastened into the left-hand side of this A-file, on top, was a warrant of deportation signed by my district director. On top of the right side of the file was a lined pink sheet that I wrote on and dated my notes every time I handled this case. The last two entries were the same: "Subject uncooperative. Refused to provide biographic information during consular interview."

I always documented when an alien was uncooperative because aliens who refused to assist us in obtaining their travel documents were legally ineligible for release. In practice, this rule was usually ignored, and uncooperative aliens were liberated just the same. Nearly every alien in our custody resisted getting a TD. Virtually all of them had records of nationality in their home countries. Most had birth certificates and copies of old passports in their A-files. Since there was no mystery surrounding their citizenship, it would have been simple for them or their families to acquire valid passports by writing their embassies. That's what a lot of our criminals had done back in the days when we'd detained them indefinitely in our no-frills Louisiana jails. But such cooperative behavior had ceased when the releases had begun. Few aliens willingly provided their own passports anymore, not with light at the end of the tunnel.

The fresh memory of Rodolfo overtook me, and I winced. Rodolfo was one, and he may have been the one to snap my spirit, but his weight pressed only with the concerted force of the others. In recent days I had liberated a drive-by shooter I should have sent to Laos. I'd let go a Pakistani racketeer (what was he financing?) rather than deport him. I had ached to remove a child molester to his native Czech Republic, but instead I'd put him on a public bus to Atlantic City. I saw their faces in a crowd behind Rodolfo. The criminal aliens I released didn't disappear. They haunted me.

From the top of the pink page, I read the phone number for the PRC consulate in Houston while I punched it into the phone. There was no Chinese TD-issue authority in New Orleans. The Houston consulate handled our cases. After two rings a secretary answered. I told her the vice-consul was expecting my call, and she put me on hold to track him down.

"Here goes," I said to Phil, who was standing by. He winked from the other side of the desk. This was a daunting mission, but New Orleans had gotten lucky a few times. We'd shipped three Chinese home this year, and in our business, when it came to the PRC, that was running hot.

The receiver was picked up: "Hello?"

"Mr. Ji, this is Ames Holbrook out of New Orleans. How are you, sir?"

"My good friend Officer Holbrook," he answered. Though the tones said it had been cultivated outside America, his English was outstanding. I'd always enjoyed his avoidance of contractions. "I am fine. I am glad you called. How have you been?"

"Excellent, sir."

"So, you have Mr. Tse there to talk to me?"

"I do, sir, and I've brought one more in also."

"Oh, and who is that?"

"Wareng Chow."

Phil smiled at my dramatic name pronunciation that now struck me as more appropriate for a celebrated head of state than a criminal deviant.

Vice-Consul Ji chuckled. Maybe he felt the same way. "Well, let us talk to him then. Is he ready?"

Phil took off for the cells while the vice-consul and I made small talk. In the large cast of consular officers I dealt with, Ji Wen was one of my favorites. The slow rate of issue from his office notwithstanding, Mr. Ji had never lied to get me off his back. When prospects were bleak, as they normally were, Mr. Ji told me so. When he told me a TD was on the way, I booked the flights to Beijing. In the business of consular liaison, as DOs call it, having a diplomat like Ji on your case was a blessing.

Phil pushed Wareng Chow into the interview room. Wareng, a strapping 170-pound man in a blue sweat suit, leg irons, and a belly chain, was well rehearsed in the consular interview drill. He feigned ignorance just the same. "What's going on?" he shouted. "What is this?"

I pushed the intercom button on the phone. "We have your consulate on speaker," I told him. Mr. Ji introduced himself in Mandarin.

"I don't speak no Chinese," Wareng said. "I been in America since I was ten."

"So, half your life in China, but you don't know the language." As Phil spoke, he placed a biographical information sheet and a pencil on the desk in front of Wareng. "Fill this out."

Mr. Ji said something else in Chinese.

"I got nothing to say to you." Wareng stretched his cuffed wrists against the belly chain and swept the form off the desk. "I ain't going back to China. I don't know nobody there."

Phil said, "You are aware that you can be federally prosecuted for not completing that form. You will remain in jai—"

"I don't care about that form. Fuck you." Wareng stood up and yelled at the telephone: "They got me all in shackles like I'm not even human. I already completed my sentence and paid my debts, but these Immigration assholes want to keep me locked up."

"He's done." Phil pulled Wareng out of the interview room. "I'll get the other dude."

I lifted the receiver. "Sorry about that, sir."

"He is a difficult case," Mr. Ji said, meaning there would be no travel document forthcoming. I knew Mr. Ji had his orders from higher PRC command to issue as few travel documents on criminals as possible. With no testimony on file, Wareng was an easy out for them.

In a somewhat troubled tone, the vice-consul spoke again. "So, Officer Holbrook, is he really tied in chains?"

"Yes, sir," I answered honestly. "They all are. Our office is in a non-secure public building. If it's an issue to you, I can unhook them while they're talking to you, but I'll put the chains back on as soon as they leave the interview room. Given that Wareng has two murders to his credit and an escape attempt in which an officer was hurt, that's about the best I can give you."

"Your policy is reasonable. It only surprised me that they have completed their sentences and they are still treated like prisoners."

"Sir, I'll let you in on a secret of the deportation business. A lot of our detainees never completed their sentences."

"No?"

"Wareng's a perfect example." I opened the fat A-file to his court papers and confirmed what I knew. "He served just three years on a twenty-year sentence."

"Parole?"

"Not quite, Mr. Ji. What happens is this: When we have a deportable alien serving state time, we file a detainer with the jail so the jailers know not to release the guy to the streets, where he could go fugitive again, but to release him directly to us for deportation. Well, the state sees the detainer and says, 'This guy's going to get deported anyway, so why not help our budget by turning him over to Immigration early?' So they call us up and say, 'Take him.' The problem is, we can't always deport the alien. We end up having to set him free. So now we have America's communities filling with criminals who would still be serving their time if only Immigration hadn't come to their rescue."

"This is unfortunate."

"Yes, sir."

"Officer Holbrook, how many Chinese criminals do you have in your facilities?"

"Forty, sir. Thirty-two mainland and eight Hong Kong."

"Ah, it seems we have a lot of work to do."

"It'll be a pleasure working with you, sir."

"For me too." Mr. Ji paused. When he continued, I noticed something in his tone had begun to change, as if he were no longer toeing the party line but speaking his mind: "This problem will keep going. We will do our best, but when we have addressed this forty, we will have another forty to replace them."

"Maybe not, sir," I replied. "Your economy's set to overtake ours. Pick up a little more freedom to go with the prosperity . . . pretty soon China's the place to be. You'll be calling me from Beijing, asking me for help deporting bad Americans."

That got a belly laugh from the vice-consul. "I'm afraid, Officer Holbrook, that we have too many people. But you are right, things are getting better in my country."

"Good. Good for the whole world."

"You think so?"

"Sure, sir. I always think it's better to have power spread out, don't you? I love my country, but unlimited power isn't good for us. It's not good for anybody. I look forward to seeing China up on center stage with America, along with anybody else who's up for the challenge. It's going to be exciting."

"I agree. It will be awhile, but perhaps our countries will work well together, just the way you and I do, Officer Holbrook."

I glanced up and saw Phil in the doorway, looking as if he weren't sure whether to believe his ears. My conversation with Ji had strayed far off the standard DO-diplomat script. I waved Phil in, and he entered with the detainee he'd had in a holding pattern.

"You've interviewed Mr. Tse already, right, sir? Do you need more information?"

"I have all the information I need. But I have talked to his family, and I would like to talk directly to him."

I extended the receiver to the detainee. He accepted it cautiously. He announced himself to his vice-consul, and the two conversed for several minutes before Tse handed the phone back to me.

"Are you finished with him, Mr. Ji?"

"I have had a good conversation with Mr. Tse. Now, Officer Holbrook, I would like to discuss the matter with you."

I signaled Phil, and he escorted the detainee out. "Absolutely, sir."

"Mr. Tse appears truly reformed. Do you think there is any chance he could remain in your country?"

I was stunned. At first I didn't answer.

"Forgive me, Officer Holbrook. I hope I am not taking advantage of our friendship. I understand that in most cases you and I work together on the cases of Chinese citizens who could not properly adjust to your society. I have talked to Mr. Tse's family and to Mr. Tse, and they have convinced me he is the exception. He is sorry for his great crime with the drug, and he has made a pledge that he will work hard and honestly for the rest of his life. He has a wife and two children. I am sorry if I am being too forward."

"No, sir. It's just that I don't have the authority to release a felon." I was walking the minefield now. At stake was my rapport with the vice-consul. "That decision comes from my district director or headquarters."

"Yes, Officer Holbrook. The story with Mr. Tse . . . if you will permit me to share my Chinese perspective . . ."

"I'd love to hear it, sir."

"We agree that these are good times for my country, but China and America are still very different."

"Yes, sir."

"I think Mr. Tse has been here so long with his family, he has picked up the American way of life, the American values—aside from his great mistake. I think he will not be able to adjust back to life in China. And since his character is good, I think we have to think about his life. In some cases, Officer Holbrook, we have to be human."

"I agree with you, sir." I was liking Ji more all the time. But what he was asking me for was unheard of. It was my job to deport criminal aliens, even if this alien's offense (possession of a great amount of opium) did not rate high on my personal roster of damaging crimes. It was hard enough that my government ordered me to liberate foreign criminals. To release one at the request of a resident diplomat was a level beyond that.

But Mr. Ji's polite request gave me pause. The reason no other consular officers had ever asked me to release a criminal was that they knew they didn't have to. Consulates were getting wise to the changes in the wind, the budding policies that had us kicking hardheads out the door. If Mr. Ji hadn't been so forthright, he'd have said nothing to me, just let the clock tick and waited for me to get the letter from my higher-ups that would force me to do the same thing he was instead asking me to do, respectfully, man to man.

My heart was racing. The action I was considering was illegal. DOs do not honor the requests of foreign governments; those kinds of deals weren't a matter of our discretion. And we were never, under any circumstance, to treat one kind of criminal alien differently from another. But what I was looking at was the record of Hu-Kit Tse, and I knew this record by heart. I was looking at a man who'd been found with a pound of opium in his work locker, but whose history was otherwise spotless, a family man in all other regards, a man who was not disposed to resume a life of crime, who did not even have, in a customary sense, a life of crime to return to, a man I would not be afraid to have living next door to my parents. I flipped through the stack of papers on the desk, and then I was looking at the history of an altogether different kind of man.

"Mr. Ji," I said, "I appreciate that you had confidence enough to discuss this with me." I measured each word. If I offended him, it was in his power to blockade the whole New Orleans district. He may have sent us only three TDs this year, but three was a whole lot better than zero. Three thugs sent to China are three thugs not set loose here, and to the future victims in America that distinction can be as precious as life itself. I took my releases personally. Unleashing a hard-core felon was like firing a rocket into a downtown office building. Maybe no one would get hurt, maybe the rocket would go in one window and out another to explode harmlessly in the sky, but there was no way of knowing. You had no control once you squeezed the trigger.

I went on: "And I appreciate what you say about Mr. Tse. I hope that we can consider his case in the balance of another case . . . like Wareng Chow. We see, on one hand, a man who can adjust to American life and, on the other, a man who cannot. Perhaps we can do the best for both." It was the groundwork for a treaty, and it was against all the rules. I couldn't stop myself.

I was hanging my soul out in more ways than one. Beyond the ethical considerations, my bid itself was shaky. I knew very well I had no leverage. At the rate my own government was operating, both Tse and Wareng Chow would be on Bourbon Street in three months. If Ji hung up the phone right now, he'd get his wish and then some. I had nothing to offer. I was gambling with air.

The vice-consul spoke: "Ah, Wareng Chow is difficult. Beijing does not have enough information."

"Sir, I don't technically have the authority to release Mr. Tse, but I can make it happen."

Mr. Ji said, "Yes."

I had never been part of a negotiation like that, a high-stakes bargain spoken in code between two men backed into the shadows of their respective government machines. I was a virgin to any form of political negotiation, but I knew Ji's yes meant we had a deal. I knew it the way a man pushing a plug into a socket knows he has his fingers on the tines. The yes snapped when I heard it, and I thrilled at what might come next.

I looked up and saw Phil in the doorway again. His eyes were wide. Phil had been my training officer from the day I'd started this job. He was now a journeyman, a GS-12 in bureaucratic pay grade speak, and I was a middling GS-9. He was my partner. These days I couldn't look at Phil without a little sadness because our partnership was soon set to expire. His sideways transfer from Deportation to the more manageable existence of Investigations had been approved. For recondite reasons of federal funding, we did not know when the transfer would occur. Next month? Next fiscal year? We knew only that one day he would exit, leaving me in sole possession of New Orleans's infamous aggravated felon docket. First and foremost, I was sad when I anticipated the end of my partnership with Phil. But I was also scared.

Phil sat in the chair on the other side of the desk from me. My pulse was still rapid as my conversation with Mr. Ji moved beyond the arrangement. I assumed we'd concluded all but the civilities until Mr. Ji said, "I hope I can see you."

"Yes, sir?"

"We will be recognizing the anniversary of China's diplomatic representation to the United States. I would like to send you a formal invitation from our consulate."

"Wow. Terrific, sir."

"Officer Holbrook, are you married?"

"Pretty soon, sir. I am engaged to be married."

"Ah, congratulations."

"Thank you, sir."

"Please tell me the name of your fiancée, and I will address the invitation to you both."

When the call reached its conclusion and I secured the telephone receiver in its cradle, a moment of reflective silence elapsed.

Then Phil said, "Shit, dude. What have you done?"

Invitations to consular functions were not in themselves rare. Management got invited to the local diplomats' soirees. Phil himself had attended all the lakefront parties thrown by the Japanese ever since he'd impressed them with his handling of a rampaging Nagoya man who'd punched through the walls of his hotel. On the surface, the only odd aspect to my invitation was its Texas setting and the fact that it came from the historically icy PRC. But Phil and I knew that what gave the invitation its weight was what had preceded it. The invitation was an acknowledgment of a bond and a pact between men. There would have been no invitation without the pact, of which I dared not speak.

I didn't have to speak to Phil. He had heard only my end of the conversation, and only some of that, but as the consummate law enforcement partner he possessed an intuitive sense of what I knew. I knew that the rules had been rewritten in an instant. In the system of TD acquisition, I had just moved beyond my government's policy of asking and not getting. I had entered the business of trading lives, sending a redeemable man to his freedom, while shipping an incorrigible man to his hell. And it was up to me to decide who was redeemable and who was not.

The Ji pact, I understand now, was the turning point in my Deportation career. There would be times ahead, and soon, when I would analyze a stratagem and wonder if it was worthy of the gleaming badge I wore and later, more desperate times, when I eschewed looking inward at all. The stress was unnecessary. I'd chosen my road the day I'd traded Tse for Chow. That was the moment I ceased to be one kind of deportation officer and started to be a different kind altogether.

Phil lifted his thick frame out of his chair and turned toward the exit. For a moment I didn't know if he wanted me to follow or if he was separating himself from me.

Suddenly before our eyes Hortense appeared. Hortense was the head of Deportation for the entire five-state district. She'd come to check on us, prowling from her office on the other side of the floor. Her apparition made me sick to my stomach all over again because she had been the one to override my "continue detention" recommendation and had ordered the release of Rodolfo. We had argued at length.

If a reader is curious about what kind of agent I was at that stage, whether I was good or bad in a functional sense (as in a good doctor cures the patient, a bad doctor does not), I don't know. That's hard to measure, and the answer would certainly vary depending on who was asked. If someone were to ask Hortense, my boss's boss until her retirement, I don't think she would have said I was a good DO. Of that I'm pretty sure.

Hortense leaned into our small room and asked, "What are you doing?"

"Building bridges with the Chinese," Phil answered. "The vice-consul just invited Ames to a big event in Houston. Better get ready to sign off on his travel authorization, including one night's stay at the Four Seasons."

"No."

Phil and I looked at Hortense.

"No?" I asked.

Hortense looked at me. Her face indicated she thought my traveling to Houston to meet with the Chinese was outlandish, maybe the worst idea she'd heard.

"You're not going to Houston," Hortense said, shaking her head. She turned around to leave us.

Phil replied, "That's stupid." Hortense was Phil's boss's boss too, but he called it as he saw it. Hortense ignored him. In a moment she was gone.

I looked to Phil, my jaw hanging.

"That sucks," Phil said.

"I can't *not* go. I'm helping our agency." I struggled to recover. "This is saving people. I'm going. I'll just pay my own way."

"Well, if you do go, you'll get fired," Phil stated simply, "and then you won't be able to save *anybody*."

THREE

Phil and the House of Death

When I was seventeen years old, I was voted Troublemaker by my high school class. As I made my way to the front of the student assembly, weaving through the field of palms slapping me, with the familiar voices intoning my name, I elbowed the palms out of my way. My classmates probably took the scowl on my face as a sign of projected toughness, an attitude to match the certificate, but I was thinking about my mom's heart breaking. No mother wants her son to earn that kind of distinction, least of all at a three-thousand-plus-enrollment public city high school with no shortage of real delinquents in the mix. I certainly hadn't voted for myself, and I wanted to knock somebody's head off. I overheard one teacher define my award as "the opposite of Most Likely to Succeed." The teacher and his snickering circle saw the contrast between the two titles, but I eventually came to realize what they had in common: the curse of expectations. If you win Most Likely to Succeed, you will never live up to it. If you win Troublemaker, you will struggle for years not to.

If you leave home at seventeen to make your own tracks in the world, that Troublemaker will cast a shadow on nearly everything you achieve. If you get a scholarship to a prestigious university, you will soon find yourself on quadruple campus probation and performing community service. A transfer to another school on a new army scholarship will lull you into thinking you have outrun the curse. But when you enter the regular army, following the proud footsteps of your father and grandfathers and great-grandfathers, you will find the shadow of the Troublemaker intruding again. If you are handpicked for a top-secret unit and you train for a spectacular combat mission, you will never be sent on that mission. Your army decorations for leadership and combat readiness will be offset by a greater number of counseling statements and letters of reprimand from superiors who see you as a poor fit for the modern force. As much as you need a chance to prove yourself in battle as your father and grandfathers did, one shot to do something meaningful, to override the Troublemaker once and for all, that chance will elude you. You will never see enemy fire, even though American soldiers will die in major engagements on two continents while you train for stillborn missions.

Believe me when I say that it is hard to escape the Troublemaker tag. For half a decade after I got out of the army, the shadow was there. I endured a sinister loop of bosses who disliked me, hostile terminations and resignations, unfortunate breaks, and bad reputations. Until this.

In my DO life the monkey was completely off my back. From the first day of the seventeen-week academy training I believed in what I was doing. Two years later I still woke up excited in the morning. I made residents of my country and my beloved city safer by removing criminal threats from their lives. I earned the highest professional appraisals. I won cash bonuses and time-off awards for overall service and crises in the field. The guys I respected at work wanted to have me around. I got the call for every hot mission that came up, and I promised myself I'd never let anyone down. My Troublemaker identity was gone.

Now I was going after the troublemakers.

"Fucking knotheads!" Phil hung up his government cell with such violence that I thought his thumb might come through the back of the phone. He stomped the accelerator and barreled toward Orleans Parish Prison, where, we'd just been told, a deputy in one of the Immigration tanks had been assaulted.

"Hit her with a lunch tray and broke her nose," Phil said. He raced through a changing light.

"Who?"

"Can't you fucking guess?" Phil asked.

I laughed. The joke wasn't that there was an obvious candidate. It was the opposite. In our detained alien population there were way too many likely suspects even to think about guessing who hit a corrections officer with a food tray.

We came down to the rough end of Poydras Street, and the g-ride (government vehicle) started bouncing on the chewed-up grid. The river end of Poydras might as well have been our town's miracle mile. It was a glassy canyon of slick high-rises, including New Orleans's tallest, the fifty-one-story marble white Shell Building. This side was a different story, a dead terminus under the Broad Street overpass, broken auto glass, and more potholes than road. The chief residents of this area couldn't drive anyway. They were caged.

We pulled into the shadows of Orleans Parish Prison, what I'd been told was the fifth-biggest criminal warehouse in the nation. The complex stretched across a dozen blocks in my Mid-City zip code and contained several distinct prisons, most of which we used. As close to the Deportation office as it was to my apartment, a couple of miles either way, OPP was a particularly convenient place to stash aliens we wanted access to.

A third of our agg felon docket resided in OPP's heavily fortified Templeman III Prison for high-risk detainees. Conchetta contained a limited number of our female offenders, as the South White facility did juveniles. At the light end of the spectrum was the Community Correctional Center, containing medium- and low-risk detainees, most of whom Phil and I had nothing to do with.

We docked along the LAW ENFORCEMENT curb, secured our guns in the vehicle safe, and set out for the House of Detention. HOD was a relative skyscraper in the OPP family, and we could see it over the other structures from our car. It was easily identifiable by the dingy vertical slats running from the second floor to the roof, suggesting that even the structure itself was behind bars. It was less hospitable inside.

We picked up visitor badges downstairs and walked up one flight to the administration area, where the warden and crew lit up upon seeing us. "You-all come to talk to ya boys?" the warden asked in that local New Orleans–cum–New Jersey accent widespread among the jail staff.

"We came to kick the shit out of whoever broke your deputy's nose," said Phil.

"Augustin!" the warden said.

"Shit."

"He on nine." The warden sent a deputy in the black corrections uniform to take us up on the elevator. "Da soona you deport dat asshole, da betta."

"Working on it," I said. As soon as I said it, I wished I could take it back. It seemed like a lie. Augustin was Cuban. Cuba was a nonstarter. Phil and I had in fact engineered an inspiring deportation scheme for another Cuban earlier in the year, but it had been shut down at the last minute by Hortense on the grounds that it had never been tried and "we don't deport Cubans."

The elevator stopped at three, and a young deputy stepped on with a wild-bearded white guy. "Have him face the back. Always," our escorting deputy said. "He's got AIDS, and he bites." The young deputy did as told, but without much feeling. The elevator continued up. There were no buttons in the car. It was all intercom and cameras to prevent escape.

HOD was a natural home for many of our maximum-risk and disciplinary cases. They'd once resided alongside state and local inmates of the same character, but now we kept enough aliens in here to populate several wings. On the tenth floor was a special medical division where some of our criminally insane aliens rested in five-point restraints.

We got off the elevator, and our escort announced us to the personnel on the floor. I felt the humidity of the place before I took my first step. The tiers in HOD were in quadrants, with a thick common wall splitting the cells lengthwise and the "free area" in the center of the building where we stood talking with the deputies. The victim of the assault wasn't here, but the others discussed the incident.

"Where's fucking Augustin?" Phil asked.

"He with the doctor," a French-named deputy answered in the local accent. "Should be up in five."

"Well, let's talk to these idiots." Phil jerked his head at the tier.

"Yeah. Maybe you can find out what's eatin' they ass." The deputy walked over to the gate on our right and turned his giant key in the lock. The cells quieted. We stepped in, and I heard the bolt click as the deputy secured the gate behind us. All the aliens were locked in following the assault. Standing next to the shower, Phil and I looked down the long row. Every cell faced a window just five feet beyond its barred door, but the windows were covered by grating on the inside, and those giant slats on the exterior of the building prevented any stunning sunsets. There was no air conditioning. A large gunmetal fan blew full blast, transforming the corridor into a wind tunnel. Hot currents rippled our clothes and hair as we advanced.

Augustin's outburst had forced the timing, but visiting face-to-face with our detained population was something we did anyway. It was supposed to give them an outlet, loosen the lid on the boiling kettle a little. Phil and I put a thousand miles on the g-ride odometer some weeks, visiting all our remote jails. Nastiness still happened: assaults like Augustin's, and the big melees with mop handles and flying batteries, and the all-out riots that brought out the fire hoses and battle gear. You could visit these boys every week, join them in their flint dorms, answer their questions for hours till you dripped with shower humidity and the industrial disinfectant seared your sinuses, but the best you could achieve was a little more time between uprisings. These were top-shelf hardheads who wanted to stay in America but were destined for hell, and they were sure to explode before long.

At the first cell a stocky youth from the Dominican Republic thrust his face at the bars. He startled me a little. We had tracked him down on the street only the day before, and his sudden appearance took me right back to that heart-pounding pursuit and arrest. (For you curious readers, four days had elapsed between my release of Rodolfo and this prison visit. I should note that Phil and I had also escorted a homicidal Indian back to Mumbai during the interval. DOs generally spend considerable time apprehending criminal aliens and flying them home, but since this story lies in that cryptic deportation territory *between* apprehension and removal, I will resist straying either way. When you sense missing time anywhere in this book, you may assume I have spent it on the streets or in the airplanes. The story loses nothing for the omission.)

"Get me out of here!" the stocky Dominican pleaded.

"As soon as we get your TD," Phil said.

"You shouldn't keep us in here!" the Dominican exclaimed. "You know inmates call this the House of Death!"

"That may be so," Phil declared. "Fortunately, we assign no meaning to the creative recasting of acronyms by *fucking criminals.*"

The Dominican's cellmate, an old Slovak, laughed. Phil had a way of working a crowd, something for everyone in his blend of advanced degree lofty oration and factory hometown street bluster. Phil moved past the Dominican, who had knifed a tourist in the French Quarter and left him for dead.

Next door a pair of blond drug dealers named Ivan and Igor spouted complaints in Spanish. The agg felon docket included several in their category, offspring of Soviet soldiers stationed in Cuba. Ivan and Igor protested passionately against the HOD meals, which they said consisted of only bologna and hard-boiled eggs, always served cold.

Phil informed them that Fidel Castro would die long before HOD offered appetizing cuisine.

I stepped nearer a detainee who had been here since my first year on the job. Archimedes Daye was a convicted armed robber who claimed he was from the U.S. Virgin Islands and therefore a U.S. citizen. Our accent and dialect people, along with the immigration judge who'd ordered him deported, all believed he was Jamaican.

"Hello, Mr. Daye," I said.

"Hello, Officer Holbrook."

"Where are you from today?"

"St. Thomas, of the Virgin Islands of the United States," said Archimedes Daye. He leaned his muscular frame into the bars, eyes the same level as mine, but he weighed probably 220 to my 195.

"All right, Mr. Daye. You're free to waste your life in here, but if one morning you wake up and realize you are actually from Jamaica, get the word to me."

"All right." He sat down on his bunk. Daye was a hard specimen. The House of Detention, with its claustrophobic quarters, absence of vocational programs, and infamously repetitive menu, had broken a lot of deportees. Uncooperative aliens who resisted their removal for years—provided false countries of origin, tore up passport applications, screamed curses during consular interviews, swore on their children they would never go back to their homelands—came around within days of their transfer to HOD. This elevated tomb worked magic in making criminal aliens yearn for the journey home, no matter what kind of nightmare home was. But Archimedes Daye had outlasted the rough years, and he probably knew it. Deportation was starting to let people out, and he figured his number would come soon.

"Officer Miller, I'm sick," a voice squeaked weakly to my partner. Peering into the shadows past the bars, I saw the voice belonged to little Hosa Gabresallie, a petty thief of Eritrean citizenship. Normally an alien with his record would have been kept in OPP's Community Correctional Center, but Gabresallie owned the honor of being the only alien ever to have escaped from OPP. He'd pulled it off in a brazen intercom bluff of the elevator and gate controllers at the CCC facility, after which he'd torn off his prisoner bracelet and fled into the busy throng outside the adjacent court building. But Gabresallie was such a shifty-eyed character that he'd drawn notice even among the probation and bail bonds crowd, and police had stopped him on general appearance after only five minutes of freedom.

"I'm sick. I'm shaking." Gabresallie held his hands up and shook them wildly. "I need to see the nurse at the other jail."

"No," Phil answered.

Gabresallie dropped his hands to his sides, where they ceased to shake.

A Russian strong-arm extortionist pounded his cell door. "I am a Jewish refugee. This is wrong!"

"Yes. There is very little about you that isn't wrong," Phil told him, eyeing the unkempt detainee.

"You persecute me because I am Jewish. I am branded, just like the

Nazis branded me in the camps." The Russian grimaced and pointed to ink in his skin.

"Nice gulag tattoos, asshole. You think you're the first Russian gangster we've laid eyes on? Holy fucking bananas!" Phil yelled across the cells, "Do we have any real Jews on this floor? We have a thirty-year-old survivor of the Holocaust over here." Howls resounded in the corridor.

"I need a kosher menu," the Russian persisted.

"Why? What does *kosher* mean? Tell me something else about Judaism."

The Russian swept the stringy hair from his face, buying seconds to formulate his response: "Kosher is the food for the Jewish people . . . that tastes better than bologna."

"That's what I thought," Phil said, walking on. "This guy's about as Jewish as Officer Holbrook."

"But less Jewish than you?" I asked.

"At least I slept with some Jewish girls in college. I researched the culture, goddamn." Phil shot a glimpse backward at the Russian, his glimpse seeming to damn our strong-arm extortionist along with the rest of his bunch our country had absorbed and whom it was now our job to handle.

In the early 1990s, following the Soviet Union's collapse, the U.S. government had welcomed hundreds of thousands of Jewish refugees from the fallen empire. Taking a page from Fidel Castro, who had allowed rafts of criminals and lunatics to drift to Florida a decade before, leaders of the former Soviet states used our government's charity as an opportunity to empty their jails and infuse America's refugee pipeline with innumerable hard-core gangsters, Jewish and otherwise.

A Vietnamese man, Anh Dang, was kneeling when we crossed his cell. "I pray you officers will have mercy. I need to get out to take care of my daughter. She has no mother. I am all she has."

Phil looked down at the kneeling, praying man. "As long as your daughter lives outside the U.S., I will deliver you to her."

"She lives in New Orleans. Please, I pray—"

"Then tell her to bring your passport to our office." Phil walked on, ignoring Anh Dang's continuing prayers.

"By the way, Mr. Dang's daughter doesn't have a mom because he killed her," I told my partner. "He cut his wife's throat in bed and left her for the daughter to find."

Phil stopped in his tracks. "And he quotes the effect of his crime as the reason we should let him out. That takes some fucking stones." I saw Phil was perspiring now. An incendiary mood brewed in him, and his face grew rosy in the bracket of his beard.

We moved up the line, checking out the rest of them. The Angolan mugger who had beaten people even after they'd given him their money. The Canadian who'd molested children at a day care center. The four-fingered Lao who'd taken a whole gas station hostage until police marksmen shot the gun out of his hand. The Macedonian carjacker who had made the passengers stay in the vehicle for days while he forced them to withdraw their savings from ATMs. The Haitian who had walked into an office downtown, pressed a knife to the company president's neck, and requested a job in the mailroom.

They complained. The food, the conditions, the deputies: None of it met their approval. Phil's answers got shorter.

We reached the end of the corridor. From the last cell a dreadlocked Liberian exclaimed, "This is ridiculous!"

"Undoubtedly," Phil said. I observed that my partner's collared shirt was damp and his face flushed. The latent red in his beard came out like sparks.

"This is inhuman treatment. You people lock us up in here and don't care about our individual story. We're not all criminals."

"Yes, you are," Phil said.

"Oh, right, in the eyes of the law, yes." The Liberian flipped his head back and forth while he spoke. "I admit that. I stabbed some innocent people. I lost my fuse. They reminded me of someone else. But then you got to put me through all this?"

I always studied Phil when we worked together. In this instant I thought I saw the textbook demonstration of a man running out of patience.

"What I'm saying is," the Liberian said, "where's my second chance?"

"Jesus fucking Christ!" Phil exclaimed. He charged back down the corridor and called to a deputy, "Will you open these goddamn cell doors!"

"Uh." The deputy gulped. "Captain says it's lockdown, because of what happened. You want me to call him?"

"Forget it!" Phil said. "I'll just have to fucking yell." Phil realized the fan was competing with his vocals, but the socket was in the free area, on the other side of the bars. He twice jerked the rubber cord to pull the plug out and, failing, gave up on that too. He centered himself on the cells, his back to the outside wall, and he addressed the aliens.

"Most of you motherfuckers don't get it," Phil announced. "You've had your last chance in our country."

The cells fell quiet. From my position backed against the outside wall, a few steps from my partner, I could see the aliens' wide eyes from one end to the other. The hot fan air rushed by Phil. Rather than drown him out, the currents seemed to lift his booming voice and thrust it into the ears of our aliens.

"You're not going to get a second chance from us any more than your victims got one from you. You did bad things to people in America, and you have to go. You want a fresh start? Get us a goddamn valid passport, and we'll give you a start somewhere else."

A voice from the recesses sputtered, "We can't."

"Can't get your passport? Bullshit!" Phil thundered. "Ninety percent of you have your passport at your family's house, and they could mail it in tomorrow. The rest of you have records and birth certificates in your home countries, and you can get a passport as easily as asking. Your governments jack *us* off because they don't want fifty planeloads of assholes like you coming home all at once to fuck it up, but getting your passport individually is a piece of fucking cake."

Our strange scene set me suddenly in a storm: the ugly shadows, heavy atmospheric pressure, violently swirling air. Phil's clothes stuck to him as if drenched by rain, and he shouted at the aliens in the tempest.

"Someone on your tier assaulted a deputy today. That's serious. I hope they charge him and make him serve his sentence in the HOD basement. But whatever happens to Augustin, his fucking stunt got our attention, and

32

this whole goddamn tier just moved to the top of our get the fuck out list. You probably heard some alien felons are getting released now. Well, it's not going to be anyone in here. If you're resisting us, if you're thinking you'll hold out long enough that we'll give up and release you in this country, you're wrong. If you don't believe it, watch. Officer Holbrook and I will start taking you out, one or two next week, a few more the week after. And one of these months or years we'll come in here and get you, and all you will have gotten for your resistance is older and more broken down."

Phil's tempest speech inspired me. I saw the scene he described, the attrition of the thugs, our turning back the tide. It was awesome. Hearing him say it, I knew we could really succeed.

My partner's barrel chest rose and sank as he surveyed the detainees amid the roaring currents. "We didn't pull you off the street just so we could set you right back in our neighborhoods. HOD is your last stop in our country. It's not supposed to be nice. If you have to get out of this place, get us your passport. We'll have you home in two weeks. That's my personal guarantee."

Phil started to march away. The detainees clamored immediately for his attention. "Will you finish up with them, please?" Phil asked me. "Numb-nuts just showed up."

I nodded and watched as the deputy turned the lock for Phil. Beyond the gate was Augustin, his wrists cuffed in front of him. He stood rigid and manic.

My finishing up with the aliens consisted largely of listening to individual apologies for their not having made themselves properly understood, followed by enthusiastic statements of concurrence with everything Officer Miller had said, and then a confiding postscript on why he who was talking to me at the time was the single necessary exception to our plan. Of course officers Miller and Holbrook had to ship everybody out, just not in this one case because of the very special circumstances involved. But these eternal wheedlers now constituted a fraction of the tier. The majority of the aliens sulked and said nothing to me, and I took that to mean Phil's speech had hit.

The old Slovak called me over to his cell. He surprised me by handing over his passport. "Two weeks, right?" he said.

I leafed through the document. It appeared legitimate, and it still had three years on it. I looked at the picture on the second page, and then I looked at the Slovak murderer in front of me. I answered, "At the latest."

"Okay, I trust you."

I said, "Thanks."

At that a darkness overran his face, the result of that protective reflex in the prison world, where kindness means weakness and compliments come from punks. "I don't like you," he said, "but you don't lie."

I pocketed the passport and made my way to the gate.

The staff locked up behind me, and at last I took my partner's side in confronting our alien of the hour. Augustin, a light-haired Cuban with gold teeth and a "Live Thug or Die" tattoo across his sculpted abdominals, was naked from the waist up, except for the handcuffs. He had some red marks on the side of his head, but my impression was that the jail staff had exercised uncommon restraint in dealing with one who had assaulted their own. Augustin seemed to be coming down in adrenaline, and so did Phil. While I was finishing up my rounds on the tier, I'd heard Phil explode at the Cuban, whose record abounded with battery convictions, and I'd glanced through the gate bars to see Augustin suffer the tirade with clenched fists and wildly darting eyes. They were in some new zone now.

"This was the last one for sure," Augustin said earnestly.

"How are we supposed to believe that?" Phil asked. "You say that every goddamn time. Officer Holbrook and I sat there in your custody interview listening to you swear to us that you had your temper under control, and now look."

"But she wouldn't give me my pills. I told her I had migraine, they know I get migraine headaches, but where's my pills? It's my *min'* they fucking with. It's pain in my *min'.*"

"Your mind is fucking irrelevant," Phil said. "You can't assault a deputy for any reason. That has consequences."

"I know." Augustin's eyes shot left and right. "Are you getting me out of here?"

"No," Phil answered.

"Why not?"

"Chances are you're going to roll off our docket for a while. I think they're going to charge you: assault on a corrections officer. You might do some state time. We'll file a detainer so you'll come back to Deportation custody when you're done. You'll start over with us right here."

"But my *min'!*" Augustin protested. With the chain taut between his wrists, he clustered his fingertips and rapped them on his temples. "It's my *min'*. My *min'!*"

"Well, this is pointless." Phil turned to me and tipped his head to the elevators. We thanked the jail staff. On our way out of the building we asked the warden to get us copies of the incident report, charges pending against Augustin, and dispositions as they came. "That fucking simpleton will never get straight," Phil stated obviously.

When we finally hit the sunshine, I heard Phil gulp in the air of freedom. Although I didn't object to the jail visits as much as other DOs did, I did feel that weightlessness upon leaving. To compound the pleasure of the moment, I presented my partner with the Slovakia passport.

"Holy shit!"

"Your tempest address was a knockout. He's ready to go home."

Phil marveled. "The old dude believed me."

"I believed you," I said. "We can't be stopped."

Phil snapped the buzzing pager off his hip and scanned the message. It came from Craig, our immediate supervisor and the lone buffer between us and Hortense. Craig wanted us at the office, so we drove straight there.

We caught sight of Craig as soon as we pushed through the ninth-floor tinted doors. He was at the far end of the central hallway, and he stepped toward us. The heels of his black dress shoes clicked the floor. Craig strode tall with perfect posture, attired in the white shirt and black slacks he favored. His customary maroon necktie flattened against his chest as he approached.

"Let's have a talk," Craig said.

We followed our handsome black supervisor as he hooked assuredly into the deportation bay. I remembered when Craig used to take his team running at lunchtime. The other DOs had dropped out, one by one, until it had just been me and Craig, running all the way out to the Mississippi, around the Riverwalk fountain, through the streams of jazz pouring from the open doors and windows.

"Have a seat." Craig locked us in his office. He stared at me in silence for what seemed like half a minute. I started to worry he had something on me. Craig was a very ethical man, and he expected his officers to be ethical too.

"I understand you had an extraordinary conversation with the PRC vice-consul in Houston," Craig said. He gripped his jaw, keeping me tracked with his intelligent eyes.

I answered, "Yes, sir."

"And you've been invited to a social engagement."

"That's right, sir."

"The mission is a go."

"What?"

"Get your travel paperwork to me. I want you at that function."

"Awesome!"

Phil raised an eyebrow at our boss. "Standing up to Hortense. Has Craig forgotten his professional health?"

I was thrilled. I'd considered going covertly, but I now had my government's imprimatur, not to mention overtime pay and per diem. Craig was putting faith in me, as he had many times before. He'd been the supervisor to interview and hire me, even though I'd been what they call an off-the-street applicant, with no law enforcement experience, vying for a coveted federal job with a big salary in an inexpensive city. And now he was sending me on a solo mission to engage the challenging PRC.

Our leader took a breath and held it. He regarded Phil now. When he released his breath, his speech followed in an all-business delivery: "Phil, your obligations to the deportation program are over. The rest of the day is yours to clear your desk and move down the hall to Investigations."

"Wow," I uttered.

Craig continued, still looking at my partner. "Your responsibility for your docket ends now and is assumed entirely by Ames."

Phil moved his hand up and across my body, in a baptismal ritual. My heart pounded. I knew the territory, there was no good reason for my nerves to be twanging, but I felt the force of the power shift right away. When it came to managing New Orleans's aggravated felons, riding shot-gun with Phil was completely different from taking charge. This was, by some accounts, the biggest, nastiest docket in the nation, and I would be the most junior officer ever to run it.

"Ames, I can't afford to give you anyone now," Craig said, "but when we pick up another officer, I'll see that you get some help."

"All right, boss. Cool."

Craig smiled ruefully at Phil and shook his head. He had nothing else to say to his former star DO.

Phil and I glanced at each other. I don't know what he was thinking, but on my mind was the difference he had made. As luck had it—luck being so much a part of a DO's life and death—Phil had been my train-ing officer. He had taught me innumerable lessons and imbued me with a work ethic I would never lose. Phil was like Craig in that he possessed an unwavering sense of right and wrong that was very much in keeping with the rules that governed our profession. But the DO scene was changing. I would have to take all of Phil's lessons and all his passion and sense of duty and spin them with my own ballistic groove.

I still say Phil was the greatest Deportation Officer in the field. He didn't lower himself to the level of the alien criminals we managed or the entrenched entities in our government and other governments that deceived us. He was circumspect and principled.

Nothing that happens from this point on would have been possible had Phil remained my partner.

FOUR

Jacqueline and the Dozen Predators on the Loose

Ninth floor. Meeting. Craig's office. Every last DO out of the field.

Our 701 Loyola work area had been buzzing since morning, and by now the noise was overwhelming. The walls echoed inharmoniously. It seemed crowded in here, and the sound was wrong, as if I were hearing things through a stethoscope. For a moment I wondered if one of us had gone down. The mood was that weird.

We were too many to fit into Craig's office, so he held court outside his door. Among the secretaries' desks he addressed us, standing tall and upright as ever. I saw right away that we were all accounted for and that my fears of *local* tragedy were off the mark. What struck me then was how light we were as a unit. It was rare to have us all assembled, but here we were, standing around our leader. New Orleans's entire force, holding down the dirty Gulf Coast, we were charged with the apprehension and removal of all deportable aliens between Texas and Florida, and their numbers measured in the ten thousands. Looking at my fellow street-level agents, I counted six heads.

Craig's bench was lean to the extreme. We had not yet received the replacement for Phil, or even for Tammy, a pretty clever DO who had been in government-provided therapy over the stress of the job and had finally shut down for good.

I hadn't seen Tammy on the day she actually quit, but I'd seen her in the week leading up to it. She'd sought me out. I don't know why. She was certainly closer to other agents, like Phil. She talked to me about the pressures of the job ruining her life, her mental health. She leaned in close and told me she had tried to turn her gun and badge in downstairs. She'd slid her gun and badge across the district director's desk, and the DD had slid them back. That story shocked me somewhat. If I'd been the DD, I would not have slid the items back. If an unstable person on the edge of breakdown ever tried to hand me a weapon, I would take it.

Tammy told me about the counseling programs she was in. "They're helpful," she said. While she spoke, I could not help thinking about the boxes of ammunition and service pistol and high-capacity magazines she still had.

"The programs are free." She went on, not once blinking her clear, light eyes. "And they're confidential. Management isn't allowed to use your attendance against you in promotions." Tammy smiled in a state of unnatural calm, and I felt my nervousness mount. Her advocacy of the programs took on an evangelical air, and I started to see the programs themselves as fringe cults. I imagined others in the office were hearing Tammy confide in me, and they were linking us as two damaged agents with emotional problems: crackpot and crackpot disciple. Tammy offered to give me the number to the programs. I thanked her, but I got up to leave. She pulled in closer, stopping me with her crystal eyes. "Ames, you're not stupid," she said. "You do the same job I do, and you feel the same stress. The only difference is I've been doing it longer."

The next week she was gone. Months later Phil was gone too, and the mission remained. Now our boss told us how much harder it was going to get.

"As of this minute, headquarters has seized custody authority from the districts," Craig said. "Beyond six months we have no power to detain any alien, regardless of the threat he poses. That authority will henceforth come from DC, and in their bid to comply with the Supreme Court's *Zadvy-*

das decision, headquarters will apply continued detention only in specific exceptional cases."

I scanned the assemblage of DOs around me. Some of their eyes met mine for an instant, while others stayed locked on Craig.

"Expect to execute a lot of releases," Craig pronounced. "We should begin to receive the paperwork from DC this week."

I thought I picked up something special in Craig's tone, an investment in this whole business. As our supervisor he betrayed no discontent; he was simply explaining the new situation and how we were going to handle it. What I got from his voice, though, was that Craig took our mission personally.

When the meeting ended and we all flowed away from our boss's white-shirted nucleus, I drifted to the fire exit stairwell. I took the rest of the stairs up, ten landings' worth, and stepped out onto the roof. This was the spot I came to when I needed to breathe. Craig had pulled all his officers into the meeting, but in fact I was the DO most affected. Aliens judged compliant and not dangerous to society weren't detained beyond six months. In accordance with Immigration detention standards, mine were the only long-term cases—100 percent of them aggravated felons, escape risks, and terrorist suspects—so it was my aliens whom headquarters planned to set free. And it was my signature that was going to fill the release lines.

I stepped near the edge of the roof and looked out over Interstate 10, then down Earhart Expressway, past the Calliope housing projects, swinging toward my Mid-City apartment. Standing between me and my home was the OPP complex. How soon would it be before I had to drive over to that prison to let some menace out? At the high-rise edge, I felt like a lightning rod for the perfect immigration storm heading for us. I had no allies. Agencies like the U.S. State Department that could help me by exerting pressure on the defiant nations refused to do so. The Supreme Court had just hung me out, stripping me of my power to detain dangerous aliens. The White House would not stand up for me but was actively fueling my problem with a de facto amnesty proposal, the mere whisper of which ensured a continuous rush of the low-road illegals most likely to resort to crime once they got into America. All the individual storms had converged.

Two days later our mail girl dropped a manila envelope on my desk. It bore the seal of the Department of Justice (Deportation's home until the 2003 switch to Homeland Security). The envelope had already been sliced open lengthwise in the mailroom, where clerks had found it negative for anthrax and explosives. The contents in fact were liable to be more harmful than a letter bomb, which probably would have killed only me. I slid the top sheet out, seeing first the familiar I Street address for headquarters in DC, and then, on the opposite side, the name of the alien felon: Sergey Sarkisov. Below was the bold caption "Notice of Release." Then there was some text explaining, among other things, that the subject was to behave himself while at large. The date and signature of a headquarters authority at the bottom made it official. I grabbed the rest of the sheaf. There were twelve letters total, all releases, all felons. I recognized the names. I had written reports urging continued detention on eleven of them. I stood up and gathered their A-files, most of which I found in the cabinets around my area. One of the aliens was a recent transfer whose file hadn't caught up with him yet. I'd been working off a temporary folder, or T-file, a green folder I'd loaded with all his computer printouts from our Deportable Alien Control System database. A-file or no, I was bound to release him.

The next week I drove a maxivan out to Tangipahoa Parish Prison. I had only four aliens to pick up there, so a regular van would have been fine, but the rest of our transportation fleet was engaged, much of it in my rollout operation. OPP was the closest prison Deportation used, but I had aliens scattered throughout Louisiana and across the state line. They were in places like Tangipahoa, West Baton Rouge Detention Center, St. Martinville (where, two years earlier, aliens had overtaken the facility in a bloody siege, to which my DO brothers and I had responded), Vermilion Parish Prison, and Mississippi's Hancock County Jail. Today several of those facilities were seeing their inmate counts go down as the result of HQ's release order. While I drove to Tangipahoa, our transportation specialists made the runs to the other jails, a full day's work for some of them.

I drove into the rising sun on my way back across the swamp to New Orleans, the skyscrapers cropping up in the distance. My vanload of aliens laughed it up all the way. They sat sprawled in their bench seats, barely acknowledging the chains I'd suited them up with, because they knew the chains had to come off soon. This was a freedom ride.

I slid the transparent cage vent open to hear my prisoners' conversations, and I glimpsed them at intervals in the rearview. They were all swagger. Of course they were. They had beaten the system spectacularly. They had come to the land of milk and honey, taken their piece of it on their terms, and now they were being set free to take another piece. Every one of them had an enforceable warrant of deportation in his file, meaning that his conduct had been so reprehensible that he had been ordered removed from the United States of America. But today they all would walk free in America, a fabulous comeback.

A Cambodian gunrunner was in the front bench, just on the other side of the cage from me. He had gun tattoos on his arms and a teardrop permanently inscribed off the corner of his eye. He drawled to his fellow convicts that Immigration had done him a big favor by cutting him out of his state sentence for a deportation that never happened. The way he figured, Deportation Officers had given him two free years. I wanted to pull over right there, throw his door open, and rip him off his bench. I wished I could silence him by announcing that I was taking him directly to prison, where he would serve his sentence to its term, but I could not. I had in fact contacted the corrections department and the district attorney's office and been told there would be no reinstatement. Both had censured me for failing to deport the convicts.

My anger at the Cambodian gunrunner passed. He was no different from the rest of the batch. And the whole batch was no different from Rodolfo, whose image still seared my nerves. At the downtown office I unhooked the Tangipahoa quartet and poured them into the holding cell with the releases from other jails. Augustin stared at me, nodding with wordless defiance. OPP had locked him in solitary for assaulting its deputy but never formally charged him (perhaps because the prison administrators had not wished to lose the forty-six-dollar-a-day federal detention income that would have ceased had they switched him to their custody), so now he was walking free. Augustin set a clear example for his fellow detainees, as the other eleven did for theirs. The message was sounding up and down the tiers:

You too can fight the law and win. Don't give up your passport like that sucker the Slovak. Don't cooperate. Disobedience is the ticket to victory.

The holding cell steamed with victory. I closed the door on my charges, softening their noise behind the Plexiglas barrier that covered the bars. I had a lot of work to do if I was going to liberate these predators.

The release process for a criminal alien is incredibly time-consuming. I will not torture readers with all the details involved, all the computer input, phone calls, headquarters and district checklists, the skull-splitting procedures that each release entails. But here are the highlights. I had to load their profiles and criminal histories into IDENT and other active lookouts and databases. I had to photograph the aliens, two four-plates with a regular camera for the file and one computer snapshot for the database. Next I fingerprinted them electronically and with ink, put them on the phone with their state and federal probation officers, answered all their questions, and briefed each one individually on his order of supervision, the Deportation equivalent of a probation contract. If the alien spoke only Spanish, I printed the OS in Spanish and read that. If the alien spoke a language I didn't speak (I retained only some Italian and German from my old army days), I lined up an interpreter on the telephone.

It might be wishful thinking to believe that the aggravated felons I released would seek legitimate employment, but in case some eventually did, I had to give each alien an employment authorization document. There were only a few officers in our building with access to the EAD computer, and I was not one of them, as most Immigration managers, not unreasonably, failed to see that item of sensitive equipment as relevant to a *Deportation* Officer on the aggravated felon docket. So I had to find someone in the building who would punch in my alien's information and print up the layout. I inserted that layout into the special classified camera I'd signed out to take each alien's picture and laminated the Polaroids with special classified lamination. For the significant percentage of these aliens who had entered my country illegally, as opposed to those who'd had green cards that had subsequently been revoked, I had to complete parole cards, requiring another photograph and the location of special classified red-ink parole stamps.

There is more, but I take it the point has been made. With this batch of releases, I got help (with the transportation, with the employment cards, with a lot of the computer input), and still, the process consumed a day and a half of my time. No DO I ever met had a day and a half in his workweek to spare. DOs struggled to stay afloat in the first place. It was a zero-sum game, and a day and a half spent releasing criminal aliens is a day and a half taken away from another aspect of the job: You weren't out arresting fugitives on the street, you weren't pressing embassies for travel documents, and you weren't physically removing the aliens to their motherlands. You weren't doing something that you desperately needed to do.

The awareness of time lost—the seconds I heard ticking off a clock somewhere in the office—wore me down as I waited for the laminates to cool on each of this dozen EADs. But I realized with a shudder that the time wasn't simply lost. I was using it to achieve the opposite of my deportation mandate.

Imagine you are a veterinarian. On Thursday the boss comes to you on your lunch break and says, "Tell you what. When you're done with your sandwich, I've got a new assignment for you. I want you to head out to our customers' yards, grab the dogs and cats, and break their legs. Do that for the rest of the week." That's what I'd been asked to do as a DO. It was good for job security but hard on morale and mental stability.

"Thank you, Officer Holbrook," a Guinea-Bissau stickup kid told me as I walked him back to the holding cell.

"Don't thank me," I said. "This was not my idea."

"Who should I thank?"

"Well, you can thank your government for not wanting you. Thank my State Department for not applying leverage to make your country take you. The U.S. Supreme Court for saying we can't keep you detained. My headquarters for rolling over. Most of all thank my president for turning a blind eye while governments like yours put platoons of assassins on our soil—" Anger swelled in me as I enumerated, but I stopped when I saw the Bissauan was no longer listening. He was smiling to his friends in the holding cell. They knew he was last, that they were about to fly.

I unlocked the door and stepped inside, gripping the bars to pull the

Plexiglas tight behind me. I ordered the dozen to sit on the benches, and I gave them a speech to scare them straight. I had seen Craig and Phil threaten departing aliens before, put the fear of God in the delinquents before they hit the pavement, but I did not think my warning was working here. Maybe it was because these were more incorrigible aliens. Or maybe it was because they sensed I didn't believe my own speech. How could I scare them when this mass liberation proved my agency had no teeth? These screwups had done nothing to earn this. They were being released for no logical reason. They looked delirious.

As I wrapped up the scare tactics and began to explain the simple mechanics of getting out of this building and finding the bus station, I felt as if I were sleepwalking. I seemed to be watching some unfolding scene that I wasn't really a part of. As a Deportation Officer, how could I have been? Twelve more Rodolfos spread into our communities instead of shipped out to their rightful countries abroad.

My resentment of Rodolfo did not fade. A reader might ask why Rodolfo got under my skin when he was only a middling crook. It was true that Rodolfo's crimes did not stand out, but they were bad enough. I never encountered a supercriminal in my docket, nothing like a clever serial killer who had eaten the hearts of his fifty victims or a terrorist who had gassed a nursery school. I don't know how many of those there really are in the world. The aliens I dealt with were the kind who harmed innocent people every day. They devastated regular families and stole their happiness. On the end of the bench closest to me throughout my parting lecture was a Chinese citizen with a record lighter than Rodolfo's. He had only one conviction, kidnap for ransom. It didn't hold much shock value, but I wondered what that victim's family would have given to have those hours back, never to have had to pace and pray and cry for one of their kin, to relive their lives without the jabbing awareness of how fragile their existence is and that parts of themselves could, at any time, be taken forever by one lowlife thug. I objected to Rodolfo because he represented all of them. Rodolfo had been the vanguard of bad things to come.

I pushed the bars open and directed my dozen charges out of the cell. They scooped up their belongings, and I escorted them to the elevators.

Most were glib and high. Augustin was surly. He flung the hall door open in a rebellious show. Phil might have slammed him up against the wall for that, probably locked him back in the holding cell for a few hours on principle. I didn't have the stomach for it. All these guys had already beaten me. I'd just signed the liberation papers on twelve dangerous felons I was supposed to have deported. To check one of them now for a bad attitude would only have underscored the fact that he'd soon be out of my control.

I had planned to leave my charges at the elevators, but in the end I accompanied them downstairs, determined at least to get them out of the building without a crime taking place. Because several were headed to other states, for reasons of family or parole restrictions, they made their way toward the adjacent Greyhound/Amtrak station across our parking lot, and I decided it would be safer to walk with them. A pair of Vietnamese peeled off as soon as we got outside. One of them would be arrested two nights later for his part in a home invasion robbery, and the next week I would get a call from the assistant warden at OPP who would tell me about it and ask if I might think about deporting the problem child this time around. The assistant warden would be chuckling, but there would be something in his tone to question honestly what in the world I was doing on the job.

I was already questioning myself. As I watched the outbound aliens board their conveyances, highlighting the diaspora component of these criminal liberations, I asked what had happened. I'd just taken command of the New Orleans aggravated felon program (a notorious prestige position in the "worse is better" logic of the U.S. deportation universe, the devil's slot where all my fellow agents nationwide knew I would get my hands bloody, bouncing the very worst invaders, God bless America and Jesus have mercy on the criminal alien swine as Ames ships them back to the cesspools they were born in), but I was welcoming the cutthroats into American society. Please rape, murder, and rob more people in my country. All that was missing was the lei. The release process was so ridiculous in fact that a lei wouldn't have made it any more surreal, and I told myself right there that if some senators or anyone from the White House ever came to oversee this release fiasco they were responsible for, I would pay out of my own pocket for a Hawaiian girl to put leis on the predators as they walked out of my office. So this was why I'd gone to the academy? This was the consequence of my professional elevation?

I tried to calm myself down as I walked back to my building in the surreal wake of the twelve releases. It sounded like a shock headline: DOZEN DANGEROUS ALIENS ON THE LOOSE. I wished for Phil back. Somehow I couldn't imagine his taking part in this. He'd have spun the ship around. I was lost. I struggled to get it together before I emerged on the ninth floor.

I returned to my desk to find the latest mail delivery. On top was the missing A-file of the recent transfer. I'd put the alien, a Lao convicted of sexual battery and rape, on a Greyhound to Tennessee. His full record had arrived only in time for me to forward it to the gaining office. I pulled his T-file apart and consolidated it with the fatter A-file. I flipped the final product closed and tagged the cover with the destination office: MEM/ DDP (Memphis Deportation). I eyed the silver electronic wand from our file tracking system. At that point, having already sent on the corresponding alien body, I might have run the red laser wand across the back of the file, as I had for the others, and been done with it. The beep emitted when the wand read the bar code would have signaled the end of my involvement.

I reopened the A-file. A few pages under on the right side I discovered a victim notification sheet. It instructed that the subject's victim, Jacqueline Pham, be informed in the event of a release. Ms. Pham herself had written a letter to that effect. The letter was five years old. I hated the idea of reopening an old wound, one that potentially had been buried away, but I'd opened the A-file, I'd seen the notice, the case was mine. I dialed her number.

I rolled my chair to the window and faced the city. The phone was ringing.

"Hello?"

"Hel—" There was some commotion on the other end. I waited while the woman on the phone disciplined a child. Her speech issued in hard Vietnamese tones. When a break came, I continued. "Hello, this is Officer Holbrook from New Orleans Deportation. I'm trying to reach Jacqueline Pham."

The woman said nothing and laid down the phone. I waited. The voice I heard next was crystal, feminine: "Hello?"

I introduced myself again. I said, "I'm looking at a letter in a file that I have."

"Yes?"

"I think it was written by you several years ago. You asked to be notified about a case? Do you still want to be notified?"

"Yes." Her voice was tender. Between her diction and the letter in front of me, with its purple ink and the fairest of calligraphy, I had a clear picture of her in my head.

"Bounmy Xayavongsa was ordered released. I released him today."

She asked, "In Laos?"

I said, "No, I released him here."

"Where is here?"

"He's on a bus to Murfreesboro, Tennessee. I see you live in Kansas. Mr. Xayavongsa is prohibited from traveling to Kansas without first informing us—" I stopped when I heard her acute breaths. She'd begun to cry.

I stared out the window, past the Entergy Building that hulked over our high-rise, past the Superdome across the street.

"The new law—"

"How could you?" Jacqueline cut me off, and then she sobbed.

"I—I'm notifying your local law enforcement. Also the police where he's going. Plus our agents in Tennessee. We can pull him back in for any violation."

"I was a bag of bones," Jacqueline said, her words coming between wails.

I pressed myself against the pane, staring past the whole city into the clouds.

"He's going to find me," Jacqueline cried. "You promised me you'd get rid of him. You promised."

"I'm sorry."

Her crying came in waves now, convulsions from somewhere deep. I was looking at the most distant spot of ether, as far from the phone as my eyes could land, but I still saw her, the tears pouring from her. She pleaded, "You're supposed to—"

"I know," I said.

I gave her my number. I told her to call for any reason. In the end she wasn't speaking, only crying, until she hung up.

I turned around slowly and rolled my chair toward my desk. I inspected what was left in the recent mail delivery. Sliced open lengthwise was a new envelope from HQ. This one contained fifteen more letters ordering the liberation of alien felons, reminding me that in this infinite storm I had glimpsed only the smallest nimbus of the leading edge.

When the workday was over, I drove home. I took my gun off, put my badge in my drawer. I heard my fiancée talking on the phone on the back deck. I went into the kitchen and looked at her through the glass. Her eyes leaped up to meet mine, and she just radiated so bright. I turned around and walked into the bedroom.

Later, as I lay facedown on the sheets, the wooden floor beneath the door frame creaked. I could feel her looking at me. I kept my eyes closed and tried to go to sleep.

I felt her weight on the bed. She lay behind me and nestled and rubbed my head. To say I believe immigration is good for my country is to say I believe in stories like hers.

My fiancée may have no trace of an accent anymore. As a first-grade teacher she may teach natural-born Americans how to read and how to love to read. She may be as American as any of us, or *more* American (as I heard a man from Italy once claim proudly) because she *chose to be* American, but she will always be an immigrant. Her experience inspires me. I wanted it forever to mean what it meant at that moment.

The coming weekend I was traveling to Houston, the next lap in a race I was running against my own government. I had to deport dangerous men like Bounmy Xayavongsa before headquarters let them loose. I was going to take my fiancée to the PRC consulate with me, and we were going to dress up and drink and party. To cement my agreement with the Chinese diplomats, I was going to do whatever it took.

FIVE

Houston and the Gold Mine

I was well ahead of schedule, advancing west on Interstate 10 at the wheel of a California-plated ten-year-old Honda Accord sedan that was a recent gift from a friend of mine. My onetime college roommate had bought it new when he'd moved out to the Silicon Valley and landed a nice entry-level job. Back then in the dawn of our youth it had been our main vehicle for the adventures of our age. Now that my friend had arrived at the convergence of his mounting success and the car's mounting years when it was no longer reasonable, in the judgment of his relatives and his employer, to be seen in the car, he'd passed it on to me. It was a way to keep the Accord in the family, five thousand resale dollars be damned. Driving now, I was struck by the implausibility of the idea, the car that had conveyed my friend and me through so many escapades in our early twenties today being drafted into official government business on a mission of national security.

The sun blazed. We were an hour short of downtown, but the traffic was already grinding. My dog, Whiskey, stood up in the backseat and panted with his chin jutting over my shoulder. I squeezed my fiancée's hand

and tried to get comfortable as we lurched toward Houston. We'd decided to make a weekend of it and press all the way to San Antonio, where we had friends. The consulate event would be only the first stop. For me it took a little of the tension out if I could pretend the trip was about more than just my relationship with the Chinese. The nearing hours when we would be at the consulate represented uncertainty to me, and I preferred to think past them. I talked with my fiancée about what we would do in San Antonio, but my mind kept circling back to the uncertain. What was I going to do at the consulate? What was I willing to do? After all it had taken to make this happen, what would I really accomplish?

The freeway dipped beneath an overpass. I was just coming up on the far slope when the car started smoking.

My fiancée noticed. "Is that you?"

I began to think we should have flown. My eyes shot to the clock. Black smoke billowed from under the Accord hood. "It is," I replied.

"Are you going to do something about it?"

"I am. Just let me get off the freeway." I began the slow merge right. I was getting honks in the crawling traffic. Some of the motorists had angry faces, and I saw them mouth curses at me for polluting, for beclouding their gorgeous view of rush-hour Houston.

"We are *not* showing up to the consulate like this," my fiancée said. "I would be mortified."

Her utterance made me less nervous. The preoccupation that we'd suffer harsh social judgment for spewing black smoke upon arrival to the formal ball was a great distraction from my own concern, which was that we might not make it at all.

I took the exit and stopped in the first lot. I saw nothing obvious when I lifted the hood, except that there was little oil. There was nothing I could fix myself without getting the book out, and there was not enough time to have a garage look. I ran to a gas station and bought a case of oil. If the Accord was going to keep burning it, I was going to keep feeding her. Mostly I possessed the sense I had to keep moving. The traffic was bad. Our time cushion was squeezing to nothing. If I didn't make that consulate party, it would be far worse than never having gotten the invitation at all.

It would be an irrecoverable backslide, Mr. Ji writing me off and declaring shame on himself for ever having believed in an American.

I filled the oil and drove on. Our motel was not too far, although I could not yet see the Motel 6 tower sign. My colleagues would ridicule my lodging choice when the U.S. government was footing the bill, but the Motel 6 welcomed dogs. Besides, with our perilous transportation state the motel near the same freeway turnoff as the Chinese consulate was likely, in the end, to prove the piece that saved us. If anything did. If we were lucky enough to reach the motel, we'd still have to make it to the consulate.

I stopped again and put in another two quarts. My hands were filthy with oil. For a moment I was relieved that I wasn't yet wearing my formal clothes, but the relief ebbed from me as I realized that meant I still had to clean myself up, put on the nice clothes, and tie a perfect knot in my tie. Time was just too close.

At last I saw the red 6 in the sky.

I dragged up to the Motel 6 office and checked in quickly. I had a sense of impetus coming back. In the room I shaved, jumped in the shower behind my fiancée, and emerged sludge-free to don my suit. Fortunately my fiancée was always a quick change, and as I knotted my tie, she stood ready and gorgeous in a silky formal dress at the door. We left our dog comfortable on the bed and hung the PLEASE DO NOT DISTURB sign on the handle outside.

When I started the Accord in front of our downstairs room, there was an explosion of black smoke and then none at all. "It's cured!" I announced as I merged onto the street and made my way toward Montrose Boulevard.

My fiancée did not believe me, but she knew there was no harm in playing along. If the engine started smoking again, I could park us a block away from the consulate, removed from critical eyes. And if it seized altogether, we could cab it from here. We were golden, and we were right on time.

At 3417 Montrose the sidewalk swarmed with black suits. Chinese valets waved us into an enclosed lot. Security checked us out, and we parked and joined the flow of other formally attired guests into the main building. I marched into the grand reception room with my fiancée on my arm.

My ears picked up a variety of accents. Of course other consulates' officials were among the invitees. I scanned the crowd, eager to find Mr. Ji, and it occurred to me then that I had no idea what he looked like.

Oh, but here was someone bearing down on me now, no doubt tipped off by the identity checkers. He had a bald, bullet-shaped head and a regal goatee. The handsome Chinese man smiled warmly on his approach.

"Officer Holbrook, my good friend!" Mr. Ji identified himself and extended his hand.

"Nice to meet you, Mr. Ji! This is my fiancée, Soraya."

"Very good to meet you." Ji's eyes lit up more. "Are you Chinese?"

Soraya smiled. "Thai."

"Oh." Ji nodded approvingly. "Then you have Chinese blood."

"That's right!" They laughed together.

There are people in this world with a brightness that shines out from their souls through their skin, and my fiancée was one. The quality was distinct from her physical beauty. She arrested rooms when she entered. Ears tuned in when she spoke. Right now, watching Ji pull Soraya across the great room to meet his wife, I knew I could not have arrived with a better partner on this mission.

The mission. What was I doing now? Was it enough just to have appeared, to show Mr. Ji I was on his side? What other tactics was it my responsibility to employ?

Ji gave me no time to formulate answers. "I very much enjoy working with your husband," he told Soraya. "It is a very difficult job he has, but you would not know it to work with him."

I smiled internally while I watched Soraya glow and converse with our hosts. What she'd known up till now about my career was what she saw at home, her man looping his belt through handcuff and high-capacity magazine cases every morning and kissing her good-bye with a loaded sidearm on his hip and the emergency callouts after hours, her betrothed vesting up for battle and charging out the door for God knew what crisis on air, land, or sea. Tonight was so beautifully different. I was proud to be able to show Soraya a glamorous side of my career. In the months ahead, when I was in trouble, and the walls were closing, and work boiled over into my personal life, and Soraya did not like me anymore, I would remember this snapshot. The picture of her standing next to Mr. Ji and his wife would make me happy because she was smiling such a real smile and she was proud of me and all I accomplished on the job. And then the picture would make me sad because those days were gone.

While the conversation was still lively, Mr. Ji pulled us across the great room to the bar and introduced us to rice wine. Ji's face had a healthy tone, and it seemed he had the jump on us, but as a good host he was determined that we have a chance to share his homeland buzz. His countrymen laughed as I reacted to the liquor's taste and heat. Mr. Ji put his hand on my back. I thanked my host and encouraged him to break away. I knew Mr. Ji had a lot of people to see, and I did not want him to feel that he needed to be around us all night. We shook hands again, and Mr. Ji repeated to Soraya what a pleasure it had been to meet her. He seemed more impressed with her than with me, but that was neither unexpected nor inauspicious. I squeezed Soraya's hand and led her away from the bar into the festive crowd. The rice wine was in my head a little, and it joined the confidence I already had in a liaison well made.

We enjoyed the festivities from there, and we could have done only that, but there was a piece of me determined to pursue the work angle just a little more. I looked through the room, and I saw targets. I knew many of the non-Americans who populated this hall were employees of their governments' consulates. Some of those governments were creating problems for me in New Orleans. Some of those governments were putting innocent United States residents in mortal danger. Despite the social nature of the night's event, I had to keep in mind that this was my battlefield as much as the New Orleans streets I policed. Craig had sent me here to make our district and our country safer. Foremost in achieving that end had been the personal meeting with Mr. Ji, but that was done, and that was only the obvious. Craig would not want me to stop. I tried to study the crowd. It was complicated in this rich scene of ceremony and gloss, all these people in their best costumes and faces, but I did my best to x-ray through.

I ventured forward with Soraya beside me, and I struck up conversations with other guests. My instincts were sometimes proved correct, as

I picked out several consulate employees. Nothing seemed to be a windfall, though. I met Greece and Mexico, but we already had solid relationships with them in New Orleans. I met Haiti (honorary), but my own agency forced us to request Haitian TDs through headquarters in a slow and often failing process, making outside negotiation improbable (Haiti's officials would sidestep the request by citing my government's rule) and potentially job-ending, since my agency was not above firing its employees for such unauthorized foreign contact, no matter how righteous the intent. My efforts at socializing to this point would prove helpful in a case or two down the road, but I could lay claim to no great coup. The evening's first surprise treasure came to me about an hour later, in the food line.

Soraya and I, eager to sample the exotic dishes but not paying much attention to our progress toward the banquet table, were queued up with our plates. I was walking backward so I could face her in the line. Soraya was enjoying herself, I could tell. Gone, at least for tonight, was her sometimes vocal resentment of my career for its tendency to put me in harm's way. She never made a secret of her objection to this point, nor did she hide her displeasure at the jail grime, the after-hours calls, and the missions that pulled me from home for days at a time. But tonight she was pure smile. I watched that smile broaden even further at some act taking place behind me, and I instinctively turned to see what it was that Soraya found amusing. There, immediately in front of me, was a restless man in a somewhat rumpled brown suit. The man's appearance, though not altogether serious, was not in itself sufficient to have triggered Soraya's mirth, even with the rumpled suit. What caused her to beam was that the person who had been standing in front of me for the previous five minutes had been a glamorous Japanese woman in a long dress, now separated from me by the brown-suited man who was apparently too restless or hungry to start from the end of the line.

Soraya knew that I had the habit of calling people on line cutting. I was not a rule fanatic. I was not the kind of law enforcer who followed speeders to their driveways to straighten them out in my off-duty time. But I respected lines, and more often than not, so long as the offender wasn't handicapped or frail, in the capacity of regular private citizen I insisted that line integrity be maintained. Soraya was waiting for me to say something to the man, but in fact I was not about to lecture him. I recognized the act of waiting one's turn in line as an exclusively American custom, and it was not my business to force its observance here on symbolic Chinese soil. I would accept the leapfrogging with no protest, just as I had at the French ski lifts and in the Italian post offices in my army days. Still, I tapped the man on the shoulder and introduced myself.

"Oh, hello. I'm Balvir Dua!" he exclaimed with a warm smile. As soon as he released my hand, he tapped his coat for his business card supply and fished one out.

"Thank you, Mr. Dua," I said. His card identified him as Indian vice-consul here in Houston. I quickly introduced Soraya while I decided how to proceed.

"I've had occasion to work with some of your professional peers in other offices," I told Dua. "I'm a Deportation Officer from New Orleans."

"Oh, so it is not in my jurisdiction." Mr. Dua spoke quickly.

Actually it was. According to the Indian consulate's own territorial map, the entire state of Louisiana fell under the Houston purview. It was only because Houston had been such an absolute black hole for TD requests that our district office had adopted, as desperate ad hoc policy, the forwarding of all requests directly to the Indian Embassy in Washington. This had resulted in a scant improvement, say, a 10 percent issuance rate over the previous zero. Ninety percent failure meant a lot of Indian felons, many violent, were on track to hit the American streets.

For the readers here who have trouble reconciling their image of an Indian with that of a dangerous thug, I'll take this opportunity to explain the reality. No nationality has a lock on the great pain criminal aliens inflict on victims in America; neither is any nationality exempt. The matter of which countries' citizens cause trouble at any given time in America is dependent on so many factors, including timing, situation in the motherland, treatment upon arrival, economic viability, location of residence, and a thousand more circumstances of luck and background, that there is no science that works for long. At the time of our story if I'd had to assign the term *most violent* to a nationality well represented in my docket, in respect to blood spilled per capita, it would have been the Cambodians. *Least violent* would have gone to my Nigerians, whose hypereducated ranks of frauds and con artists preferred to steal from people who didn't know they were being robbed. As my career continued, I'd watch the ex-Soviets and Eastern Europeans climb toward the violence label as the Southeast Asians let go. And so the evolution runs. The criminal cycles turn the counterintuitive into standard and then those standards back into counterintuitive two years later. My aggravated felon docket contained more whites than blacks, but not many more. The Hispanics, Asians, and non-Hispanic whites and blacks maintained dependably even quarters, hovering within ten points of each other as a percentage of my detained population. The criminal alien problem was general and widespread, with most foreign countries contributing, so it was no surprise to any Deportation Officer that a nation that gave us so many upstanding and brilliant software engineers also gave us nasty predators. Indians were all over my docket. I had muscle-bound, tattooed, gold-toothed Indians (not counting the ethnic Indians from countries like Guyana, Suriname, Barbados, and Trinidad) with criminal histories so thick they needed extra A-file folders. The last Indian I had personally escorted home had stabbed a girl nine times and then shot her for good measure. At current rates, for everyone like him I managed to get home, there were another nine just as dangerous whom my government would order me to unleash. Unless I could stop it.

"New Orleans, Louisiana, Mr. Dua," I said in a helpful tone, the way he might have said, "Jodhpur, Rajasthan," to me for clarification of his country's political geography.

Suddenly, in his trademark champion form, Mr. Ji appeared. He spoke directly to the Indian vice-consul. "Officer Holbrook is my guest from New Orleans."

"Oh, very good." Mr. Dua smiled. He seemed impressed.

"He is my good friend," Mr. Ji said. "You look at him and you see this big, strong man." Ji put his hand on my shoulder (I was actually under two hundred pounds and barely over six feet). "But Officer Holbrook is extremely patient. I can say that it is easy to work with him successfully."

"Oh, yes," Mr. Dua replied to his consular peer. As the two vice-consuls spoke, they seemed to be reacting to more than each other's spoken lines. I sensed there were pieces of their conversation I was missing, some kind of diplomatic encryption that transmitted on a silent track.

Mr. Dua turned to me. By now we all had stepped out of the food line. "I'll look forward to working with you," he declared in his quick rhythm. He gestured to his card in my hand. "That second number is my direct phone."

"Thank you very much, Mr. Dua." I shook his hand. "It was very nice to have met you."

When he released my hand, the Indian vice-consul cut at once to the very front of the food line, making up for lost time by hitting the banquet table directly. I tucked his card into a very secure inside pocket of my coat and buttoned it in.

Mr. Ji whisked Soraya and me in the other direction. He brought us to the end of the grand room where the ceremonial display was set up. The Chinese consul general stood there with his wife, and Mr. Ji made introductions.

"It's an honor to meet you, sir," I told the consul general before I conveyed the same to his wife.

Our conversation was very short, but long enough for the consul general to ask me if I'd been to China.

"Not yet, sir," I answered, a little sheepish at not having visited his important homeland with its teeming cities and Great Wall. "I've been wanting to for a long time."

"I think Officer Holbrook will have the opportunity to go to China very soon," Mr. Ji told his boss.

"Good," said the consul general.

The attendant photographer lined the six of us up for a photograph. The exchange between Ji and his boss had me giddy. *The opportunity to go to China very soon.* Did that mean Wareng Chow's travel document was slated to arrive at my office? The flash lit us three men with our three women, and the shutter captured the scene for all time.

Soraya and I eventually did get back to the food line, when there wasn't really a line left. Most guests had already had their fill, and now Soraya and I joined the stragglers who arrived at the banquet table's edges and proceeded to curl around one another, filling their plates at leisure. The food was excellent. The Chinese had put on a good show all around.

The crowd was thin, I noticed, and the air was getting quiet. I took a look at my watch. Soraya would want to get back to our dog, but after that we had choices. Checking out the downtown Houston nightlife was an option. So was checking out of the Motel 6 without even spending the night and taking I-10 another three hours to San Antonio. I was ready for anything. I wanted to discuss it with Soraya, but she was involved in conversation with a couple she'd just met.

Out of the corner of my eye I saw Ji approach. He stopped short and smiled, and I signaled to Soraya that I was headed off. Intuitively I joined Ji. We were not halfway to the bar before I guessed that the night's rice wine bonding was not over.

"I am very glad you could come, Officer Holbrook," Ji said at the bar. "Thank you."

I laughed and set my glass down. "I'm the one who should be thanking you. Soraya and I had a wonderful time. You and your wife are terrific."

We talked a little more and shared some laughs. Then he said, "Before you leave with your fiancée, there is something I have for you."

"Wow. Really?"

"Yes. Before you leave."

"Great."

"The family of Mr. Tse called me. Do you remember? Mr. Tse is the case where we took initiative."

"Of course, sir." I had not forgotten the alien whose freedom I had arranged. I looked across the nearly empty floor to Soraya, who was listening to an older female. The timing was good. This was a conversation for Ji and me alone.

"His family is very happy. It should go well. I think you and I worked together to do a good thing."

"*At least one* good thing, sir."

"You are right." Ji chuckled. "So, let us keep our friendship strong and continue to take initiative when we agree it is appropriate."

"Absolutely."

I saw Soraya come across the floor toward me, an immaculate vision in her dark dress and skin. She took my arm when she arrived. She said, "Thank you for the wonderful evening, Mr. Ji."

Mr. Ji smiled. "Excuse me," he told Soraya. "I must get something for your husband from my office if you will wait one moment, please." He walked off.

His office. The festive decor had made me forget this building was where Mr. Ji worked. Soraya looked to me. "What's he getting?"

"I don't know," I said honestly.

In a few minutes Mr. Ji returned. He extended a stiff envelope, which I accepted. We shook hands all around. I didn't see his wife, so I left Mr. Ji with some words of gratitude for her too before Soraya and I turned to the exit.

We held hands walking to our car. Soraya leaned into my arm. There were few lights outside. The enclosed parking lot was quiet. Our Accord was nearly alone. I opened Soraya's door and watched her slide in before I pushed it closed.

When I got behind the wheel, I looked at her and said, "I'm guessing you want to go straight back to the motel to see Whiskey rather than check out Houston from here."

"See Whiskey first," she said.

"We can also go to San Antonio tonight," I said. I started the engine, and no smoke came out. Or maybe it was too dark to see it.

"Are you really going to drive right out of here?" she asked.

"Yeah, it's cured," I told her. "This car fixes itself."

"Right," she said. "But I was talking about the envelope. You know you want to open it."

I did. And I didn't. I'd been too nervous to reveal the present, but I had to. Here, behind the wheel of my car in the shadowed parking lot, my hands tore into it, fingers diving for the contents. My fists leaped up with the prize, covered with the clipped label in Ji's handwriting: Chow

Wareng. I slid the label aside and squeezed the turquoise book. It was the passport-quality TD that China was so famous for not issuing. I flipped the cover open to see the glowering face of Wareng Chow. His glower actually was for me; I'd taken the photograph. Good for one entry into the People's Republic of China. The book's one-year validity was eleven months and twenty days more than I needed. This turquoise ticket represented a very antisocial alien who was not going to harm another soul in my country. It represented the alternative of well-being and peace for the victims who otherwise would have been.

Mr. Ji had put it on top on purpose, not only because the Wareng Chow TD was awesome in itself, but because it was also a symbol. It was the first step on a road two men had agreed to take together. Mr. Ji had called the road Initiative.

I'd known the envelope was heavy the instant Mr. Ji had handed it to me. Now, in the dark and quiet parking lot, alone with Soraya, I pulled the sides apart and inventoried the remaining contents. Inside the envelope were ten more faultless TDs corresponding to ten more Chinese aggravated felons.

All at once I was holding more travel documents than the previous total the PRC had issued to my office in the past several years.

SIX

Wareng Chow and the Shock Wave

The next workweek I thanked Craig as soon as I returned to the office. I was going to get some pats on the back and even more beers later for breaking open the PRC, but the truth was my boss had been responsible for this. In his office, Craig laughed it off and redirected the credit, as was his style, but I knew the score. He had hung himself out to put me at that consulate. He had steamrolled Hortense's will, probably by taking the matter to the district director, and since then Hortense and anybody else who didn't like me or Craig had been waiting for this to fail, preferably in dramatic style. Craig had known he'd had little to gain professionally in contrast with much to lose if the foreign contact had somehow blown up in our faces. It still could, I knew, in the event that somehow Mr. Ji's and my Initiative came to light, but that wasn't going to happen. Right now it was all good news on the ninth floor. The doomsayers had to wait for another day.

I walked from Craig's office to my own desk. I was jumping to raid my file cabinets. First, though, I photocopied the covers and photo and information pages of all eleven new travel documents. I made extra copies of ten of them and put those pages aside (I had a plan involving them that afternoon). On the overseas escort the alien's TD stays with the escorting officer the whole time. Theoretically it has completely fulfilled its purpose at the point in a foreign land when the officer hands it over to receiving officials along with the alien himself, and there should be no further need for it or the information it contains. In practice, however, it is essential to have copies of the TD in a criminal alien's file in anticipation of two events, both of which, from time to time, do occur: (1) The TD is lost. This is rare. When it happens, it is usually an officer's mistake, but not always. There are freak accidents and thefts by contractors or others sympathetic to the criminal alien cause. (2) The criminal alien illegally reenters America. This is more usual. A DO's ability to furnish a copy of the legitimate TD a particular government printed for a deportee the last time he was kicked out of the United States is by no means a guarantee that the government will print another one to help bring its degenerate heir home again, but it doesn't hurt. It is marginally easier to shame a consulate into reissuing when you can say, "Of course he's from your country, Mr. Vice-Consul. You're looking at a copy of the travel document *you* issued on him two years ago." Marginally. There is no sure thing in the criminal alien war, least of all when your own government won't back you up, but DOs look for any edge they can get. I two-hole-punched the copies and set them in eleven stacks. I wrote the A-numbers on each photo page, along with the date.

I flipped open my file cabinets. In numeric sequence I located the A-files corresponding to my eleven new Chinese TDs and pulled them off the shelves. One at a time I flipped open the cover and clipped in the copy of the travel document, following that with the original TD in an envelope that could not be opened or removed from the file without particular effort to that end. Next I updated the local and nationwide computer screens to reflect that the TDs had been received. Finally, I took my red laser tracking wand and scanned the bar codes for all eleven files. With every beep, the system transferred a file to Departure Verification.

I loaded the files on a cart and pushed the cart down the hall. In the life of a Deportation Officer there is no feeling quite like this one. There are other parts of the job that satisfy. Apprehending criminal aliens on the street feels good, and I'd be lying if I said anything rewarded the physical senses as much as the hunt and takedown in the arena of bricks, asphalt, and open sky. But that step is so early in the deportation process that your awareness of your coming struggle smothers any sense of accomplishment you could feel. After the arrest everything can go wrong.

Now, however, this much later in the game, with only the trip left to check off, you are close enough that you allow yourself to hope. This is when hope first rushes into a DO. It is a sudden blood dope infusion that lifts the spirits like no other piece of the track. Success is possible. Success is near.

I pushed the cart through the wooden door into the detention area and onward to the left corner office. I stopped the cart at Manny's desk. Manny was used to seeing me drop files on his desk, but typically I hand-carried them. Typically I didn't need a cart.

"What do you have?" Manny asked me. His green uniform was pressed and sharp.

"Eleven Chinese."

"How many?"

"Eleven."

"Eleven *Chinese?*"

I nodded.

Manny's eyebrows lifted, and he pressed his lips together with anxiety for a moment. "How many are group threes?" He knew, because I was the officer pushing the cart, that these all were criminals. What he was asking is how many of the criminals fit into one or more special categories that required officers to escort them all the way to China. To reacquaint the reader, the categories are: violent, escape-prone, sick, and insane.

I answered, "All eleven."

For a moment Manny didn't breathe. Manny was our supervisory detention enforcement officer. Among his primary responsibilities was alien transportation, including repatriation flights. To help him handle this immense load, Manny had working for him a score or so of detention enforcement officers. DEOs were green-uniformed junior-grade officers charged with vital transportation, security, and custody functions pertaining to aliens. (Beginning in 2004, DEOs received additional training and position upgrades and were thereafter known as immigration enforcement agents.) Manny was slow to breathe because his staff was overloaded already. It wasn't Craig's Deportation Officers who took most of the trips when we finally had the aliens set to ship. There weren't enough days in our weeks for us to bring back our own aliens, even if we'd done it full-time. DOs managed escorts in the dicey cases that were predicted to require our uncommon diplomatic skills, fluency in immigration law, or other expertise thought highly developed in our line. For the remaining cases it was our fellow agents in Manny's crew who pulled the lion's share.

"How much time do we have?" Manny asked, bracing himself for a narrow window. A classic device employed by contentious governments in their quest to keep their undesirables in America was the imminent-expiration TD. Manny had seen more than his share of one-week-validity passports. A week minus however long the passport had taken to reach us in the mail. If we immigration agents didn't have enough time to schedule the trip, shame on us. Fortunately this was one tactic the PRC did not utilize.

I shared the good news with Manny: "A year." I didn't need to tell him the sooner, the better. Manny knew that. Like a significant portion of immigration agents, Manny was a naturalized U.S. citizen (in his case from Honduras), and like many naturalized U.S. citizens, he was more offended by depraved aliens than I was. He'd assign the trips to his workforce as fast as he effectively could and his DEOs, who were extremely proficient at their jobs, would execute with like speed.

I lifted up the top A-file in the cart and extended it to Manny. "This one's priority."

"Okay."

"Whoever gets it, let them know, he is a rabbit."

Manny nodded while leafing through the file of Wareng Chow. "I'll put Pullet and Boyd on this," he said, observing Wareng's history of violence and flight.

"He's at OPP," I said. "If you can pull this off without letting him see it coming, I recommend it."

"You think he'd try to escape from the jail?"

"It's been done. But more likely he'll find a lawyer to get some freeze put on his removal."

Manny shook his head. "Like a private bill or something?"

"Or a habeas petition. Or a civil suit. These guys have all the options in the world. That's why I'm staying away from him. I don't want him to read my face and know he's going back. If he stops here on the way out, though, I'd love to say good-bye."

"I'll call you," Manny said. He eyed the brown files in the cart. "What about the rest?"

"Just your average kidnappers, murderers, and triad boys. I'm going to go visit them." I walked out of Manny's office to do just that.

"Give 'em my best!" he called to me.

I hit the central corridor with a victorious step. Now, even if the letters from headquarters made it to my office, and some would, I was no longer legally obligated to release these gangsters. I was high and getting higher just thinking about what I was going to do next. I was brimming with energy, maybe too much, so I stopped by my gun locker to secure my H&K, and then I walked halfway down the hall to the ninth-floor weight room.

Deportation Officers were supposed to meet high physical standards, and to our upper management's credit, it was official policy to put us in the gym a few hours a week at full pay. It was often impractical since we DOs were out of the office much of the time and had our schedules pretty well locked up when we were here, but I took advantage of the deal when I could. The program was working for me. On the physical fitness test back at the academy I'd been able to bench 250 pounds just once, but now I could do it several times. I wasn't trying to add more weights. I just wanted to get faster. In most of the stories I heard about immigration agents getting hurt, it seemed they hadn't moved fast enough.

After the workout I showered and reholstered my .40-cal. I stepped to the vehicle key locker and pulled out the set for the blue Ford Crown Victoria. I opted not to take a government vehicle home on a daily basis. It made sense for some of my agent peers to keep a g-ride, especially the DOs who lived across Lake Pontchartrain to the north. It gave them the flexibility to go straight from home when they got called out for a far-off mission or when a sheriff's department paged them for help deep in the morning. The gas they saved on their long office commutes was a side bonus. I lived three miles from work, though. When we got the crisis order to report to 701 Loyola, I was always the first agent in. And when I was called out for a mission elsewhere that required a vehicle with a cage, it took me only five minutes to come here and switch. On the personal side, leaving work in my Accord at the end of the day gave me my own kind of flexibility to take whatever route and run whatever errands I felt like on my way home, without worrying about an OIG inspector following me and documenting my unauthorized use of a government vehicle.

I walked outside into the sunshine and marched down the sidewalk to the Macy's garage. The blue Crown Victoria was waiting for me on the fourth floor, where we contracted space for our unmarked deportation fleet. I turned the key and saw that the last agent who'd used it had left me with practically no fuel, so I cruised to the Exxon on Lee Circle to fill up before I climbed onto Interstate 10. I had ninety minutes of driving to get to Tangipahoa Parish Prison.

I tuned in the radio and settled into a favorable lane. Tangi (abbreviation pronounced "TAN-jee" by the deportation set) certainly conjured mixed emotions in me. When I drove up this freeway, I sometimes imagined I saw myself on the opposite side, coming the other direction with Rodolfo in the cage. Tangi was the prison where I'd picked him up and chauffeured him away to a life of freedom in my backyard. I couldn't think about Tangi without remembering Rodolfo for a painful instant. I also couldn't remember Rodolfo without thinking about what he symbolized: every dangerous alien going free.

Despite that searing association, there were aspects to the jail I liked a lot. It was seventy-five miles away from New Orleans, so it was just close and familiar enough to feel like home field, but not so close (like Orleans Parish Prison in my own zip code) that it felt as if these thugs were in my home. OPP had other disadvantages that overmatched its convenience factor, mainly the aliens' proximity to their big-city lawyers, who chiseled away at their deportation warrants, expunged records, enlisted congressional intervention, and played every other legal game to help their clients beat the system. By contrast, Tangipahoa was something of an island. My current run across the bayou highlighted that point. Past Louis Armstrong International Airport on 10, till well after the switch to I-55, it was all swamp and water beneath me. It was good country out here. It was the kind of place where a man could breathe God's air and get some monumental work done on his own.

By the time I made the Amite turnoff, it was the prisoners' mealtime (referred to as feed-up at this particular facility, always injecting my mind with a Wild West image I thought suited it). The jail staff didn't care for visitors during feed-up since it added one more security headache during a chaotic time, and I respected that. I decided to take a parallel lunch. I pulled into Popeyes and brought my bag in with me so I could get some preparation done while I ate my spicy chicken.

When the timing was right and I had my papers in order, I got back in the Crown Vic and doubled back on West Oak Street. I turned right at the light and curled left behind the Winn-Dixie into the jail lot.

I thought of Phil when I stepped from the sedan. I had already come several times without him, but Phil and I had spent so much time at Tangi—for alien-packed classroom briefings to explain the latest adaptations in immigration law, jail liaison, dorm visits, melees with detours to the local emergency rooms, rollouts, roll-ins, vanloads, busloads, early-morning pickups to crack-of-dawn international flights—I'd probably always miss my old partner when I swung by. But it was a new game now. I locked my gun in the safe and stared over the car roof. I regarded the Tangi fortress in a new, stark light. For the alien aggravated felons inside, this was their final stop before either deportation or liberation, depending on my success. This was the battleground upon which my personal immigration fight would be won or lost.

I walked through the entrance into the visitor waiting room and raised my credentials to the mirrored glass. The door to my immediate front released, and I pushed inside amid the painted cinder-block walls and the corrections officers in blue uniforms. I saluted the warden and assistant warden, who were talking in the administrative bay on the other side of the counter. The three of us enjoyed some small talk before Deputy Cox arrived from the dorms.

I cut back with Deputy Cox in the direction from which he'd just come, and we stopped in the last room. New Orleans Deportation kept enough aliens in here that the warden had dedicated a deputy to manage them. He'd chosen Al Cox for the job, and he'd given him this office.

"Hey, we had a little incident in Dorm Y last night," Cox said, pulling the door in for a little shield. "Your latest group of Chinese boys put a bunch of our soul brothers in the clinic."

"Shoot. Why didn't you page me?" I asked.

"It wasn't no big deal. It was funny." The deputy snickered. "Them soul brothers started it. They thought they was dealing with some of them starving Chinese stowaways you guys bring us from the ships. Decided to bust up their game of checkers."

"Oh, no," I said.

"Oh, yeah." Cox cackled. "And I guess these Chinese is real gangsters—"

"Straight out of the tongs," I said.

"Well, these boys fucked them up some American convicts." Cox howled. "There was equal numbers—all upstairs is local inmates, and all downstairs is Chinese—and when they first got into it, I was fixing to run in there, but Sarge told me just wait, so we stood there outside and watched the show. The Chinese boys ended up throwing our local inmates up the stairs in a big pile. It was like Jackie Chan in there, only they wasn't no chop sockey shit. It was just street brawling. Crazy."

"Man, please send me the report when you finish it. I need to put it in their A-files."

"Hey, no problem," Cox said. "Sorry. I would've called you, but none of the INOs got hurt." INOs were the immigration detainees. I didn't know exactly what *INO* stood for, but like *feed-up,* it was a part of Tangi's vernacular I'd picked up by context.

I said, "I need to see them today anyway. Can we do a full walk-through?"

"Everybody? Sure."

"Cool," I said. "Then afterward we'll bring the Chinese up front."

"Sounds good," said Deputy Cox. I left my bag in his office, and we stepped out together. Cox spoke into his radio, signaling ahead to the other corrections officers in the wings, and we pushed through the heavy gate into the main prison.

Aliens were all over this facility. They were mixed in with state and local offenders according to crimes. My armed robbers were housed with American armed robbers, and so on. The aliens frequently complained about this arrangement, arguing that they should have been placed with nonviolent offenders since the aliens had completed their criminal sentences already and should not have been forced to live alongside hardened convicts still serving, but I appreciated the jail policy, not least because many of my aliens hadn't completed those sentences. Besides, I'd witnessed the result with the alternative. Detention facilities in the past had succumbed to political pressure and tried the criminal alien logic in categorizing deportable aggravated felons as administrative cases and housing them with American shoplifters and traffic violators, but the result was always the same: alien felons on top running commissary extortion and other rackets while a bunch of scared local inmates serving ninety days for hot checks or marijuana forked over whatever currency they had for shower privileges, toilet paper, and their meals, among other jail-issued necessities the hardened aliens appropriated as their own to control and sell.

So in Tangi I had aliens in multiple wings, named by compass direction (e.g., north wing), and within the wings multiple dorms, distinguished by letter (e.g., U dorm). Deputy Cox knew where every one of them was in the labyrinth. I was grateful for the warden's judgment in assigning the immigration post to one of his best men. It would have been a gift to have any single contact to keep me informed about my aliens, but when that contact was as motivated as Deputy Cox, it made it even better.

Through the wings we marched. I carried my orange notebook labeled "Tangipahoa Parish Prison Liaison" from dorm to dorm. It contained documentation from my previous visits, including disciplinary reports and Polaroids from the injuries sustained in the fights, along with the question-and-answer pages that were the heart of my jail visits. The aliens had numerous questions about their cases, their rights, their money, their personal property, rumors they'd heard about their home countries or revolutions in U.S. immigration law, and a range of other topics, so every couple of weeks I'd come in here and let them ask me new ones while I gave them answers to the questions they'd submitted last time around.

From dorm to dorm aliens posed so many of the same questions that Deputy Cox was frequently able to answer them for me while I fielded the next. Cox was a force for good. As a corrections officer he knew the rules for running a stable jail, probably the most important of which was to be fair. I'd never seen him handle an inmate in his prison differently from another on the basis of anything but behavior. He applied the rules with an even hand. Cox was around six foot four, 275 pounds with no fat, so he was also the perfect guy to have on your side in the prisoner bays when the aliens were sizing you up.

And they were. More than in any other place, a DO feels the aliens watching him in prison. Outside, on the street, an alien carries an awareness that this is not his territory but yours. In jail, where the wings take on a feeling of sovereign resident soil, that sentiment is reversed. A DO is coming to *their* home when he steps into the aliens' dorms. And unlike the corrections officers, the DO is a pure visitor, far from his comfort zone.

I felt the aliens in their orange prison jumpsuits studying me, wondering if they could take me. Perhaps some of them had already decided that they could, and would, and they were only waiting for that perfect moment. I had been in prisons at times of crisis. I knew what the air felt like when aliens rose up. The unsettling thing was that that air did not differ much from this air. Those scenes of blood, shanks, and hostages and desperate aliens leveraging their tenuous control were the same scene I was in now, just fifteen seconds in the future if the aliens decided to spring. I kept my eyes open while I answered questions in the orange field. I stared back, all robot and cold water. I tried to give them nothing to read.

Tangi's dorms were two stories. Some grim-visaged aliens who had no questions and didn't care to learn anything preferred to stand behind the railings of the upper decks and stare down on me rather than join the horseshoe crowd around me on the floor. These antisocial aliens on their perches added a vertical depth to the scene that kept me scanning high as well as right and left. My eyes searched their hands for batteries, chunks of concrete, and the other missiles whose downward flight gravity would assist. After I answered the floor questions, I walked up the steps, to get a better look at the uncommunicative aliens and their cells and to appraise the perspective they'd owned when they'd been staring down at me.

Through the wings we proceeded, each dorm erupting as I approached and clinging as I left. The topic the aliens were most fervent about was their imminent releases. There was a popular rumor that they all were going to be set free. They clamored to learn about the *Zadvydas* decision, and what it meant to them. That Supreme Court action had actually come down months ago, when Phil had still been my partner, and we had brought Tangi's aliens up to the classroom, where Phil had given a clear briefing on *Zadvydas* and its ramifications for all our aliens to digest. But back then before our DC headquarters had implemented it, it must have seemed too abstract for our aliens to grasp. By now the *Zadvydas* decision was no longer abstract. It was upon us with a vengeance.

Now is as good a time as any to explain it to the reader.

The *Zadvydas remand*—technically not a decision but still referred to as the *Zadvydas* decision in immigration circles—was the product of a legal fight that began before I came on board and stretched all the way to the year of our story. The case with momentous national consequences had been born right here in the swamp, as *Zadvydas v. Underdown,* when self-claimed "stateless" alien Kestutis Zadvydas originally challenged New Orleans district director Lynne Underdown's right to detain him.

An intelligent blonde and a former Border Patrol agent, Underdown had been in charge of deportation for our five-state region (Lynne was Hortense's predecessor) before moving up to oversee a phenomenally aggressive enforcement period as New Orleans's first female district director. In Underdown's reign, criminal alien arrest rates peaked, as did detention tallies. Characteristically, Underdown refused to release career criminal Zadvydas, who'd been born in Germany to Lithuanian parents, while her DO subordinates tried to get either country to accept him. Zadvydas appealed to the courts on an assertion that our agency had no chance of removing him and that his continued detention amounted to indefinite imprisonment, a violation of his due process.

Underdown transferred (to the Border Patrol's Miami sector, where she shattered another barrier by becoming the first female chief patrol agent), and the case pushed ahead without her, taking on the names of New Orleans's subsequent district directors in a *Zadvydas v.* —————— fill-in-the-blanks exercise through its conclusion. (I served under Underdown in my first year. She'd been the authority who'd signed off on my hire after my interview with her and Craig.)

In the case of Zadvydas, the Fifth Circuit Court of Appeals finally weighed in on our side. Doubting Zadvydas's claim of nonremovability, the court denied his appeal and left us with its imprimatur to conduct business as usual.

But not for long. The notorious case came back to life when interested appellants cited a contrary judgment from the Ninth Circuit Court of Appeals (western states) in the similar case of Kim Ho Ma, a Cambodian convicted for a gang killing. As the application of U.S. immigration law was a national matter, it was inappropriate to have standards vary by region. Both items, *Zadvydas* and *Ma,* were consolidated for higher review.

This was the year the criminal aliens won. The Supreme Court remanded the case with language that effectively finished our agency's practice of keeping dangerous deportable aliens off the street until their countries took them back. The highest levels of the INS had subsequently developed a new national policy following the spirit of the Supreme Court guidance. (Upon HQ's promulgation of this policy, in which it'd wrested ultimate custody authority from the districts, a reader may remember Craig had delivered his infamous briefing to all his DOs, with the prophetic conclusion "Expect to execute a lot of releases.")

Today, from dorm to dorm, I addressed the aliens, teaching updated classes of my own, not only on the history of the *Zadvydas* decision but on its immediate meaning to the aggravated felons before me.

"How long can you keep us here?" the aliens demanded.

"I can keep you for a hundred eighty days total," I told them. "On the hundred eightieth day, headquarters takes over your custody, and I have no authority to detain or release you."

"Immigration been had me for more than one hundred eighty days!" someone always yelled.

"Then you will probably get your release letter soon," I answered. "I have no authority to detain *or release* you. You have the address for headquarters in DC. Write them."

"But you're still gonna try to get my country to take me."

"Correct. My job is to get your government to send me your travel document before my government sends me your release letter."

The groans and protests showered down after that, but as vociferous as they were, I barely heard them over my own last words resounding. The clarity of my mission statement was so magnetic that for a moment I could think of nothing else.

When at last I finished with the dorm visits and pushed through the final gate from the main prison, I turned to Deputy Cox outside his office and allowed a smile to break across my face. My smile should not have been taken for relief because what I'd just done was unpleasant. I never minded the jail tours. My smile was restless and forward-looking, driven by the coming announcement I'd been cycling in my head all day.

I shared my plan with Deputy Cox.

"They're not going to like it," he said, grinning with just a trace of anxiety.

"Do you think we should get more deputies?"

"Won't hurt." Cox called on the radio for some support. Then he flipped through his detention rosters and began radioing the respective control guards to send the detainees he named up to the classroom.

The aliens dragged in getting there, no doubt taking advantage of their rare consolidation to trade gossip and inimical plots during their fitful advance up the hallway. Within ten minutes, though, it was done. Now they pooled inside the entrance of the classroom. I stood near them. Deputy Cox was several feet behind me, next to the unoccupied teacher's desk. The student desks were arranged neatly, running wall to wall, a large sea of straight rows and surfaces scrubbed clean by the industry of jail trustees.

The desks were empty, and the Chinese looked at the desks and then at me.

I spoke to them. "No need to sit down. This'll be quick." They stopped where they were, with their backs to the light blue paint on the wall. There were nearly thirty of them in their orange jumpsuits. They included every Chinese detainee at this prison. Two had been brought in from medical cells. The first of these two was insane. He was filthy, and his own excrement coated his face. The other was so antisocial that he attacked anyone he lived with. He had shuffled in here in full body chains, eight-link leg irons keeping his steps short. The rest of them were just regular aggravated felons, legally credited with multiple rapes, homicides, intimidation schemes, protection rackets, extortions, kidnappings, and carjackings, and innumerable shattered lives between them. I looked through the reinforced glass square in the door to the right of them and saw a pair of deputies peering back my way.

"I know I just talked to you all," I told the group, "but I wanted to bring you here specially to tell you this."

I lifted my sheaf of white sheets. As I read from each, I peeled the top sheet off and rotated it to the back, and in this manner I began to identify the chosen: "Qing Ren Li. Hua Zhen. Cheng Loe Zhu. Dong Yong Chen."

As I read, something unexpected happened. The group began to laugh. They couldn't control their joy. Each name produced grips and cheers from the increasingly glowing pack.

I was confused. Then suddenly I was struck with the reason. These Chinese thought they were going to be released. I hadn't planned it this way, nor would I have, but I should have foreseen how it matched the sentiment of the hour. As I continued, I realized my unemotional mien had contributed to the misunderstanding because it allowed the aliens to read the assembly the way they wanted to. With Washington ordering so many criminals liberated, it was the natural expectation of every one of these felons that he was on his way out the door. Pretty much everyone I looked at was grinning, save for the two from the medical cells. And that twosome's reason for not reacting was not that Washington wouldn't release them. HQ released the insane and the clinically destructive as quickly as they released everyone else. Alien advocacy groups frequently petitioned for the release of such remarkable causes, initially offering sponsorship and then dropping the berserkers like hot potatoes into society at large as soon as they were free, leaving the advocacy groups to take up the next remarkable cause. No, the reason the two here were not laughing with their countrymen was that the crazy one had no particular desire to be free and the antagonistic one was so freighted with hate that there was no room for joy in his whole being.

"Bing Sheng Hoang. Gui Lin Zhao. Kun Bai Hui. Yung Shen Wu. Jing Yang. Xiang Min Lu."

I had named ten of them, fully a third of the felons before me. I looked at the blue-uniformed deputies, and then I looked back at the men in the orange jumpsuits. "You're going home," I told them. "By home, I mean China and Hong Kong. I just read your names off your travel documents."

My orange-clad audience froze, mute and white. The joy vanished from the room in a sudden suck. The extra security turned out to be superfluous because these Chinese were broken.

I wasn't sadistic, and nothing like cruelty was behind my presentation. I think I just saw I was in a war, and I thought it was best to acknowledge it. Even if the highest levels of our government were busy surrendering a piece at a time, we DOs on the front lines were digging in to fight and win. I knew what effect my announcement would have. The news hit the PRCs hard and then sent a shock wave through every other nationality in the criminal alien horde.

If the Chinese weren't safe, no one was.

SEVEN

Archimedes Daye and the Suriname Switch

"Hello, Mr. Dua. This is Ames Holbrook from New Orleans Deportation."

"Okay. Mr. Holbrook. Very nice." His speech had a quick rhythm.

"How are you today, sir?"

"Very fine, thank you."

"Excellent, Mr. Dua."

"Are there others on the line?"

"No, sir. I . . . Just one moment, please, Mr. Dua." I turned over my shoulder and pushed the vent open with a crack. "Silence! You're shrieking so loud, people think you're on the phone with me. I'll tell you when you can say another word."

I'd tried to slide my thumb over the mouthpiece for that delivery, but apparently I hadn't effected the proper seal.

Mr. Dua asked, "Where are you?"

"I'm sorry, sir. I'm driving. There are a couple of guys in the back who'll be leaving my country in the near future."

"Indians?"

"Oh, no, sir. But if you'd like to take two Italian career burglars, I'll be happy to send them to you."

"No, *thank you,*" he proclaimed decisively. We laughed together.

"I normally wouldn't call you from the car, sir, but the timing hasn't been working out lately, and I wanted to catch you before your lunch." On the basis of my efforts to reach him on previous afternoons, I surmised Mr. Dua's daily lunch lasted until he went home for dinner.

"Very good you did," he told me. "So, you received the package."

"Package, sir? Which one?"

"The two travel documents. I sent you the FedEx yesterday afternoon."

I pulled off the road to avoid crashing in excitement. "Beautiful, Mr. Dua. They're at my office then."

"Would you like me to read you the tracking numbers?"

"No need, sir. I'm sure they're waiting for me." Better to show I trusted him. Besides, the Indians would have used the prepaid return air bills I'd included with the TD requests. I had those photocopied in the files, so I could track the envelopes myself.

Vice-Consul Dua spoke again. "You'll have another one next week. I think Suman Parek. And we're still following the others."

"Thank you very much, Mr. Dua. I look forward to the others also." I tried to sound calm. I wanted to layer a combination of appreciation that I was dealing with such a professional with an accompanying expectation that this was how the process was supposed to work. I did not want Dua to think he was going beyond. I wanted him to keep cutting TDs until every deportable Indian in New Orleans was back on the subcontinent.

"No problem, Mr. Holbrook."

We traded a few lines before we hung up. I slid the vent open and told my Italians they could resume their chatter. Nothing could bother me now. I pulled back onto the road. Despite my act for Dua, I was anything but calm. I was ecstatic. The Indian consulate had been a lost cause forever. The very idea that its tap was open intoxicated me. This was another direct dividend from the Houston trip. It was the way things were working for me lately. The forbidden tree continued to yield fruit.

I rolled the Italians into Orleans Parish Prison and, returning to the g-ride, retrieved my H&K from the safe. With my head in the trunk I heard the muted ring of my phone up front. Not only did OPP prohibit guns in its facility—standard—but it also wouldn't let us bring in our cell phones. That would be another reason that not long from now, I would write this jail off. In my campaign of subterfuge, the telephone was to become my greatest tool.

I scrambled around to the front and unlocked the door. I was happy to hear the loud ring signaling the caller hadn't given up. News had been good lately, and I didn't want to miss a single bulletin. My excitement ebbed when caller ID indicated the home office and not some exotic consulate, but I answered. "This is Ames."

"Ames, Sam." Sam was my docket clerk at 701 Loyola. He was a good-natured blond youngster who would later become an agent. For now he was getting some valuable experience in the most instructive sink-or-swim docket imaginable. "Your friend Tad Thomas called."

"Wow, I haven't talked to him in a while." Tad Thomas worked out of the embassy of Jamaica. He had the power to issue TDs. Unfortunately, with New Orleans's bountiful Jamaican population providing a constant stream of aggravated felons, at some point last year Mr. Thomas seemed to have gotten tired of my unquenchable thirst for his documents. He'd referred me to a consular officer in Miami, and from that point the aggravated felon ranks had outstripped the TD issuance to the point that HQ was now springing Jamaicans out of my docket with distressing regularity.

"He said he's going to call you again Wednesday morning," Sam said. "I don't know what he wants to talk about, but it sounded good."

"It sounds great. All right, I'll prepare for Tad. And you will, right now, fill out a transportation sheet to get our six worst Jamaicans to the office on Wednesday."

"Uh . . . Six *worst* as determined by what?"

"The guys who are about to get out who you don't want living next to your mom. Check our database for all the Jamaicans we've had longer than five months and then look at their crimes."

"Sebastian Willows?" Sam asked, referring to the rare-even-in-New-Orleans combination serial rapist–serial arsonist we'd just transferred after he'd tried to set fire to his cellmate at the last facility.

"Perfect!" I said ardently. "Start with him! You've got five more."

"You don't want Archimedes Daye?"

"Absolutely not. First of all, he's just a regular armed robber, and far more important, we don't want him souring the whole pot when he swears to Tad that he's never been to Jamaica. 'I was born in the Virgin Islands of the United States.'" I pronounced the last part as Archimedes Daye himself. "We start in the box, Sam. We'll get to the wild ones."

"Won't you feel a little stupid if Tad doesn't want to talk to these guys and you brought six bad Jamaicans downtown for no reason?"

"Sam, I'd feel stupid if I *didn't* have six bad Jamaicans in the office when Tad called. What is luck, Sam?"

"Opportunity meets preparation."

"Oh, I almost forgot. Check out all the release letters from HQ and any more that come in. Any Jamaicans, add them to your six for Wednesday."

"But I thought we can't delay releases—"

"We can't," I said. "But if Tad Thomas overnights the TDs, we have a chance."

"I'm on it!" Sam said.

I hung up after Sam and slid behind the wheel, buoyed further by my docket clerk's enthusiasm. Many of Immigration's administrative workers were indifferent to our mission or, worse, saw themselves as champions of the criminal aliens. There were exceptions, and Sam was one of them. As an agent in training Sam worked zealously to advance the deportation cause. Craig had assigned the proper clerk to my nasty boys.

I merged out into Tulane Avenue traffic, thinking about Tad Thomas and happily contemplating this new age when *the diplomats called me.* It was a supernatural point on the DO timeline, and I vowed to stretch it as far as it would go.

I rode the wave of my PRC score. I kicked into high gear with other embassies, forging relationships wherever I could. Every time I set foot in the office, I stopped by my desk and dialed the 202 area code. I chipped at those embassies in DC, and when they tried to pawn me off on a consulate whose jurisdiction I was supposedly in, I made sure to get the name of someone very important at the embassy, so I could say he sent me.

Diplomatic goodwill was gold, but it wasn't the only commodity that made TDs appear. There was also luck. And the lessons luck taught. One afternoon a DO from the nondetained side came to me with a travel document for a problematic Surinamer. As soon as I saw the picture, I recognized the career mugger. I had no Suriname contacts whatsoever, and until this moment I didn't even know that Dutch-speaking patch of South America even issued.

"Where'd this come from, Rolf?" I asked.

"The consulate addressed it to me, but he's not mine. I looked him up in DACS and saw your ID."

"Yeah, he's mine. He's a violent maniac. The consulate won't even talk to me about this guy. How did you do it?"

"I didn't," Rolf said. "That's what I'm trying to tell you. I've never seen him before."

"But they sent it to you," I spoke quietly, absorbed in discovering the reason.

Rolf nodded. "Everything—the cover letter, the envelope—had my name on it. Actually, the envelope was the return envelope I addressed to myself for *my* alien."

"Wait, you asked them for a TD for another alien?"

"That's right," Rolf said. "I'm still waiting for it."

"The consulate mixed them up," I declared. I went over it for both of us. "In the past two years I must have sent forty photos of my guy in request packages. The consular officer's desk is probably covered with them. Can't you see him slapping the TD together, accidentally grabbing up one of my packets?"

"Oh, no." Rolf grimaced.

"No, this is *great*," I said. "What did your guy do?"

"Fraud marriage. Something like that."

"So, look," I said excitedly, "we're going to get rid of a psychotic criminal. Do me a favor, Rolf. Your guy's on the street already, right? And your case is current? No problems, no one's going to complain if his file sits on the shelf a little while?"

Rolf nodded to all of it.

"So leave it alone till after next week, please. I'll tell you when my mugger makes Paramaribo, and then you can phone Suriname and say you're still waiting for your TD. By then it'll be too late for them to cancel mine."

Nations did indeed revoke travel documents when they had second thoughts. Consulates sent nasty dispatches threatening that any attempt to use the document would result in the freezing of all repatriations. It was tough to have a TD in the file and not use it, but there were times when it was best to swallow your pride and drive on. Such had been my experience with Don Hankins, the honorary consul general of St. Vincent in New Orleans. I'd enjoyed a positive relationship with Hankins, and then one day he'd rebuked me for "forum shopping" because he'd learned the New York consulate had already refused to issue on a violent felon who was the case Don had just issued on. Its objection? The felon had AIDS, and he was best served by America's Medicaid system. Hankins demanded I not use the travel document, and as strongly as I disagreed with the expectation that America should underwrite AIDS therapy for the world's violent criminals, I gave in to the demand. I couldn't afford to offend Hankins, who was still more friend than foe. He issued on other felons, and from my experience with St. Vincent, that made him one of a kind.

Rolf agreed to set his Surinamer aside. That was a luxury of the non-detained docket. Aliens running free didn't file suits or create any kind of legal friction for the deportation program. Free aliens, in fact, *preferred* their Deportation Officers to forget about them. There wasn't a clock on nondetained, and those DOs didn't have to race.

But I did. My mind revved as I thought about the TD in my fingers. There was no question in my mind that Suriname had issued on a toxic citizen because it believed him harmless. I'd always known countries behaved this way, that their issue decisions were predicated on whether their sons promised to be productive or destructive in their homelands. Some countries made no secret of the system. Governments from Barbados to Cape Verde protested that they should not have to accept citizens "who learned their criminal ways in the United States." But this Suriname mismatch brought the theory right into my hand. It had answered the question, How do you get a TD for a psychotic mugger? with the solution, Downgrade his conviction to marriage fraud.

I processed the Surinamer's file and brought it to Manny. I got word the next week that the mugger had gone home quietly.

It was then, in the arena of TD acquisition, I began the practice of minimizing criminal records. At first it was just a matter of picking an alien's lightest crime. If a rapist had been convicted of trespassing along with the rape, I cited the trespassing charge when requesting a travel document. Later and deeper into the game I tried not to mention any crime at all. I downplayed or omitted criminal history to problem nations across the board. This was counter to regulation. My side had made the rules on the ground that receiving nations had a right to know the dangers posed by their returning citizens. That was a fine notion, but it had been born in another time, before we were obligated to release dangerous "nonremovables" to our own streets. Today the criminals were destined to be released, one way or another. They would be free to prey on a fresh set of victims, either in their own countries or in mine. For my part, I had not taken an oath to protect other countries. I had sworn to protect America. What I was doing now was compensating for governments that should not have been stalling in the first place. If a country did not have a backlog, I was forthright. If countries insisted on keeping their criminals in my country, then it was they who forced my hand.

The TDs came in. My relationships with the diplomats and my new tactics all were paying off. And something else happened in conjunction. I managed to develop momentum. It was a very positive kind of momentum that drove results even when I wasn't exerting them. "When it rains, it pours," the saying goes. That's how it felt. It was pouring.

The glut of TDs produced a side effect I never could have imagined: A significant number of my aliens started to play ball. Perceiving they were now more likely to be deported than not, many of the criminal aliens wanted to have a hand in their destinies. They began volunteering to talk with their consulates, to come clean and provide accurate biographic details for a change, and some even surrendered their own passports. Families were mailing passports to my office weekly, and still more passports and national identity cards were mailed directly to the jails. The jail staff, who opened and inspected all mail, usually intercepted these latter documents for me, but even a few that slipped through ended up in my hands when the aliens presented them to me during visits.

One day a Chinese detainee approached me to request a private conference. He'd been convicted of ripping off a southern casino to the tune of thirty thousand dollars.

When I had him alone, the young man said. "Officer Holbrook, I can get my passport." His English was very understandable.

"Good. Then I advise you do it."

"I have a problem." He swept his face with his hand, stalling to prepare his statement.

"Just say it, Mr. Hor."

"I can't go to Beijing."

"Well, where do you propose to go?" I immediately feared he was like so many other criminal aliens who didn't want to stay in jail but refused to go to their home countries, resulting in a net standstill. As hard as it was to get these outlaws' rightful motherlands to take them in, it was nearly impossible to find other countries willing to accept them. So a criminal alien's offer to be sent anywhere except where he came from was the emptiest possible gift.

"Anywhere you send me. I just can't go to Beijing."

I assumed he'd intended Beijing as a symbol for all of China. I replied facetiously: "I'll fly you into Shanghai then."

"Can you do that?"

I blinked at the unexpected response. "What? No, Beijing, but yes, Shanghai?"

"Yes, Shanghai," he said.

"Why is that so different?"

"You don't understand. The cops in China . . . they are very bad. In Beijing they throw us in jail. They beat us bad. All of us when we go back." As he spoke, his eyes nervously searched our empty room, as if he expected Chinese police to crash in at any moment to beat him. "They take our money. I have money. I don't want to lose it. You don't understand how China is different. In America cops A Number One!" He jabbed both thumbs up enthusiastically at this pronouncement. "In China cops very bad. They beat us and steal."

"Okay. But if the problem is *Chinese* cops, how will Shanghai be any better than Beijing?"

"All the Chinese deport from America back to Beijing. In Beijing they wait for us. It's a business. Beat us, jail us, steal us. No money left. Cops get all money from all Chinese deport in Beijing."

"If you go to Shanghai, there's no guarantee it'll be any different," I said.

"No one ever deport to Shanghai," the young man stated positively. "They don't expect. I have a chance."

I said, "I'll bring you to Shanghai."

"Thank you, Officer Holbrook." He squeezed his hands together in front of his face and bowed. He seemed close to tears. "Thank you. Thank you."

"Don't thank me," I said. "I'm just trying to get you out of my country."

"I know, but you're not doing it mean."

"Hey, Mr. Hor, you still could be beaten and robbed in Shanghai. And if you think I can stop it, you're wrong. U.S. officers have no control once we land."

What I said was fact. Some foreign airport authorities went out of their way to demonstrate the impotence of U.S. enforcers on their soil. I'd had my steel handcuffs taken from me enough times that I now traveled with string restraints. And my trials had been trivial. Some peers had been injected with syringes under duress in outland airports and then forced to pay cash for the dubious immunizations. Still other American officers had been arrested outright. "If Shanghai cops beat you and take your fortune in front of my eyes, there's nothing I can do. You understand?"

He answered not in words but by reaching into his waistband and pulling out his passport.

I would end up being the lead officer to escort Mr. Hor back. Managers would sign off on the use of my valuable DO time to pioneer the route since Shanghai was an untried handoff point. The route would work like a charm. An exuberant Mr. Hor would catch up with me outside the airport and offer to treat me and my fellow officer to a Chinese feast. I would decline and wish him luck.

From the beginning I suspected Hor's stash might have been part of the ill-gotten thirty-thousand-dollar casino money that had never been recovered, but I knew any attempt to dig into that stood to derail his return to China, perhaps eternally. The way I saw it, if the casino got its money back, it'd also get Mr. Hor back to rip it off again. And Hor was apt to become an unlawful but nonetheless permanent resident of the United States. The decision of whether to miss a window of removal for a criminal alien for the purpose of further investigation or prosecution was one DOs had to weigh frequently, and I consistently opted to get the alien out when I could.

My docket was loaded with aliens who had been caught carrying drugs into America's airports. Rather than send this class of alien back on the same plane straightaway (a legal burden imposed upon international carriers), airport inspectors followed procedure and prosecuted the invading offenders. After the drug mule had served his year or two in prison, deportation programs then attempted to effect the accompanying removal order, only to find that the airline was no longer in business, the alien's identity and nationality were in question, or other manner of obstacle stood in the way of the drug mule's repatriation. The mule was then released to the American streets, whereupon he would demonstrate that smuggling drugs was only the most wholesome sample of his criminal behavior. The drugs had been a way in, but at heart the alien was really a car thief, terrorist, bank robber, child molester, or even a combination, and since no country was claiming him, he'd be here in America for the long haul. Those airport mule cases had disillusioned me for life.

The lagniappe of Mr. Hor's trip to Shanghai was that he became what we DOs referred to as a multiplier. He wrote his friends in prison to report the shocking absence of corrupt and sadistic authorities at the Shanghai airport, and those with the most to lose approached me for the same deal. Had Mr. Ji at the PRC consulate not been sending travel documents to me concurrently, this would not have happened. Only because the aliens calculated they stood to be deported one way or another did they decide it was safer to steer their own ships.

I offered a deal across the board, not just to my Chinese but to all my aliens, regardless of nationality, since there was plenty of anecdotal evidence to suggest that airport intimidation spanned the globe. The deal was: Get me your passport, pick your airport. The aliens terrified by the likes of Beijing, Zagreb, or Tegucigalpa were welcome to touch down in Guangzhou, Dubrovnik, or San Pedro Sula if only they got me TDs. Those who failed to assist me, I promised, would be thrown to the dogs.

At that instant of my professional flight, it seemed as if I were in a tornado of TDs. I had only to snatch them out of the air.

Then, in the eye of the whirlwind, I got a call that stopped my pulse.

"My good friend, Officer Holbrook. How have you been?"

"I'm terrific, Mr. Ji. How are you, sir?"

"I am fine. I have your passport here."

He didn't mean a Chinese national's passport for me. He meant *my* passport, the special red-jacketed passport my government had issued me for official travel. I said, "Wonderful, sir."

"So I will put the official visa inside and send it in your envelope so you will get it tomorrow."

"Thank you, Mr. Ji."

"I hope that you will enjoy my country."

"I'm sure I will, sir. I'm going to take some extra days."

"Good." Ji sighed. I knew he had something else to say, but it was a long time before it came. "It has been a great pleasure to work with you, Officer Holbrook," he said at last. "I have taken a new position, and I am afraid I will not have the privilege to continue working with you so closely."

Suddenly it was I who had trouble finding words. I managed to say, "Congratulations, sir."

"Thank you."

I struggled on. "I hope we can stay in touch."

"Of course!" he asserted. "I consider you my good friend. I will be here in Houston still. Please call me anytime there is something you wish to speak to me about."

"You *are* a good friend, sir. Please call me too, for anything. My contacts run far and wide."

"I am sure of that." Mr. Ji chuckled. "So, may I take this opportunity to introduce you to my successor?"

I sat up alertly in my chair. "Absolutely!"

"I have prepared Mr. Cai for the unique challenges presented by your special cases. New Orleans, I have told him, has no shortage of lawbreakers, very exceptional lawbreakers."

I laughed aloud at his delicate phrasing. "Thanks a lot, Mr. Ji."

"I have also told Mr. Cai of our close relationship. He is looking forward to working with you as successfully as we have together. Good-bye, Officer Holbrook. Here is Mr. Cai."

"Good-bye, Mr. Ji."

"Hello?" came the fresh voice on the line. "Officer Holbrook?"

And so the torch was passed.

I was incredibly nervous about Cai. I dreaded more than anything going back to the old days of once-in-a-blue-moon travel document issue from the PRC. As a breed once considered nonremovable but now flying out of my docket, the Chinese aggravated felons were an integral part of my momentum. I thought about speeding down the freeway in fifth gear and suddenly shifting into reverse. Out drops the transmission. If the Chinese stopped now, it would break everything.

My fears turned out to be unfounded. I stayed in touch with Ji for special cases. Even more important, Mr. Cai proved just as ready to deal. And once Cai had given me enough to believe in him, I broke into newer territory still by orchestrating his historic diplomatic visit to New Orleans. I got headquarters to fund business-class air connections for the new vice-consul and a suite at the Hyatt Regency across the street from our office.

Over the days he was in town, I had every Chinese criminal in our system brought into the office, and I watched with satisfaction as Mr. Cai interviewed each one personally. Within a few months most of them were home in China.

My results got attention. I received accolades at work. Craig put me in for a performance incentive award, all the more affecting because I knew those rare, precious prizes of money or paid vacation required thorough written justification on the part of the supervisor who submitted the requests to headquarters. That Craig had devoted his important time to my enrichment meant a lot to me.

But more than anything, I loved watching the criminals fly. When I wasn't escorting them myself, I loved passing through the detention area and seeing TDs I'd acquired hanging on chrome clips on the magnetic assignment board, like glitter on a Christmas tree, and I loved when my fellow agents walked up and grabbed those trips off the board and confidently headed out the door to execute another warrant of deportation and close out another A-file to be shipped to the National Records Center in Missouri, where, with any luck, the file would sit for a hundred years until its destruction. And I loved when I received a letter from headquarters in DC ordering the liberation of an aggravated felon who was airborne at the very instant I read his name on the notice of release.

I loved when Tad Thomas called that following Wednesday and offered to start clearing New Orleans's long-term Jamaicans. I told Mr. Thomas I had seven Jamaicans in the holding cells at that moment. He interviewed them all—our six worst, as picked by Sam, and another who'd just come up on the HQ release list—and pledged to send their TDs by FedEx the next day. I expressed my gratitude to the high-placed Washington diplomat, who replied that he'd be happy to take care of any problematic Jamaicans for me in the future.

After I had said good-bye to Mr. Thomas, I informed the Jamaicans in the cells that they would be going home. I answered any questions they had: money, property, and the rest.

"Officer Holbrook," said one middle-aged Jamaican who had spent most of his life in jail.

"Yes, Mr. Curtis." I kept the cell door open and faced him.

"Do you remember when you told Archimedes Daye that when he wakes up one morning and realizes he's Jamaican, he should tell you?"

"Yes."

"He did, Mr. Holbrook. He woke up. He wants to talk to you."

Like that, it kept *pouring*.

I was sure I could win. I was sure I could do it all.

EIGHT

Africa and the King of the Beasts

Soraya was a surfer. She was on her board the first day I met her. I watched her radiating form glide across the icy fronts of the gray Pacific waves. I was in the waves too, but bodysurfing, a swordless knight in a realm where the true gods stood with both bare feet on boards.

She'd been eighteen, my goddess had, that day I first saw her in the waves.

Neither one of us would remember exactly when we'd fallen in love with the other, but it had not been long after that. The courtship took place in the ensuing months in the city that raised us both. We cruised the streets of San Francisco, sometimes with her surfboard on the roof. I laughed when out-of-town surfers rolled by and honked their horns on my side of the car and gave me the fraternal thumbs-up. Soraya fumed every time this happened, so hotly did she object to being mistaken for the girlfriend of the surfer instead of the surfer herself. It was a stereotype of another time.

San Francisco then was different from San Francisco now. Ocean Beach lacked parking signs, and throughout the year few cars sat along it, except during a handful of rare weather days when it was comfortable to strip down. The surfing scene was small. The few females who regularly paddled out on their surfboards to take on San Francisco's notorious refrigerator sets enjoyed a special brand of local fame. In fact, if you spent much time on Ocean Beach between the late 1980s and early 1990s, you probably laid eyes on Soraya, and chances are you remember her.

On this visit to our old hometown, more than ten years after I'd first glimpsed her in the water, she had already been recognized. I'd smiled when the young man pointed and said, "I remember you surfed Ocean Beach." His was a refrain I'd heard delivered by old volleyballers, and SF Irish drunks who used to watch her over bonfires, and the surfers who'd inhaled the icy salt spray alongside her at spots like Kelly's, VFW, Sloat, and #18.

Today Soraya and I looked out over our old hometown as we walked down the aisle. With that backdrop, we slid on our platinum bands. Our wedding was the greatest moment of my life.

My best man, Kishore, gave a moving toast afterward, from the ballroom of Sausalito's Alta Mira Hotel, with its lofty view across the bay. Though he did not mention it, Kishore was the friend who had given me my Honda Accord, the sedan whose polluting engine had sent our pulses pounding on the way to Houston on the imperiled official mission to the consulate of the PRC. The Accord had survived. It remained my primary vehicle, was still the car I drove to work every day. Kishore had been my roommate at the University of Hawaii. He was an immigrant from India.

Forty percent of the guys who'd stood for me were immigrants—two foreign-born groomsmen beside the three whose Irish, German, and Mexican paternal lines had landed in America at least a generation before. Julius, born in the Philippines, came my way now in his groomsman jacket of purple Thai rain silk. He bear-hugged me without saying a word. His eyes were redder than mine.

The string quartet that played out in the sunshine packed up at my signal. A jazz band began to play upstairs. Another wave of toasts sprang out. Before long it was my turn to speak. I'd contributed some emotional words at the rehearsal dinner at the Ocean Beach–overlooking Cliff House the night before, so I steered toward mirth today, albeit with some deceptively deep setups. I felt overwhelming gratitude as I looked into the crowd of more than one hundred. My eyes found two immigration agent friends on the balcony outside. Eddy Wang and Sam Chung had been my closest pals in the basic training course, though we had branched off into separate curricula for a portion of our training. Like most DOs, I'd gone through the academy with only a handful of others bound for the recondite battlefield of Deportation (the rest of my class had headed for Investigations). With a maintained stock of fewer than 600 agents worldwide, we U.S. Deportation Officers were recognized as the smallest enforcement division in our agency (for a comparative example, there are roughly 11,600 FBI agents on duty). I'd never heard of a full Deportation Officer academy class. Had such an influx come along, the single class would have constituted nearly a 10 percent increase in the DO ranks, and Congress certainly had not signed off on anything like that.

Eddy and Sam were star agents. Their Chinese-speaking households had engendered Eddy's command of Mandarin and Sam's fluency in both Mandarin and Cantonese, which added tremendous investigative value to their units. The other member of our academy quartet, Chris Siouris, had grown up reading and speaking Greek. That so many immigration enforcers were immigrants, or children of immigrants, made sense. Applicants with foreign-language proficiency and an understanding of different cultural backgrounds should have received preference in hiring when all other factors were equal. But more significantly, many of that type sought out the job because they believed in the objective. I'd witnessed an attitude shared by many whose families had immigrated to America and sacrificed much in honest pursuit of the American Dream: That dream belonged to those who earned it.

I led my audience's eyes toward Sam and made up a story about him. Sam smiled back at me from the balcony, taking the tall tale good-naturedly as the audience matched his face to the yarn I spun. I sat down amid the typical wedding applause for a bridegroom. My family was with me, and I met their eyes around our table with warmth and pride.

When I saw a burly form come my way from an adjacent table, I sprang back to my feet. It was Phil. We grabbed each other, and then Phil introduced himself to my parents.

"Oh, we know you," my mother declared. "You used to be Ames's partner, didn't you? Boy, I know he misses you."

I studied Phil, and for a sinking moment I was overcome by the tangent my professional life had taken since he'd left. Phil and I still hung out in New Orleans. Our friendship off the job had not changed. But my work and how I felt about myself on the job did not resemble what I recalled from the days Phil and I had worked together. That had been another era, and everything I remembered from then was tinged with some distinct hue I couldn't place. It was as if those memories had been shot on different film.

I watched Phil talk to my father. They seemed men cut from the same cloth. My father had served thirty years as an infantryman in the United States Army. I had not the faintest doubt that my old man had conducted himself with honor for every minute of those thirty years. He had upheld the Laws of War. He had followed the Geneva Convention. No less in combat. No less in his most excruciating hour in Vietnam. And in the present, in the immigration war, I was sure that whatever Phil was doing now he was doing with a high sense of moral responsibility.

The man who'd trained me for my career now spoke with the man who had trained me for my life. I tried to shake the feeling I wasn't worthy of either.

My father had taught me to follow the rules. He was living proof that a person who did that could accomplish his goals, take care of his family, and sleep at night, content in his lot. When I strayed, my father had belted me. More times than I could remember, he had put fast leather to my skin to impart his lesson. I would always be grateful for that.

Phil, with utmost care, had taught me the rules that governed one of the most critical posts in the security of the United States of America. He had given me the perfect foundation in the greatest job I'd ever have. Sometimes Phil had yelled at me to drive his instruction points home. Other times, like the day I nearly got us killed, he'd used quiet.

On a routine jail pickup Phil parked the government Jeep Cherokee outside the CCC facility of OPP. Laughingly we noted that recent modifications had made the vehicle less than suited to transporting criminals. The author of the modifications was the SDEO of the time, a tobacco-chewing maverick named Adam who had previously asked to take the Jeep to Texas on official business. Adam had invested the front console of our government Cherokee with an expansive panel of switches that corresponded to numerous special effects of sound and illumination. Concurrent with the panel's placement, our locking gun safe had been removed, or since the new panel of switches now overran the space where the gun safe had been bolted, it is theoretically possible that the panel had been screwed in *over* the gun safe, and that the gun safe remained, just hidden and inaccessible beneath the futuristic panel.

The other item to disappear from the Cherokee as part of the upgrade was the cage, a rigid construction of steel and bulletproof glass bolted behind the front seats, designed to protect the law enforcement officers who rode up front from the frequently desperate criminals in back. Since Adam's newly installed *Star Wars* panel stopped at the seat belt joints between the front seats, a few inches short of where the cage had been bolted, the reason for the cage's removal was not immediately apparent. The cage would not have interfered in any way with the free flicking of all switches on the new panel. Phil was the first to remark that what the cage *had* interfered with was the reclining of the front seats.

So Phil and I dismounted the vehicle outside the jail and pondered the circumstance of having no box in which to lock our guns. This was significant inasmuch as we were not allowed to bring our guns into the jail while we retrieved our prisoner. This prohibition on guns in prisons is a given. It applies to every law enforcement officer, every state, every jail I've ever heard of. I have personally experienced the lifting of this prohibition only once, at a prison in St. Martinville, Louisiana, in December 1999, and that prison was under siege. A handful of Cubans and a lunatic Bahamian had taken over. They'd beaten the warden ruthlessly and had several deputies hostage at the points of their shanks. Phil and I had gone in there with our guns and every spare high-capacity magazine topped off, and the deputies had buzzed us straight in.

But CCC was not going to welcome us like this. The deputies would scream at us, order us out, and call our district director before we made it through the door. We would not be allowed on OPP grounds again, and our usefulness as New Orleans Deportation Officers would take a recurring lifetime hit.

"Just put them under the seat," Phil said at last. "We'll lock the doors and hope Adam's fucking switchboard has a security system built in." We slid our loaded .40-cals (at the time Berettas; plainclothes agents would soon be issued H&Ks) under the seats, and we both realized at about the same time that our pistols were rolling. In the next instant we also discovered what the pistols had been rolling on, expended shell casings. Phil and I carefully collected the shells. We recognized spent brass from our own law enforcement round as well as some longer, slender samples I associated with rifle hunting. There were not a lot of casings, just a handful that had probably eluded a vacuuming and a pickup of larger debris such as cans.

Now, before I even commence an isolated instance of speculation in this book, I want to warn the reader that is what I'm doing. Phil and I were not with Adam, a standout supervisor well liked by his troops, on his reported official business trip to his home state of Texas. For all we actually knew, Adam had used the Jeep only for necessary government travel, or maybe he had found some other way to Texas and hadn't used the Jeep at all. That was possible, just as it was possible that the new light and sound capabilities Adam had endowed in our Jeep had some job-related applications beyond those of the simple flasher and siren it had already carried before the upgrade. But the picture Phil and I carried in our heads, the one we talked about all the way into the jail, was that of Adam and his Texas buddies deep in the woods in our Jeep, with the seats comfortably reclined, long rifles popping out the windows, two cases of Lone Star beer and the H-E-B grocery receipts fluttering, several sacks of Whataburgers, good ol' boy hoots and snickers punctuated by the rifle cracks and the occasional blasts from Adam's duty revolver, all accompanied by the intoxicated flicking of switches for the most fantastic, magic sound-and-light spectacle the Texas backwoods had ever seen.

It was more than Phil and I could get our heads around. We let our smiles fade into our jail faces as we headed inside for our rollout, a Costa

Rican with a ten-year-old drug conviction, not in our docket. We were picking him up for another DO.

We got up to the immigration section, and the place erupted as it always did. I went in all business. No smile in greeting the alien as I proceeded to twist his sweat suit in a diligent body search. Monotone commands as I snapped him into his leg irons, belly chains, handcuffs. Phil had the paperwork, and we were off, leaving the frenzied alien cries behind.

I seated the Costa Rican in the back of the Jeep and buckled him in. We slid up front, Phil started the engine, and we rolled.

About a minute later the Costa Rican said, "Excuse me, officers. Uh, you might want to do something about this gun."

I spun around and saw my black service pistol on the floor behind me. Phil pulled to the shoulder and slammed on the brakes, a tactical move that sent my weapon sliding forward, under the front seat where I'd left it. I hopped down and snatched the pistol. I shoved it into my holster on my hip. Phil, who had his service weapon already, who had not made the mistake I'd made, sat patiently, waiting for me to take my seat again and close my door. He rolled us away. I turned around to regard the prisoner, who was enjoying his moral high ground. He knew we both knew my whole cool act was destroyed. My dry greeting, professional search, overkill with the shackles all had added up to minus territory because in the end I'd given him access to my duty weapon, bullet in the chamber, eleven more in the clip. The Costa Rican's eyes were already on me. He'd been waiting for me to turn around. He said, "You're lucky I'm not one of those other guys."

I knew the other guys he meant. Another deportable alien, say, a Rodolfo, one of those thugs who care about nothing. The chains wouldn't have made a difference. Prisoners can eat in those belly chains. A prisoner could certainly snap quietly out of the seat belt, drop on the pistol on the Jeep floor, roll faceup, and drill two successive high-angle shots, one through the passenger seat and one through the driver's. TV forensics shows live off scenarios like that: *The bullets entered both victims through the lower back, then traveled on an upward trajectory* . . . followed by a demonstration of a hollow tip round's chaotic influence on the internal organs of two federal agents.

I looked the Costa Rican in the eye. "You're right."

Phil said nothing. He did not dress me down in the Jeep. He was not saving an outburst for later either because he never brought up the incident. Not in ten minutes, once we'd delivered the prisoner. Not that evening.

Not today at my wedding, even though the story of the time I almost got us killed would have made a memorable toast. For the life-and-death deportation lessons, Phil maintained crushing silence eternally, so as never to interrupt my own brain's exclamation of the moral that had broadcast within me since the instant I'd screwed up.

Phil slapped my back at the table on his way out. He had a good buzz that brought me back to the joy of the occasion. Things were beautiful after all. I caught Soraya's eyes, and they crinkled up in a smile for me. Just that quickly I was in a frictionless glide, feeling perfect, better than I'd ever felt, and looking forward at greater brightness still.

The honeymoon suite at San Francisco's Fairmont Hotel was next. And then the honeymoon itself, the trip set up to top all the trips we'd ever taken. We traveled a lot. I earned twenty days of vacation a year, not including sick days that the government allotted in a separate account. It was twenty pure fun days that, when connected to weekends and government holidays, expanded to forty-five days of vacation to see the world, and Soraya and I did that. We saw the world so often that despite the rapid accumulation of leave, I had a current account balance of zero. Our wedding and honeymoon should not have been possible except for the fact that Craig had requested and received a special headquarters authorization to let me go thirty annual leave days in the hole. I would have to pay it back—the leave I earned upon my return would be sucked straight out of my account every month—but just the same, the advanced leave grant was so rare that it had elicited a degree of grumbling from a couple of workers in our office, who charged that Craig treated different employees differently. That charge was true. Craig did his best to reward his subordinates he perceived worked hard for him, didn't lie to him, and never turned down an assignment. The others Craig did his best not to reward.

As I coasted with Soraya through this vacation that should not have been possible, I maintained a reservoir of gratitude for Craig. It was a reservoir that increased in content every awesome day.

After our night in the Fairmont, Soraya and I checked in at the San Francisco airport and had a Bloody Mary in the international terminal to burn off the champagne hangover before it hit. Virgin put us on a seven-hour layover in London, enough time to see the sights. The sky was open, and it was the hottest London day anyone we ran into could remember. Soraya and I loved it. It wasn't part of our scripted honeymoon, just a fluke of scheduling, so we treated London like the gift that it was, the gift on top of the gift, and we maximized every minute until we had to fly again.

Our next plane touched down in Pretoria, South Africa. A fellow DO at 701 Loyola had given us a night's stay there at a haunt of his for a wedding present. It was a legitimate hotel and also a real live crocodile farm and a nice way to begin.

From there Soraya and I were top-of-the-line every step. Our honeymoon was three weeks of safari. We were whisked between luxury lodges in the Okavango Delta. We canoed the Zambezi River for a week, and every time we disembarked, our tent was already set up with champagne, bed linen and pillows, and a hot-water shower as good as in a fixed hotel. There was always a host waiting for us when we landed at a new place. We never caught a cab. There were sedan transfers to our two brick-and-mortar hotels, in Harare and in Victoria Falls, but aside from that we got around in the wild in open safari wagons, our own prop airplanes, or a helicopter.

The animals were glorious. To see the herds of zebras and giraffes gallop across a field with grace like blowing wheat was one miracle. To witness the same herds sense a lion and reverse course together like darting schools of fish was another. It all seemed like miracles down there, south of the equator, with the elephants trumpeting directly into our faces, the hippos splashing to escape us and hiding behind trees that didn't conceal even both their eyes, and the endless horizons the sunrise set flame to, oxygenated air, and bluest skies that transitioned into clearest nights and the Southern Cross.

Soraya and I set out on a private hike with our rifle-toting guide. His eyes were all over the ground that surrounded us. He was a native Botswanan named Finley, and even when he halted to show us some aspect of the land, or a survival tip, or an animal we hadn't seen, his eyes did not cease searching for the predators that could charge us and kill us if he did not get off a shot. He crouched by a sage bush at the base of a low hill and pulled a leaf off. He folded the leaf so it snapped, and he handed it to me. I inhaled it. I wanted to share it right away, so I thrust it to Soraya and watched her inhale. She drew through her nostrils and smiled and closed her eyes and rolled her head back, and I knew she was feeling exactly what I had. It was all of Africa in one leaf, the sage leaf, whose freshness you could breathe in and drink and trap inside you. To Soraya and me it smelled like heaven.

At the crest of the hillock Finley halted us again and pointed at a water hole. On the edge near us a lion pawed his freshly killed impala.

Quietly Finley asked, "Do you know who is the king of the beasts?"

"The lion," I answered.

Finley appeared to nod slightly. He looked back toward the scene of the kill. "Behind the lion," he said.

Behind the lion was only the pool from which the impala had surely been drinking in his final seconds of life, before the lion had seized him. I didn't know what Finley meant.

"I saw a scene like this, but with many lions," Finley said. "They were eating an antelope. Suddenly there was a splash from the water. Like this, the kill was twenty feet away. The lions looked up when a crocodile came out of the water. The crocodile walked toward them, and the lions ran. The crocodile walked to the antelope. He grabbed the antelope in its mouth, then turned around and dragged it back to the water. The lions just watched from a distance. They licked their chops and walked away."

"Wow," I said.

Finley looked at me and nodded. "That's why I say the crocodile is the real king of the beasts."

From then on I noticed that the lions didn't sleep next to the water. They even pulled back on a chase when their prey ran into the water to escape. Lions knew about goring buffalo horns and giraffe kicks that could split their rib cages and punch holes in their hearts. But they didn't fear those animals. Lions still treated them as prey. It was the enemy they didn't expect that scared the lions. The prehistoric relics that spent most of their days in the same place, submerged to their eyeballs in the very resource every animal in the jungle needed to live, those unevolved old guards the lions could never match.

The revelation brought my mind back to work. This vacation had been a spectacular escape, and I really hadn't been thinking about the job. Notwithstanding a few circumstances occasioning fond thoughts of my professional associates (the workmate who'd paid for our night at the Crocodile Lodge, the fellow agents who'd traveled to make the ceremony, and the boss who'd gotten me the thirty days), out here in the African wild it was easy to get pulled away with Soraya into the breathtaking new surroundings and think of nothing that had happened before. But Finley's story of the real king of the beasts jarred me with the similarity between this dangerous land full of surprises and the professional arena that awaited my return. A DO's obvious adversary was his prey, the criminal aliens he had to hunt and dispatch. But just as the giraffes, zebras, impalas, and the rest of the warm-blooded prey that the lions had to take down in order to live weren't the lions' true insuperable nemesis, so neither were the aliens ours. The lions had their crocodiles. We Deportation Officers had our leaders—HQ on up. It was the U.S. government that derailed us, helped itself to our prey, and otherwise became our unconquerable adversary in the struggle against the criminal alien tide.

I looked out across the delta at the lion eating his impala. I found myself pulling for the lions, against the crocodiles. Where I had earlier felt a professional bond with my rifle-toting guide, I was down now with the beasts. Here the animals fended for themselves in the wild, and at home DOs had to survive in a political jungle on their own.

Finley resumed our walk, and I shook it all off. I tried not to think of work anymore. For the most part I succeeded, until the very end, when I was overcome with a different emotion, gratitude, for the boss and the paycheck that had granted me this experience of a lifetime. It really seemed beyond what I should have encountered at this early stage of my life.

I could imagine some OIG inspectors getting wind of my vacation and following me the whole way to document the street-level agent living high on the hog. They'd snap pictures of the opulent wedding and of the Fairmont suite in San Francisco, and then they'd follow us on the Virgin flight to South Africa, into the Okavango Delta, our private plane jaunts around the region: Botswana, Zambia, and Zimbabwe, this three-week safari in the five-star luxury camps, where even the breakfasts were banquets and prestige-label alcohol poured from sunset on. It was true I'd paid for the wedding, the honeymoon, all of it. Those OIG inspectors would be sure I was crooked. There were a million ways for a DO to make a million dollars after all, from importing contraband or people on the back end of deports to setting aliens free—through administrative manipulation or by vanishing them in thin air on escorts—and a lot of document whips in between. Out here in Africa I would certainly appear to be overshooting my federal agent income, even with the supplement of Soraya's New Orleans public schoolteacher's salary. The OIG boys would be congratulating each other, smacking their backs with smug delight. But then they would follow us home to New Orleans, where they would see our battered apartment in the 70119, the decades-old stereo with the wooden tower speakers, the TV set with the pliers, and the Honda Accord sedan that a friend had given us, and those OIG inspectors would fall dispiritedly to their knees.

They could never get anything on me. I was as clean as they came. Whenever I heard about the rare agent who defiled his badge and abused his power for his own profit, I was sickened. I despised a dirty agent.

Standing back from it all now, I suppose some good agents will finish this book and feel the same way about me.

NINE

Tangipahoa and the Forced Migration

I entered the ninth-floor conference room with the stragglers and looked for a seat in the rear. Every Immigration employee in the building was supposed to be in here, but on the Deportation side there were agents on fugitive ops, agents on escorts, somebody watching the holding cells, someone else conferencing an embassy VIP, etc., while the Investigations side had its own field alibis, along with the odd investigator who was so deep undercover he hadn't been anywhere near 701 Loyola in a year. So the mandatory morning ceremony was light on enforcers, as the ceremonies always were, and heavy on administrative types. I saw a sampling of workers from other offices in our district too. Their type was always drifting through from around our five-state jurisdiction.

I had a habit of missing these conference room assemblies, but not this time. I'd returned from my African honeymoon only to go straight out to the field for days running, and by now I'd been away from my desk for so long that my clerk, Sam, had paged me, saying it was time to come in and listen to my voice mails or else he was getting a transfer.

I dropped into a brown-upholstered chair a row behind Fenwick Johnson and John Seright across from the exit. John was the guy who'd given me the night at the Crocodile Lodge in South Africa. I thanked him for it again, and we traded a few lines about the friends of his who ran the place, characters.

Fenwick and John were the frontline detained DOs, which meant they got the files of New Orleans's locked-down aliens as soon as they came into the system. Their docket was not as loaded as mine, but that was because their population turned over constantly. In the busy Deportation universe, cases raced in and out of the frontline docket so that while they rarely had as many aliens as I had to tend to at any given instant, over the space of several months they handled more A-files. My cases came in and out more slowly, stayed longer.

Splitting responsibility for the frontline detained docket down the middle by A-numbers, Fenwick and John followed the new cases and then either released the detained aliens who won in court or arranged deportation for the detained aliens the immigration judge ordered removed. For that latter group, Fenwick and John initiated TD requests, and in 80 percent of the cases they had success. Fenwick and John were renowned for getting TDs, even on criminals. It was they who made New Orleans's name as the office that shipped the criminal aliens home. Those two individually acquired far more TDs than I did. Even at my current extraordinary pace, I didn't match either of them in numbers of passports hauled in. Fenwick and John were a good complement, often trading nationalities across their desks to make use of each other's particular relationships and strengths. They had many approaches, all legitimate and aboveboard, but generally (and for the purpose of instruction I write in general terms throughout this mechanics-laden chapter) John got to know the consular officials on a personal level, developing rapport by demonstrating a genuine interest in their lives, whereas Fenwick was more scientific, mastering the diplomats' professional preferences in order to frame his TD requests in ways that promised success.

In that minority of cases where they came up short, when Fenwick and John did not secure a TD for a particular alien within three months of

that alien's final order of removal by an immigration judge, they had to recommend custody determinations. If the alien was not dangerous, Fenwick
and John had him kicked out the door. If the alien was a grave threat to
society, they transferred the file to me. Actually, "Aggravated Felon Docket"
hadn't been an official title for almost two years. The technical label now
was "Post-Order Custody Review," referring to that evaluation process the
long-term detained aliens received. But since virtually all the aliens who
failed the release evaluation were aggravated felons, the agg felon nickname
didn't seem likely to die.

All the aliens I received had been filtered two ways—for their behavior
and for their governments' propensity to have them back—and they'd been
found on the least promising end of both. It would have been defensible,
from a human resources standpoint, to have no one in my position (most
Deportation offices around the country did not have an exclusive aggravated felon docket for long-term cases, preferring instead to put all their
detained officers on the frontline docket and divide the misery). After all,
if second-to-none DOs Fenwick and John hadn't managed to deport an
alien, then that alien had fairly earned the label "nonremovable." But Craig
saw the value in spreading his officers vertically instead of horizontally. It
minimized case burnout, for one thing, when a frontline DO could pass
his alien to someone else. For another, it allowed for new methods to be
applied when the new officer took over.

Most significantly, it turned the DO at the end of the line into a spe-
cialist for end-of-the-line aliens. The cases Fenwick and John gave me were,
by definition, broken. I was a fixer.

This is the reason I was considered a success: I brought dead cases back
to life.

I heard my name called, and I gripped the steel frames of Fenwick's and
John's seat backs in order to lift myself from my brown-upholstered chair. I
sidestepped to the center aisle and made my way up the blue carpet to the
front of the conference room. The district director shook my hand.

"Well done," the DD said,

I accepted the Outstanding Performance Award from the DD's hand
while someone snapped a picture. I smiled as I walked back down the aisle,

clutching my certificate, scanning the clapping audience of Immigration employees from the ninth and eighth floors. I knew most of them. It was a good family. I found my seat again and cheered the other employees who got awards.

When the ceremony ended, people filed forward to an ad hoc dessert table by the lectern. I hadn't taken three steps when young Sam clamped my shoulder. He was wearing a black polo shirt. His blond locks appeared to have received a recent trim.

Sam asked, "You're going to your desk now to check your messages, right?"

"Hey, my man. Actually, I was—"

"You're going to your desk now to check your messages, right?" Sam repeated.

"Yes, I am."

Sam escorted me across the hall to the Deportation bay. We paralleled the gray-rug cubicle walls until we reached the end.

"People are calling *me* to ask why you haven't returned their calls," Sam said. He was smiling, but his was a nervous smile, and I felt the urgency of his desire that I get caught up as soon as possible. It was a hard enough existence for Sam when I was in control. He didn't have the time to deal with my spillover.

"Thanks, Sam."

There we were between his desk and my cubicle. That Sam's and my workstations stood very last in the respective lines of clerks and DOs seemed a poetic match for the end-of-the-line aliens we handled. Perhaps Craig had designed it this way.

Sam watched me curl around my cube wall. I took a seat in my rolling chair, grabbed a pad and government pen, and accessed my loaded voice mail.

"You're dead," stated the first message. I replayed it again because it wasn't clear, but that remained my best interpretation. Nearly every DO had menacing curses and fatwas heaped on him as part of the job. The message could have been from someone (or a relative or fellow gang member of someone) I'd arrested, handled, deported—pick one. That was actually a great way to start, and I skipped to the next message with a jolt of optimism. If half my messages were death threats, it was possible I'd finish this up before lunchtime.

No such luck. I slogged through messages from diplomats, aliens' attorneys, plaintive girlfriends of aliens, tipsters, other law enforcement agencies, officers in my own agency, and the motley remainder, all the while jotting down abbreviated substance and diagramming my response and priority. When I played one message, though, my pen fell from my hand. It was a woman crying. There were no words, but halfway through the message my blood froze as I remembered the time I'd heard those sobs before.

The crying on the tape was weeks old. I called back at once, but her number now blocked my desk from calling in. I tried on my government cell, but no one answered. Jacqueline Pham had come as close to me as any of the victims I'd encountered on this job, and now I couldn't even reach out a helping hand. I could feel her fading into the crowd of thousands of shattered lives the villains in my docket had made. I would never hear from her again.

Maybe crying was all Jacqueline Pham would have conveyed to me had I been here to pick up her call those weeks ago. It could have been that Bounmy Xayavongsa found her. Or it could have been that her attacker had not reentered her life in any physical way but that the fact he roamed free in America continued to terrify her to tears.

I bolted from my chair and hit the central hallway.

"Ames, where are you going?"

I heard someone ask that, but my head was so full of anguished noise that I didn't know who, and I pushed the door to the fire exit and escaped inside. I climbed the flights of stairs in solitude until I hit the roof.

The sky was gray, and I stood on the roof edge wondering how I could have deluded myself into thinking I was effecting change. My TDs barely scratched the surface. I was still losing more cases than I could count. In my head I heard Jacqueline's tears falling, and I was sad. But even when I pulled myself away from her sobs, when I escaped the loaded emotions that pull at every human's heartstrings, I was still sad. Maybe the rapist Bounmy Xayavongsa hadn't found Jacqueline Pham. Maybe she had won the lottery, erased her memory, and now lived in a fortress in Hawaii where no harm could ever come to her again. Even if I believed those conditions, there was one absolute I could not deny: Bounmy Xayavongsa was going to find *somebody*. Praying for Jacqueline Pham's safety, even if my prayers were answered, would not stop the rapist from exacting his toll. There would be victims, that was for sure. It was tragic. And then I remembered Bounmy Xayavongsa was only one criminal. I had released dozens. And I had a never-ending number on deck to go free next.

The high wind gusted, and I leaned into it. My recent "success" had served only to engender a false sense of pride. I had made progress, but it was in the way a man who tears a clump of grass in his fingers has made progress in mowing his lawn. I had not come close to turning the corner on the scourge. With hundreds of criminal aliens still in the nonremovable category, I would have to do a lot more if I intended to make a meaningful difference. I had been anguished. Now I was fed up.

I looked out over my city, my river, and my people, and I said that I would do more. I spoke the words, and the wind carried them out like a promise from nature to the land.

I descended to the ninth floor. I turned on my computer and opened the aggravated felon database and hit "print." I printed every page. I walked to the big central printer and watched the pages cascade. I watched the names and A-numbers drop out in neat columns in the laser black etching, followed by the other columns that I would use for my own matrix. There were FBI numbers, crimes, gang affiliations, aliases, and all kinds of details on my subjects, each note laid out in those razor black columns on white stock for clear reference, but I was waiting for the most important one, nationality. There it came.

When it all had printed out, I grabbed the solid stack and walked it across the hall to the conference room. The great room where I'd accepted my award today was now deserted. The huge conference table was empty, and I slid my stack across its hard mahogany surface like a card dealer showing the entire deck on the green felt.

The countries stared at me from the pages: many, many countries from every politically mapped continent on the globe, except Australia.

Yes, Australia was unrepresented in my ill-famed docket. The reason for the omission was not that Australians were such great souls. It was that the Australian government had never balked at receiving its criminal citizens. I silently thanked the Aussie administrators and cursed all the countries whose names I saw before me now.

But, I reminded myself, it was not those other governments I had to worry about. Not really. They were but a second-level foe, and now I had to consider them only in relation to the true king of the beasts. I was going to figure out how to get a lot more of these vicious criminals out of my country, and when I did, those rogue foreign governments wouldn't block me. I knew it was the federal government of the United States of America that would strike down my plans every chance it got.

So I look at these countries and ask myself: Whom can I remove without drawing heat from higher? That's my only question this minute. It's all that matters. I'm not yet sure how I am going to remove any of the deportable aliens, but I am confident the stratagems will come to me, and if not, I'll shut myself in until they do. In any event the how will have to wait. Given my situation, I have no choice but to work this problem backward. There's no point in devising the perfect scheme to return criminals to their homelands if irrelevant of the scheme, the very fact that criminals are returning to particular homelands sets off an alarm that leads my government to shut me down.

I've seen entities in my government crush so many repatriation plans that no act of command betrayal can surprise me. It happens any time, anywhere, for any reason. If you get permission from one authority, you are still open to having your legs cut from under you by another. If you work hard on an unconventional plan, you must remind yourself that all the work might be for nothing in the end.

This was the case when John Seright solved the Afghanistan problem.

Afghanistan had been bewitching DOs for as long as any of us remembered. Nearly two hundred countries fed the criminal alien tide in America, each with its own challenge for enforcers, but Afghanistan stood out as a nation we could count on to generate a new problem every time the last one was solved.

Ninety-nine percent of the final order aliens who languished in Immigration custody did so because their countries failed to issue travel documents. The citizens of Afghanistan were in a different boat entirely. The Taliban had effectively controlled much of the country since the 1990s, ruling a territory so dangerous that the Federal Aviation Administration had issued a blanket flight prohibition, rendering it impossible for anyone in the United States to purchase air passage to Afghanistan, even for official government business.

That prohibition had frozen the return of Afghan criminals for about a year until some sharp DOs in Philadelphia had figured out that airline tickets to Kabul were like Cuban cigars, not legal for sale in the United States but readily available at foreign airports. I joined the pioneering DOs who began flying dangerous Afghans into Dubai, Delhi, and Rome, then purchasing the follow-on transfers at those airports, fittingly consummating the removals aboard the deportees' national carrier, Ariana Afghan Airlines. Dozens of public enemies left America that way, and hundreds more were slated to go, until things got even worse in the motherland.

By late 2000 Afghanistan's militant Islamic set was wreaking havoc on a Godzilla scale. Not complacent after shuttering in women and knocking the economy back into the barter age, the Taliban launched into full harasser mode, cattle-branding non-Muslims, dynamiting irreplaceable icons, and rubbing out any representation of Western thought or technology. High on that latter list was the Kabul international airport and the air travel that went with it. Ariana ceased to fly.

The Afghanistan Embassy in DC, still staffed with non-Taliban hangers-on from the old regime, became an island, cut off from the homeland and starved for cash. It cranked out new Afghanistan passports at a high velocity for anyone who could mail in fifty dollars and a set of photographs, as a simple matter of survival. In New Orleans we had a valid passport for every one of the dozen or so Afghan criminals in our jails.

But *how to get them home?* No district in the country had solved that one yet. Without air service as an option, the outlook was bleak. It wasn't as if we could *bus* these people out like Mexicans or Canadians.

And then one day John asked me for my official passport. When he gave it back to me a few days later, it sported a visa for the country of Turkmenistan. This was the fruit of a relationship John had developed over a year. John had applied his natural people talents, and the Turkmen ambassador to the United States had invited him to fly our Afghan criminals into Ashgabat and then drive them overland to the Afghanistan border. There we would hand the deportees to the Turkmen officials and let them complete the transfer. It was going to be a hellish escort, but weren't they all? Craig got a visa too. He was going with us on the first mission.

"Headquarters cleared this?" I asked John.

"Oh, yeah." John chuckled. "The DC brass is taking credit for the idea."

That was the last chuckle we shared over it. The next thing we knew, the U.S. ambassador to Pakistan (who exercised authority over the nearby 'stans) issued a statement officially forbidding our operation on the ground that we could potentially offend the countries involved. Actually, it was clear that we were going to offend our Turkmen hosts by *declining* their generous invitation, but the American ambassador to Pakistan was apparently not worried about that, so long as we did not risk hurting the feelings of the Taliban across the border. For years State had failed to intervene on our behalf when it could have compelled rogue nations to take their criminals back, and now it finally did intervene: to make sure one nation didn't get a chance to take its criminals back even if it wanted them. Well, no one could say the State Department wasn't consistent, at least in its commitment to keep foreign criminals on U.S. soil.

Just like that, players in high positions of public trust in our government routinely break the framework of repatriations that DOs have spent months or years to orchestrate. Other times they leave the framework intact but take away the reason.

Phil and I once obtained a rare Havana-issued passport with valid reentry tag for a deportable Cuban. The Cuban, who had been convicted here of felony weapons and drugs charges, had left America voluntarily to visit Cuba and then had been arrested by inspectors upon returning to the

United States. We went immediately to HQ with the request: Can we try to ship this one back? It took HQ awhile, but it surprised us by giving us its blessing. We put together a Plan A (an approved charter flight out of Miami) as well as a Plan B (via Mexico) even though our Plan A looked like a sure thing. From the start Hortense, the head of Deportation for our five-state district, was turned off by the idea of deporting a Cuban. It was politically touchy. But she knew she could not prohibit a repatriation that had the endorsement of her own superiors. So officially she never did cancel our mission. Instead, two weeks short of our operation, Hortense simply had the Cuban criminal let out of jail.

With that memory in my mind in the deserted conference room, I uncap a red Magic Marker. On the entrance side of the conference room, a wall runs its length between the front and back doors. The doors are closed, making me feel secure. The window side is naked, and I can look down on the postal parking lot and the Greyhound/Amtrak station and the interstate, but I am up high on the ninth floor, and no one can observe me. I turn inward again to my aggravated felon sheets spread across the surface of the great mahogany table. I focus on the sharp black nationality columns on the white stock printouts. As I navigate the edges of the table, I run my red Magic Marker across every citizen of Cuba.

Cubans are safe.

Next is Vietnam. I make even more red lines between the boxed columns on my white stock. When I get to the letter *N*, as in Nguyen, I line and line and line, and I have to rotate the Magic Marker to keep the tip from going dry. Vietnamese are safe.

I move on to the Cambodians and the Laos. When I have finished putting red lines through them, I see I have put a significant portion of my docket off-limits to myself. But it is what I have to do. The four governments whose criminals I have just made safe have transparent histories of refusing repatriations. If I deport a felon to one of those four countries, I will draw scrutiny from important people in my government. And while I have not yet figured out how I'll deport anyone on my printout, I know that whatever the how turns out to be, it will not stand up to scrutiny from important people in my government.

Now I have taken care of bars by nationality, but I am not finished paring my list. There are other restrictions, and the biggest is relief from removal. Aliens convicted of particular heinous crimes, the kind of crimes blanketing my white stock, are not eligible for regular asylum relief. This does not mean that immigration judges do not find a way to assign relief.

The Executive Office for Immigration Review is home to the justices who render immigration decisions. The EOIR and its appellate division, the political appointee–staffed Board of Immigration Appeals, are maintained as separate entities from my agency. This is designed to avoid conflict of interest. What is not designed, but can result, is a clash between Immigration district counsels (the prosecutors in the immigration law arena) and the immigration judges (many of whom see themselves as protectors of the aliens). This is a clash the IJ can win, one way or another, because the judge has the last word in his courtroom. Though aliens' criminal convictions leave IJs no legal choice but to sign off on their removal orders, there is much more leeway when it comes to granting relief from those same orders.

This is the odd story of the aliens I am now lining through with my red Magic Marker. These are toxic men in limbo, decreed unfit for American society and ordered deported by immigration judges, yet fenced into the United States with holds placed on their deportation orders, also by immigration judges.

Withholding of Removal. Deferral of Removal. Convention Against Torture. You do not need to know these terms. You need only know that if I deport an alien who has been awarded one of these forms of relief, then I will lose my badge. I am taking some professional risks already, and I will take more, but I will never deliberately get fired. Right now I have too much to accomplish as a DO. Right now I'm too angry to let go.

When I get to the *Z*s, where many Chinese fall, I run a red line through the antisocial Chinese who lives in a medical cell in Tangi because he attacks everyone he lays eyes on. He has Withholding of Removal because the IJ thought he might be imprisoned without trial upon his return to China.

The antisocial Chinese is safe. My government will liberate him here in New Orleans.

Finally I cap my red Magic Marker. The bad part is over. Everyone else on the white stock is fair game. What I have before me are the dead cases that I can still get out under the radar. There are plenty.

When I walked out of that conference room and left it completely deserted again, I already knew what my first step had to be. I met with Sam over his desk, and I handed him half the sheets from the aggravated felon printout. Sam smiled wryly as he leafed through his sheets.

"What are the red lines?" he asked.

"They're lost causes."

"Oh, as opposed to the rest of our aliens that are such winners?"

"That's right. We're going to make winners out of them. Winners of a trip home."

"I like it. How does this start?"

"We write up the paperwork and transfer them to Tangi."

"Can we do that?"

"Can we transfer aliens between jails, Sam?"

"I mean, can we do so many?"

"Let's spread it out over the next few weeks. You request no more than five a day, and I'll request about the same."

Sam asked, "Won't the wardens at the other jails get pissed off if they lose that many Immigration bodies?"

His was a good question. The contract facilities offered us a place to put our aliens, even in huge quantities after roundups, in exchange for our stocking a detained population there, giving them a dependable stream of federal dollars. If we emptied too many beds at once, they would surely call somebody up high to report it. I'd already considered that. "While we're transferring aliens into Tangi, we need to transfer other aliens out of Tangi back into those same jails to match the loss. Give them the red-line aliens who are in Tangi."

"Do the numbers match?" Sam asked.

"It's pretty close. Close enough that no one's going to pick up the phone. If we end up going light anywhere, I'll make it OPP." We kept aliens at OPP for the shortest amount of time, so I didn't think they'd be noticed.

"So we're rolling aliens in and out of all our jails, every day, on top of the roll-ins and rollouts we already do," Sam said. "Are you putting your initials on the transfer requests?"

"Of course. This is legal, remember. I'm just consolidating my aliens so I can visit them all at once. Otherwise I have to drive to eight jails. But we're still bringing our sheets down the hall separately. I'm hoping Manny misses my initials and thinks you're doing some project for Craig."

"Okay, Ames," Sam said. "That's a lot of gasoline."

"Our tax money well spent."

Sam took another look at his pages. "What about the girls?" he asked.

"Wow," I replied.

"Wow what?"

"I hadn't thought of that. Tangi doesn't take our females." I paused and came out with a weighty decision: "Don't move the females."

Sam grinned. "So the girls now have red lines through them."

Girls were safe. I was not going to win all my cases. That was the nature of my problem. I had to make choices. I knew I had bad ladies: robbers, poisoners, blackmailers, and the one who had dropped a live TV on the face of a sleeping man. But the males were larger and commanded bigger pools of prey. To make that distinction would be once more a violation of the rule against treating one criminal alien differently from another, but it was a distinction I lived by. From that point on I never obtained another travel document for a female. From that point on I never tried to.

I drove some vanloads over the next few weeks, when Manny's staff was stretched, but for the most part they took care of it. I saw the vans pulling in and out at all hours. I saw the aliens go from brown hospital cotton or blue sweats to orange jumpsuits and vice versa, with street clothes in between. I peered at the aliens through the windows of the vehicles. When I saw the marked Immigration vans on the roads and highways, I would wave to the officers up front, and then I would speak to the thugs inside. The thugs couldn't hear me since we sped by each other, but I'd still say something. I would say, "Good-bye, criminal Vietnamese, Cubans, Cambodians, and Laos. I'll see you on your release date." Or: "Hello, criminal Salvadorans, Chinese, Russians, Koreans, Indians, Italians, Guyanese, Guatemalans,

Frenchmen, Byelorussians, Belizeans, Pakistanis, Poles, Colombians, Cro-
ats, Germans, Angolans, Armenians, Togolese, Dutch Antilleans, Hungar-
ians, Burkinans, Irishmen, Jordanians, Romanians, Iranians, Sri Lankans,
Trinidadians, Egyptians, Estonians, Algerians, Argentines, Macedonians,
Moroccans, Uruguayans, Ukrainians, Bolivians, Antiguans, Vincentians,
Bangladeshis. . . . You are on your way home."

My mind was off. I was pushing too hard, and I knew it. Sometimes
when I saw the vans roll, on the black road, on a black evening, I squeezed
my head in my hands because I was overwhelmed. It was beyond quantify-
ing; the nasty freight, the poor victims, and now the gasoline.

Back and forth the trucks rolled, on all the interstates of Louisiana,
sometimes reaching across the state line. In a few weeks the flow was something like normal again. The engine blocks had a chance to cool. The grit
settled on the road.

And Tangipahoa Parish Prison was now my personal warehouse, filled
with cursed cases.

Ten

Suicide Simmons and the Coercion, Forgeries, and Lies

There was never any traffic after Louis Armstrong International, where the western shelf of the New Orleans metropolis seemed to drop off the end of the runway into the swamp. I pulled the Crown Victoria off I-55 at the Amite exit, hooked a left around the Winn-Dixie supermarket, and coasted into the prison lot. By now I could've driven to Tangi in my sleep.

I checked my odometer and saw the reading I'd predicted. It was a rare constant of the job that gave satisfaction to my ambush- and land mine–conditioned psyche. You went from one cataclysm to the next when you carried the DO badge, so the things that didn't change drew your attention. I found it riveting that Tangipahoa Parish Prison stayed firmly planted right here, waiting for me every time I curled around Winn-Dixie.

Inside, things did change. Al Cox was no longer here. He'd been hired away for better pay at a private security post at one of the refineries. He'd called me when it happened, and we'd thanked each other and exchanged bittersweet good-byes. I'd been trying to get the standout deputy on our immigration team, but my agency didn't permit direct hires for law enforcement positions. No matter how great a fit they'd be for your unit, local applicants still had to take the written exam along with every other applicant in the country. Al had never gotten the score he'd needed. The test is supposedly designed to identify people with the special traits required of federal law enforcement professionals. In truth the test is worthless. Some people can't ever pass the test, even though they'd be perfect for the job. I took the test once and received the highest score possible. So there you have it.

Cox's replacement, Stan Bid, showed me the immigration board in his office. He had about fifteen prisoners who wanted to see me. Their inmate numbers were written in dry erase in a neat column on the right. Bid had previously taught me how to call them up from the dorms using jail code on the spare radio he always left.

"Oh, Claude Simmons wanted to see you too. You can get him out of the suicide cell."

"Suicide!" I exclaimed.

"Oh, no, it ain't like that," Bid said quickly, waving his hand. "You got us so many of these new guys, warden's still figuring out where to put 'em. Simmons's just been in that cell an hour."

"Oh, good. You know you need to call me if someone tries to kill himself, right?"

"Of course. He'll be out by feed-up. We're just moving 'em around." Bid was a good deputy. The warden had continued the tradition of putting one of his brightest on the immigration post, and Cox's big shoes had been filled. But Bid operated differently from Cox. He usually gave me an initial report and then left me on my own. Part of that was his style. Another part was that he didn't have the time to spend with me, now that I was visiting more often and especially now that I'd loaded his jail with untested characters who required his attention in the tiers. "You need anything else?" Bid asked.

"No. Thanks a lot."

"All right. Call me if you need me." We shook hands, and he was gone. I watched the door swing shut.

This is how it was. The office was not all that much bigger than a janitor's closet, but it had everything I needed, including a solid metal desk and a phone line. The sky blue–painted cinder block all the way around was the right combination of business and salve. Next to the door was a filing cabinet full of inmate records on my aliens. Tangi maintained paperwork in the folders we handed them with each of our roll-ins, so an alien's biographic sheet was stapled inside the front cover of each. This basic on-site library was extremely helpful to me. It let me pursue the mission without hauling in sensitive alien data from 701 Loyola. Most of the time I came in here with only a page of notes.

Convictions were included. That was important because particular criminal behavior was one way I hadn't subdivided my aliens at the office. It was necessary here since at least until I caught up with the headquarters release machine—if that day ever came—I was going to keep receiving orders to set some criminals free. I had to look at every criminal alien in here as a name on a release letter in some HQ bureaucrat's computer. If that bureaucrat printed and mailed all those letters to me next week, whom would I most want to have airborne already?

My opinions came into play. I ignored drug offenders and others I did not consider threatening enough, relatively, to warrant my special attention. In this race against my own government, losses were guaranteed, and so prioritizing became paramount. Time spent on the case of a felony drunk driver was time not spent trying to remove a rapist, and so on. If the U.S. government was going to liberate criminal aliens on American soil, then I owed it to the people I protected to ensure that the aliens released were the least dangerous ones. It was not that I was excited to scatter identity thieves, drug dealers, and insurance scammers into local communities, but when the alternative was assaultive robbers, kidnappers, and child molesters, the decision was easy.

That day there was a random circumstance that had dropped into my lap. My mind had been revolving it since Deputy Bid's mention. I glanced at the inmate numbers on the board and the radio I used to call the aliens out of the dorms. That would come. Right now there was this idea I had to act on.

I pulled a folder out of the cabinet and flipped it open: Claude Simmons, citizen of Antigua and Barbuda, strong-arm robbery. Antigua had been thwarting me even more severely than the frustrating Caribbean as a whole. I'd sent multiple TD requests to the Antiguan consular sections in Miami, New York, and DC and had received nothing for my efforts. But the Miami diplomats had gotten so tired of hearing from me that the last time they'd admitted the decision to issue was made not by them but by the chief of police in the island state.

I dialed my government international calling card on the jail phone. I had my government cell, which surprisingly worked in this cinder block chamber, but I liked to save the battery since the jail had been kind enough to let me access its outside line for toll-free calls. Oftentimes, when I had aliens in here with me, I'd run both phones at once.

At the prompt I punched in the 268 prefix, followed by the last number I'd copied at the top of Simmons's sheet. The computer voice told me, "Thank you." After several rings someone picked up.

"Office of the Chief of Police, may I help you?"

"Yes, please, ma'am. This is Deportation Officer Holbrook calling from the United States for Chief Barclay."

"Oh, from the United States?" Her island accent was warm.

"Yes, ma'am. I think I spoke with you last week. Unfortunately now I have an emergency to report to Chief Barclay."

"Oh, no. Just a minute, please."

I waited.

"Hello, Officer Holbrook," Chief Barclay said. His island accent was firm, not warm. He was a busy man.

"Hello, Chief. I was hoping we'd talk on better terms, but I'm sorry to report a bad situation."

"Is this about the citizens you are trying to send here?"

"Well, one of them: Claude Simmons. He's on suicide watch."

"Suicide?"

"He's in the suicide cell right now, Chief. He's depressed that his own country won't take him back. He thinks he'll spend the rest of his life in jail, so he might as well end it."

"That isn't the case," Barclay said. "The consulate in Miami is working on his return. That's who you should be speaking with."

"They told me to talk to you." They had not. Miami's consulate had mentioned the chief of police in the abstract, so as to convince me its hands were tied. "You are the authority, aren't you, Chief?"

He didn't answer, so I continued. "In any case, Chief, I'm required by my government to notify the top authority for an emergency of this magnitude."

"This is serious?"

"Yes, sir. And it gets more serious until Mr. Simmons is back in Antigua. I'm sure you know better than I do, Chief, that people who want to kill themselves keep trying until they succeed. His life in here is not getting better now. Other detainees call him Suicide Simmons."

"That's bad," Chief Barclay said. "May I talk to him?"

"Yes, Chief, of course." I tried to sound eager. "We can set up a conference for this afternoon if that fits your schedule." Chief Barclay didn't know I was forty feet away from Simmons. I had to temporize in order to think this through. Simmons might say he wasn't really suicidal, though Chief Barclay wouldn't necessarily believe him. More problematic would be Simmons's expressing a vehement opposition to an Antigua return.

Chief Barclay sighed. "We'll see."

Running with that sentiment, I said, "He's already spoken with the Miami consulate. They have his birth certificate, photographs, the full package. They know he's Antiguan. They say they just need you to sign off."

"But it takes time to verify that Claude Simmons has a home to return to in Antigua."

I rejected that assertion on two grounds. First, it did not matter if Simmons had a home to return to. That was his own country's responsibility, not America's, and if Simmons spent his first days home on the beach catching fish, that was simply the situation he'd carved for himself. My second objection to Chief Barclay's claim that he needed time to verify *anything* was that the population of his whole country was less than the Superdome attendance during a Saints game, and I had a feeling the chief of police could have located the Simmons family in five minutes.

I said, "Well, Chief, you know what you have to do. And I know that I have to put the substance of this call in writing for my headquarters in Washington DC."

"Why?"

"Headquarters says we have to, Chief. They don't like bad publicity, and Claude Simmons's killing himself will be bad international publicity. DC wants the record to show we mailed the initial passport request, with his Antigua birth certificate, over one hundred days before his death, and still you did not issue the travel document on your own citizen, Claude Simmons, may he rest in peace."

"You'd better tell Claude Simmons he's coming home," said Chief Barclay.

I paused, wanting to make sure I understood. "If I tell him, I'd better bring him home, Chief."

"You will. Miami has his photographs?"

"Yes, Chief. And a prepaid FedEx envelope to ship the travel document straight to my desk at U.S. government expense."

"Good enough. Tell Claude Simmons we'll see him next week."

"Thank you. Hey, Chief Barclay, I hope I can get you out here for Mardi Gras one of these days."

He said good-bye, and I put the phone down. I'd been on my feet, pacing the office, stretching the phone cord along cinder block walls through the entire shaky conversation, and now I fell back in the chair.

I trusted Chief Barclay. I thought of him as a fellow protector, another law enforcer trying to take care of the people in his country. He was not my enemy, and I did not blame him for having resisted the return of dangerous criminals to his land. With the U.S. government's granting amnesty to all nations that refused to take back their criminals, I could almost recognize a nation's responsibility, in the interests of its residents, to take advantage of the amnesty. I was at odds with my own government for implementing the amnesty, not with other governments for accepting America's self-destructive offer.

I propelled myself into the rest of the day's work at Tangipahoa with an eye toward the angles, the possibilities that existed. Even as I radioed the tiers and read the inmate numbers off the board to call the aliens to me in successive marches from their dorms, I dreamed up solutions. No case was a write-off. Everyone had a vulnerability to be exploited. My mind was swimming when I called it a day.

I said good-bye to the jail staff and then went out to the Crown Victoria, holstered my sidearm, and settled in behind the wheel for the late-afternoon drive home. The sun was shining through the branches of the swamp trees, challenging my eyes to adapt to the alternating light and shade across the windshield. About thirty minutes out over the elevated freeway track I spotted a gas station I had never visited before.

I rolled down the steep exit onto the strip of dry land below. I stopped the sedan next to a pump and hopped out. The air was full of the diesel rumble of big rigs idling all around. Across the Crown Victoria roof I regarded a huge earthen lot that could have held more than a dozen trucks on busy nights. I went in and paid for the gas with the government credit card.

Outside, I drove my topped-off car into the earthen lot, parked in a desolate patch, got out, and shut the door. I put my elbows on the Crown Victoria roof and leaned forward. From its place on my hip, the rear sight of my H&K pistol rapped the driver window.

I assessed the forlorn gas station property. This place was as stagnant as the swamp around us. The wetland wasn't healthy for the business, and in reciprocation the business contributed enough diesel exhaust to neutralize the fresh air that people in the middle of nowhere could otherwise count on. I pulled the cellophane off a pack of five cigars I'd bought, retrieved a cigar, and then pulled the cellophane off that too. I put the cigar in my mouth and struck a match to light it. I drew in several times as the match flared. I exhaled, regarding the gas station property through a drift of smoke, and I decided it was fabulous swamp after all. This polluted, disagreeable lowland was the perfect place to think about my job.

Today I needed to consider what I'd done and, more important, apply it to what I had yet to accomplish. It went against my grain to lie to officials on the phone, but I'd known at the moment I secured Claude Simmons's passage to Antigua that I would soon report suicidal citizens to consulates representing countries all around the globe. In the deportation world, where too often you find your gears toothless and your tools broken, when something works for you, you use it. Telling diplomats that the blood of their suicidal citizens would be on the diplomats' hands was a tactic that produced TDs, and I was going to run that tactic into the ground.

I did not stop there. Just as I refused to let my progress end with the Chinese and the other international relationships I cultivated to effect deportations, I also set no limits on the trickery I employed to the same end.

I continued to report suicide attempts that never happened, even when no suicide cell was involved. The drawback to the tactic was that its use was limited to one suicide report per consulate. Any more than one, and I'd put the credibility of the report in jeopardy, or worse, I'd turn the focus on me and my suspect jails that were driving multiple detainees to suicidal depths. Out of necessity, I diversified.

I began hitting problem embassies on multiple fronts, with coercion, forgeries, and lies. I manufactured faxes from family members appealing for their loved ones to be returned to their motherlands soon rather than rot in jail. At 701 Loyola I dictated quick lines here and there that female secretaries wrote for me on blank pieces of paper upon which I subsequently printed other pleading family letters. I was sure the feminine script would be above suspicion, and I could not imagine a line like "Please send Papa home" in a girl's cursive wouldn't tug at the heart of even a world-weary diplomat.

I claimed to be in charge of a list of special headquarters cases that consulates had to issue on lest they suffer punitive action from Washington. To lend reliability to the list, I usually left off one or two of a country's cases so it would not look like a housecleaning, but the excepted cases were always the least threatening offenders. This tactic worked so well with Russia that every time I called about any case, they would interrupt me to ask, "Is this one on the list?" Sometimes I intentionally conceded that no, this one was not on the special headquarters list yet, and I let them rope-a-dope me for a month or so before I called to report, "He made the list!" In that same phone call I would volunteer that we also had two new Russians, at which time the consul would cut me off abruptly and proclaim, "Only the one on the list today."

I spared no workable idea, not even one devised by an Indian convicted of practicing medicine without a license. At his removal hearing the quack had presented the IJ with a letter on White House stationery extending a presidential pardon for the Indian's harmful surgeries and other medical misconduct. I photocopied the White House letterhead and applied it to a memorandum of my own concoction, equally counterfeit to that of the "doctor," in which the White House proposed harsh consequences for governments refusing to issue travel documents. I scribbled an alien's name and A-number on top. In the margins I affected notes from White House personnel, meant to convey they'd passed the memo back and forth: "J, Think Yemen will still give us trouble?" "If they do, D, we'll come down on them like a hammer." Then I hit a random spot on the letter with a glue stick and slapped it on the back of my TD request sheaf so it looked as if it had gotten stuck there by accident, and I mailed it off.

I enjoyed great success, success quantified by passports landing in my mailbox. And each success encouraged me to try even harder to manipulate the system to make it work for what I considered the greater good. I kept numerous outrageous schemes going at all times.

It was one of my earliest, almost forgotten tactics that came back to bite me.

I got a call from the Romanian consulate first thing in the morning. As a DO you know that consulates rarely telephone you, and if they do, the call does not come first thing in the morning. You are not that high on their list of priorities. So the call itself scared me even before I picked up the anger in the consular officer's voice. I already felt the line of questioning was going to be threatening to my professional life.

"Mr. Holbrook," demanded the Romanian consul, "is it your policy that you are sending two officers for accompanying a citizen to their home country if you are not finding that citizen dangerous?"

"Our escort policy varies, sir. The decision to send two officers is based on the circumstances of the deportee. Violence is one factor to consider, as are escape history and physical and mental health."

"But if that is applying, if *any* of that is applying, your rules are requiring you to inform the consulate, yes?"

"Yes, sir."

"So we are being clear on this: If you are sending two officers, there is a reason?"

"There should be."

"Thank you, Mr. Holbrook. I will please speak to your supervisor now."

"Absolutely, sir. Just a minute, please." I hit the hold button and stared out my window. I did not want this stickler to talk to my supervisor. Romania didn't sound any personal alarms right now, but this guy obviously thought he had a legitimate grievance. I really wanted to know what it was. I hit the hold button again to release it. "Hello, sir. Mr. Seright has stepped out of his office. Would you like me to have him call you when he comes back? That should be within fifteen minutes." I was banking on fifteen minutes being enough time for me to brief John Seright, who was not my supervisor but who possessed the uncommon people skills to defuse this Romanian nightmare if anyone could.

"I'll call back," said the Romanian consular officer.

"Or maybe I can help you, sir. Do you want to tell me what the issue is?"

"The issue?" he snapped. "You were making no mention of violence or any other factors when you were requesting a passport from us for Alexandru cel Cumplit. But this week two of your officers are requesting official clearance for escorting him."

"Oh." In a lightning flash I saw the drawback to my stratagem, and I vowed in that instant to restrict its future use. For my initial TD request I had reported Alexandru cel Cumplit as a noncriminal. In fact he was a violent sociopath who necessitated full escort. I could not back off that latter part now because there was no way in the world that I'd inflict an unguarded Alexandru cel Cumplit on a commercial airliner. However I tried to extricate myself, it had to validate the two escorts. "I know why that is, sir."

"Oh, you do?" the consular officer replied. "Please, I hope you are telling me now."

"There was a large fight at the detention facility recently. It involved a lot of detainees, and Mr. cel Cumplit was one of the ones mentioned in the report. As you know, sir, our escort rules are very strict. Standards call for a two-officer escort if there's *any* violence in the subject's file. Unfortunately the jail report is in Mr. cel Cumplit's file, so we have no leeway on that technicality. We have to send two officers all the way to Bucureşti, even though it's a waste."

"Aaaah." The consular officer sounded his satisfaction. "I didn't know you were having such technicalities."

"I wish we weren't."

"Wait!" the Romanian consul exclaimed. His tone suggested he'd switched back to stickler. "You were saying the report from the jail is in his folder, yes? Is it possible you are faxing this to me?"

"Fax you the jail report from the fight, sir?"

"Yes. When I'm receiving the fax, I'm approving the clearance."

"Why don't I let you go right now then, sir, and I can fax it to you in the next few minutes? That's no problem." It really wasn't. If cel Cumplit hadn't been in at least three fights this month, I was a monkey's uncle. My only challenge would be finding a report that didn't demonstrate what a menace to the world cel Cumplit was.

I sent the fax off, and the clearance came through. It was a bullet dodged. I'd never considered that these long-lunch consuls might possess the attention span to compare a TD request with an escort wire weeks later. The experience showed me that there were traps out there.

If I hoped to survive them, I'd have to get even more devious.

Eleven

Philadelphia and the Fifty-three Bastards

I walked the halls at work expecting to get busted at any moment. I knew my fellow agents would consider my conduct unworthy of the badge. I respected those agents. I even respected them for what I imagined would be their disapproval of me.

At this point I just couldn't stop myself.

I lied easily those days, to pretty much anyone I met along the deportation trail. People used to say I couldn't lie, but now that was far from true. This job had turned me into a master fabricator. It was unexpected because in the law enforcement arena the Deportation Officer was widely thought of as a straight-ahead post. Some people make great law enforcers but can't stomach the parts of the mission that require them to violate their own character standards: lying to suspects, facilitating criminal activity in stings, building bonds with scumbags in order to take them down harder later, and every manner of undercover and quasi-undercover operation. The enforcement-minded plain folks who bristled at that side of law enforcement were able to find their natural home in Deportation. I was one of those who had been drawn by the directness of the job.

DOs didn't go undercover. DOs didn't need to build trust with suspects to make cases. A DO's cases were already made. The fugitives a DO went after were already deportable. They'd previously done dirt, and there was no need to convict them of doing any more dirt in order to send them home. In fact DOs referred to their wanted men with the shorthand B&B. This stood for "bag" (apprehend the alien) and "baggage" (let the alien pack one suitcase for his flight home). A DO had only to grab his fugitives and ship them. With a mission that straightforward, to whom would you need to lie?

As it turned out, my answer was: just about everyone. It was the cursed middle territory that made it necessary. On the front and back ends, arrest and removal, sure, a DO could be effective without falsification. But in between? On my docket? Good luck.

I lived in a false universe. I headed numerous false units: Long-term Cases Division, Special Cases Division, Problem Consulate Division, HQ List Enforcement Squad, Special Liaison to the White House—whatever I thought was worth a try. I conveyed false dispatches of menace and censure from false commanders. My false professional existence made sense to me because it was the only professional existence that was compatible with my professional leadership. If you are a Deportation Officer charged by your government with the removal of your country's most dangerous personae non gratae, and your government is releasing them into your country in direct opposition to you and the laws it is charging you to execute, you will take some measure to reconcile the contradiction. The measure I took was extreme. I twisted everything in the middle so that the contradiction didn't matter. If one part of a statement is false, I'd learned in grade school, the whole statement is false. I made my piece of the deportation mechanism false to render the release machine untrue.

And then one of the weirdest things that could have happened to someone in my situation happened to me. I was given a fresh DO and told to train him.

Craig made good on his former promise to provide me help when new talent came on board. The day Tyrone, a longtime DEO from down the hall, was elevated to Deportation Officer our boss paired him with me.

Craig gave me instructions to bring Tyrone up to speed on the complexities of the assignment and to get him off to a proper start as a DO. By all appearances it was a great move.

Craig was to be commended for attaching Tyrone to me, thereby putting two streetwise officers together on New Orleans's aggravated felons. It also made sense for Craig to place his up-and-comer Tyrone where the learning curve was steepest. Nothing better for a new troop than to hit the ground at full speed.

Craig also knew we got along well. Tyrone and I had plenty in common, starting with our zip code in the city. On the job we'd already worked some missions together, including the first raid I'd participated in after the academy, an alien-smuggling enterprise run by a shotgun-wielding U.S. citizen named Cooter. It had been an Investigations-led operation, but the special agents had enlisted Tyrone and me for extra muscle. Since then we'd teamed up a few times, and it had always been positive.

Tyrone joining Ames on the end-of-the-line detained docket probably looked to most observers like the perfect union.

The problem was Tyrone was supposed to learn from me. I was expected to show him the right way to do things, but I did nothing by the book. I couldn't very well teach Tyrone by my example. It would have been an overwhelming bad dream for a beginner DO. The job is difficult enough to master when you stay in the boundaries. Try getting a handle on it when your training officer designates as "suicidal" one violent felon from each country, sends forged faxes from two-dollar-a-page corner stores in the city so the Deportation phone number won't be recognized, willingly sends aliens home on fake documents, and alternates fantastic job titles depending on which consulate he's calling.

There was no way. With everything else Deportation made me juggle, I now had to conceal my vocational techniques from my apprentice.

My efforts to lead a work life separate from Tyrone were somewhat rooted in my fear of getting caught. By this time I was paranoid enough to wonder if Tyrone had been told to keep an eye on me and report his findings. It could have been crafty engineering on Craig's part to assign the last person I'd suspect to spy. But my main motivation for keeping Tyrone at a distance was that I liked him, and I was doing everything I could not to corrupt him. I carried the sense now, somewhere in the back of my mind, that I was going down the pipes. I had to make sure I didn't drag Tyrone down with me. The unfortunate consequence was that I was a poor training officer. Tyrone learned almost everything on his own. When he asked me questions, I tried to give him by-the-book answers, but I barely remembered the book anymore. I'd twisted my work life up so many ways that I didn't know what would get us in trouble and what wouldn't. I left Tyrone adrift. Guilt pressed on me when I contrasted my performance as a trainer with that of my own training officer, Phil, who had been such an awesome mentor. I wanted to tell Tyrone I was sorry. I still feel like telling him now.

Tyrone and I had a loaded schedule this day. Two U.S. marshals' flights were inbound from Philadelphia, and we were to meet one at Louis Armstrong. On the airplanes were 160 final order aliens for us to scatter into our jails. I haven't yet explained to readers this aspect of our job, but now is a good time.

Not only did we at New Orleans Deportation have our own criminal aliens to deal with, but we accepted shipment of criminal aliens from other parts of the United States. Louisiana had the cheapest lockdown facilities in the nation, charging the feds a mere $46 per day compared with $184 in pricey northeastern locales. Given the finite budget of the Immigration organization, there was no arguing the benefit of housing four aggravated felons for the price of one. And there was always room in Louisiana. Not that the Bayou State had trouble filling its own jails—Louisiana actually owned the number one incarceration rate in the country—but parish jails were paid only $22 a day for every state inmate and as little as $9 each for local offenders. Sheriffs know their math: better to kick out a state or parish inmate prematurely than to miss out on a $17,000-a-year federal detainee. So the river of bad apples kept flowing south, amassing eternally in the brick and concertina delta of Louisiana's detention facilities.

The A-files came with the bodies, and we in the New Orleans district took ownership of the cases. This was the structure of our incomparable two-pronged misery. New Orleans, being the fugitive mecca that it was, kept us up to our ears in our own extraordinary criminal alien population.

Adding to that, our cheap lockdown facilities made us the end-of-the-line dumping ground for the rest of the nation's problem cases. We had it all.

Tyrone and I rolled up to the perimeter gate on the west side of Louis Armstrong. I slid my airport badge through the reader from the driver's side. The gate opened, and I moved up so the rear bumper just cleared the gate. While we waited for the wire gate to close behind us, Tyrone and I peeled the fifteen-inch-diameter magnetic agency seals off the metal panel behind our seats and slapped them on our painted sedan doors. We had to be marked on airport property. When the gate closed behind us, ensuring no one else could sneak in on our card, I drove on.

It was a clear, sunny day, and even with big planes taxiing across our line of sight, the expanse of this concrete table seemed huge. On escort missions we'd turn right at this point to bring our prisoners to their commercial flight gates. Today I turned left.

"We're not the first ones here," Tyrone said, indicating some peers congregated around the staff shack ahead of us on the baking tarmac. We parked with the other Deportation rides, a mix of take-home sedans and transport trucks, and walked over to join our crew. One DO passed out cigars, and I took one. A half dozen of us sat in tipped-back chairs on the flight line, laughing and smoking.

"There it is," somebody said as the minimally marked marshals' plane dropped through the blue sky. We went to work.

We raced out in our vehicles to meet the aircraft. We jumped out all at once and ran toward our stations. The tarmac was noisy even after the plane stopped moving. Bobby Smith, a journeyman DO and our top fugitive hunter, took perimeter duty, posing under a wingtip with his Remington 870 pump shotgun racked for combat. I would have loved being the shotgun guy on perimeter, but today I had to climb the steps. Since I'd gone out of my way to divide the incoming alien roster in advance along the lines of destination prisons (I'd wanted to get particular cases into Tangi), I'd been nominated to read my own roll call when time came to deplane the bad boys. The aircraft interior looked as colorful as I thought it would. Drawing from more than thirty countries, the manifest represented more than 15 percent of the nations in the world.

I grabbed the microphone for the PA system. I'd hardly started to read when one marshal interrupted. "Fuck that, man. Just get 'em off the plane."

"No. I'm reading them in my order."

"Fuck! This is gonna take forever. Why?"

"You're the one who's two hours late," I said. "Don't jump on me for taking ten minutes instead of five."

Another marshal calmed down the first. He nodded to me, and I proceeded. There were high-strung officers in every agency. I wasn't bothered.

One thing I liked about my reading role was that I got to see every alien face-to-face as he walked down the aisle and past me to exit. If I picked up an extremely negative vibe, I marked his name on my page. I'd check his file later to see if he warranted elevated repatriation priority.

I heard a commotion outside, and I looked below out the back hatch to discover that no alien was the cause. The aliens had flown shackled, as was the rule, but in a routine interagency spectacle, the marshals were now accusing Deportation of having brought "twice as old" handcuffs and leg irons to exchange. A shouting match resulted. No middle ground was found among the enforcer brethren, so now the marshals were unhooking every criminal alien who stepped off the plane and the Deportation Officers were immediately reshackling them with their own identical equipment. I smiled at my partner, Tyrone, who was down in the action. He shook his head.

I resumed calling the names into the microphone, a little more deliberately than before. I was no longer the slow link, thanks to the unhooking and hooking below, and I was able to match the aliens to their crimes on my roster and make an assessment of each man as he passed. Sometimes they stopped to make assessments of me.

"Where I go?" exclaimed a bearded Syrian convicted of intimidation with a deadly weapon. He leaned into my space. He seemed the type who was angry by nature.

"Keep moving," I said.

"You tell me first where I go!" Spittle flew off his beard.

I made sure my finger was off the microphone before I spoke into his ear: "You go down the steps. You go by yourself right now, or I can help."

"I go by myself and I say you helped!"

"That's okay too," I said.

He cursed me in his language as he turned and headed down the steps. I pointed him out to the enforcers below, so they'd know to be careful when they switched chains. His name got a mark.

This was a bang-up procession, as expected. In a tradition well recognized by our office, every other district sent aliens to New Orleans after a process of careful selection to ensure we received its biggest headaches. Philly had cherry-picked these standouts straight from its notorious York and Berks county contract facilities. York and Berks were the closest thing that part of the country had to our immigration contract jails in Louisiana, which is to say they were dumping grounds for the eastern seaboard, and their handpicked losers were all-star deportation freaks to a man. Philadelphia had shipped the boys straight to their natural home, and we in turn welcomed them to their destiny. Devils like these always wound up in New Orleans.

After I'd called the last one off, I walked the aisle with a marshal to make sure we didn't have an escape artist hiding under the seats. Our check was negative. I shook a couple of marshals' hands and headed down the steps to the flight line where Tyrone had our boys corralled.

Our boys were headed for Tangipahoa Parish Prison. Just as Philadelphia had conscientiously airfreighted us its worst, I with equal diligence had selected the most worthy to enter my warehouse. Vans were already rolling off the airport property in all directions, spreading Philly's gift into detention facilities across Louisiana and western Mississippi. Absent from those vans were the fifty-three I'd kept for myself. The majority of Philly's most fiendish did not quite merit cobilling with New Orleans's most fiendish, but these fifty-three showed that kind of promise. I directed their linear formation into the big bus I had on loan from the Border Patrol, checking them off my final list as they got on.

We had the bodies. Tyrone confirmed we had the A-files. We were ready to go. I boarded the bus last and greeted the uniformed on-loan drivers.

"Do you know how to get there?" asked the one behind the wheel.

"I do. But you'll be able to follow him." I pointed through the wind-shield. Tyrone looped in front of us in the sedan with the blue light flashing and a trio of alien heads swaying in unison in the rear glass. Tyrone had three of our fifty-three locked down with him.

I stepped toward the bus aliens, eyeing them all. "We're going to a facility more than an hour away," I announced. "I'll answer your questions when we get there. You will get dinner tonight, and the food is good."

I joined the shackled prisoners in general seating, and we rolled. The drivers were forward of the locked cage door, and I was on this side with the felons. I sat sideways in the front seat with my back to the skin of the bus so I could watch the men, who were watching me. Their eyes rolled off me and found each other. As they sized up their company, they could not help comprehending on some level that they had arrived in this group on this bus not by chance but as the result of meticulous consideration, and they might have read in my eyes that I had been part of the process.

I had a plan for them. I had the same simple plan for them that I had for all my aliens at Tangi. I planned to get them out of my country.

I allowed a glance over my shoulder, and I saw Tyrone right in front of us, speeding in the left lane. Motorists responded to Tyrone's blue flasher. Ahead of him cars drifted in continual peels to the right. Tyrone's being with me but separate from me, in a vehicle of his own, seemed to capture our professional pairing.

We made the Amite exit, the same exit I always took, and Tyrone raced ahead to block the intersection where we turned. He stopped broadside in the oncoming traffic lane, and we passed him there as my bus took the left unimpeded. People craned their necks out of car windows to see what was in our bus, but every bus window was caged. It was also dark in here, and there was no penetrating the shroud. We hissed to a halt at the sally port and a driver unlocked the cage door. I told the aliens to stay seated. I hopped out to confer with Tyrone.

The jail staff poured out of the facility. A heavy shift was in effect to process our roll-ins. I'd notified them these were Tyrone and Ames standard hardheads, and they came out now in a fitting show of force.

We realized the bus was too big to park inside the low-covered sally port, so we rolled it adjacent and had the aliens step off and through the gate. We watched them closely on those ten steps between the bus and the wire fence. I saw looks in the eyes of some head-cracking deputies that let me know they wouldn't be upset at all if someone stepped out of line, but the aliens were behaving, typical of new prison arrivals. For my part I tried to get the aliens inside quickly. You could count on that new arrival/good behavior syndrome for about five minutes.

When the last man was in, I climbed back on the bus to perform the same escape artist check I had on the airplane. I looked behind and under every seat. Negative again. I turned to the drivers and ascertained they were the same immigration agents I'd met at the airport and not two of my aliens in their uniforms. I thanked both drivers and sent them off.

Inside the jail I joined the deputies in unhooking the arrivals. Tyrone presented the multipage roll-in form to the desk sergeant, who signed for the receipt of all fifty-three. If one of the hooligans got away now, Tangi would take the hit for it. But even up here in the administration area, the closest way out was through two reinforced metal doors with rigid dead bolts. We were past the point of likely escape. We had much left to do. Some parts of in processing the prison could take care of later. The parts involving security, like photographs and registration, the prison wanted done immediately. Tyrone and I helped where we were needed. This was a long process. Though we couldn't see it through the walls, we could sense the daylight disappear and the night turn black outside.

When we finally had the aliens in the classroom, all the desks occupied and numerous aliens leaning against the walls, there were impulses of impatience and agitation I could feel. We all were breathing each other's air in this crowded room, and all of us resented each other for it. No one was satisfied and no one would be, and half of me wanted to send everyone to his dorm right now. But if I didn't answer the questions they'd been saving, the jail was liable to see an uprising.

I walked to the front of the class and introduced myself. I introduced Tyrone. I told the aliens that we were their Deportation Officers, and I gave them the address where they could write us. I assured them we would visit often and be available to anyone who needed to ask us about his case.

"But," I told them, "in our eyes, your cases are over."

"What does that mean?" interrupted an alien with a childish voice. He had a fixed sneer I'd noticed on the bus. "You're just gonna leave us here and ignore us?"

I stopped talking and regarded the man in the rear. As a DO you expect some agitators in every crop to confront you. The agitators try to embarrass you at events like this, your debut with the new felons. Here troublemakers score maximum damage with minimum risk. They sabotage your authority from the first, yet enjoy security in the knowledge that only the most impetuous officer would respond with physical violence in this scene. If for a moment you consider force, you quickly check that instinct. You have been trained extensively to meet violent action with the minimum level of violent reaction necessary to subdue it. You do not employ any force on a man who is simply heckling you, no matter how inconvenient the heckling. If you are that impetuous one-in-a-hundred agent who does dive over the desks to flatten this loudmouthed whoreson to the tile for his having come to your country and hurt innocent people and followed that with his unimaginable nerve to interrupt you while you were trying to provide helpful information to a roomful of foreign criminals, then your time carrying the badge will be short. Depending on the situation, your time on this earth might be short too. Tonight, in the classroom of Tangipahoa Parish Prison, you are one of five unarmed law enforcers in the company of more than ten times as many violent criminals. If you initiate violence in this tinderbox, your fellow enforcers in the room will fight valiantly against the uprising alien horde that you have set off. And if your peers survive the hour, if their reinforcements arrive in time to stream into the classroom in their riot gear and push back your foes, and the ascendancy of the enforcers is restored, those peers will then turn their beatings on you.

I responded to the agitator calmly, for the benefit of the whole crop: "No, it doesn't mean we're going to ignore you. It means the opposite. Since all your appeals are exhausted and your removal order is final, I'm going to give you my full attention while I figure out how to get you to your home country."

The agitator with his fixed sneer jumped back again in a shrill tone.

"You ain't gonna get me to my country! Motherfuckers always try to get me to my country, and motherfuckers always fail. I—"

"Who are you?"

"What?" he asked disingenuously. "I can't hear shit in here. This place sucks." I knew he'd heard my simple question perfectly well. He was still trying to fluster me.

I fondly remembered how Phil used to respond to aliens like this. Phil would blow his top and jump down the alien's throat, and I always loved it. The only drawback was, we could never carry on from there. After Phil had finished lambasting the alien, he'd tear out of the building in a trail of profanities. In a situation like this, once you let your temper go, it's gone, and you just have to call the whole assembly off. I drew a restorative breath of air before resuming. "What's your name?"

Kept on the spot, the alien suddenly clammed up. He folded his arms and pushed out his big jaw in defiance.

I turned to a pair of deputies behind me. "Can you match this guy off his photo or bracelet or something and tell me who he is?"

I thought one of them would head straight for the door for the information, but instead both deputies eagerly moved on the troublemaker and pulled him out of his seat. From there they hauled him out of the classroom.

I took several steps toward a stringy-haired blond youth who wore a psychotic stare. He was seated beside the agitator's empty chair. "You were talking to him as if you were friends. What do you call him?"

"Hambrick," answered the stringy-haired blond.

I referenced my list. "Hambrick Ramkishun from Guyana." I studied the aliens. "Is anybody else in here Hambrick Ramkishun from Guyana?"

Most of the room stayed silent. A few said, "No, sir."

"All right, so that's the guy." I was now able to put a sneering face to the name I remembered from my prearrival culling phase. Hambrick Ramkishun's life in America had consisted of violent assaults alternating with prison sentences resulting from those assaults. In other words, he was typical of the audience I was addressing. I continued. "Mr. Ramkishun is convinced we won't be able to get him back home, but I promise you all right now that I will." I paced the classroom, eyeing every member of my audience. "As you all know, New Orleans Deportation gets criminal aliens home. We have the number one removal rate in the country. We take our job seriously. We take our job especially seriously when our government brings you here from somewhere else in America. The problem there for us is that unless we get you home, our government is going to let you out. And when you get out, we know from experience, many of you will choose to stay in New Orleans. My fellow officers and I live in New Orleans, and we have enough trouble with the criminals who come to our city for their own reasons. The last thing we need is our government making our problems worse by picking up felons from the rest of the country and dumping you in our city. You understand?"

Silent contemplation from most, and a few yes, sir's.

I resumed. "If you really want us to ship you home before you get released by headquarters, then please let us know the way Mr. Ramkishun did. We can make you a priority as well."

With my pen I marked Hambrick Ramkishun's name on my list. I continued my monologue without interruption. The jail staff served the aliens their dinner here in the classroom, and the aliens listened while they ate. My oration was not loud or dramatic like the knockout speeches I'd heard from the diaphragms of Phil and Craig. I did not put a lot into my deliveries because my mind was spinning too hard on how I would get these thugs home. It was not important that I shock or even impress these aliens. They were not my adversaries, any more than the lambs were the wolf's adversaries on the ranch. The wolf had to worry about the sheepdog more than the lambs. I had to worry about my leaders more than the aliens.

When I opened the floor to questions, they came nonstop.

There were serious property issues. More than twenty of the aliens in here had not seen their property since *before* they'd been transferred to Philadelphia. They had receipts from the previous district. It was excruciating to consider, but Tyrone and I were going to have to devote many hours to tracking that property down. Deportable aliens had a right to their property. We could not deprive even the most heinous criminals of their belongings or allow anyone else in the chain of immigration custody to so deprive them. We were not the Beijing police.

It was after midnight when Tyrone and I finally wrapped up. We told the aliens we'd visit soon. The stringy-haired blond, who'd heated up at the end with a string of unconventional questions, somehow thought of more and caught up with Tyrone and me in the hall.

"How do you rate this jail culturally?" he asked.

"Very good," Tyrone said.

"So, they don't restrict your freedom?"

"It's a jail."

He swept his stringy hair from his face. "I know, but I mean freedom of expression. I believe in this important freedom, which is why I'm drawn to America. I'm going to stay in America."

"Maybe next time. Not this time."

The man's intense eyes seemed to be in a state of constant search. "Why next time?" he asked.

"We have to execute your deportation warrant," I said. "After we deport you, you're welcome to apply at the U.S. Embassy for a waiver of your crimes, and, knowing the State Department, they'll probably give you a visa to come back here. That's what we mean by next time."

"You think the embassy will give me a waiver even for the aggravated battery of a law enforcement officer?"

"Especially for that one," I said.

He nodded. "Then that will be my Plan B, in the event that my asylum petition is denied. I consider myself culturally an American."

Tyrone and I stopped at the entrance to the administration area. I heard the click from the released dead bolt and I pushed the steel door. "Good night," I said.

"Just so you know"—the man spoke through the closing door—"I refuse to go back to Iceland."

I tested the door to make sure it was secure between us. His behavior seemed appropriate for a criminal who'd escaped a Reykjavik insane asylum and fled to America. I did not mark the Icelander's name. He did have a pending asylum claim, and I could not deport him before that was decided. He would eventually lose that case, and I would escort him to Iceland, where trench-coated security police would appear in the jetway and the whole group of us would bring him in a secure vehicle to the same Reykjavik insane asylum from which he'd escaped. Several months later the Icelandic security police would e-mail John Seright, my partner on the Reykjavik mission, to notify us that the man had escaped from the insane asylum again and we should keep our eyes open.

Tyrone and I stepped outside the prison into the dark night and headed home. An hour later we passed the exit for Louis Armstrong International Airport, and I thought of our arriving there, coming the other way in this vehicle, and smoking cigars in the squint-inducing sun on the flight line while we'd sat in tipped-back chairs. It seemed like a memory from another age.

The next time we convened at the office, there were several dozen new A-files piled around our work areas. These A-files corresponded to the new arrivals in our docket, a lot more than just the group we'd rolled into Tangi. The first thing I did with Tyrone was contact the Guyana Embassy to follow up on the request for Hambrick Ramkishun's TD. I had promised fifty-two alien aggravated felons in that classroom that I would get Hambrick Ramkishun back to his motherland. Now I had to succeed. I reviewed the A-file carefully with Tyrone, so we could tell Guyana when previous TD requests had been made and exactly what had been sent with those previous requests and so we could answer any question the embassy had about any biographic detail pertaining to its citizen. With Tyrone watching, I performed it all as I imagined the book said I should. We made no headway whatsoever. Six months earlier we would have, but today Guyana was a nightmare that the State Department had helped create. I hung up the phone and smiled weakly at Tyrone, and I said something lame about how we'd have to be persistent.

Good God, Guyana. The readers will learn all they need to on the Guyana front soon enough, when I relate what I did with Guyana and precisely what I did to Hambrick Ramkishun in one of my most low-down moments as a DO.

But that day with Tyrone, it went no further. We'd asked the embassy, "May we send back Hambrick Ramkishun?" and the embassy had answered no, and then we'd set down the phone. It was only the first A-file we'd cracked out of what looked like a hundred A-files recently spilled around our desks, all fresh aliens, all plucked from elsewhere but looking to set up illicit shop in our beloved New Orleans if Tyrone and I failed. Honestly, we had no chance to win this.

Dishonestly, I thought I had glimmer of a shot.

Twelve

Dragan Madunic and the Tense Checkpoint

A s a DO you counted yourself lucky when you got to see a case through to its conclusion. Escorting a dangerous alien home was one of the most gratifying pieces of the business. You paid for that gratification in sweat and hot-wire tension every inch of the way.

Once a final order alien had a travel document and all holds were cleared, it was your job to determine how far the alien needed to be accompanied. A simple white-collar criminal was seen only as far as his last connection and let go there, in a process known as departure verification, in which officers watched the plane door close and the bird take off with the alien inside.

The criminal aliens who had to be accompanied to their ultimate destinations typically fell into one or more special categories we have discussed: violent boys, escape artists, the insane, and the sick. Most of them were repatriated by DEOs, the transportation specialists in the business. It was the extraordinary cases, those likely to incur contact with foreign officials and demand such skills as diplomacy and knowledge of the law, that remained the responsibility of Deportation Officers till the very end. When you got one of those cases, every detail of the trip was yours to handle.

Just getting on the plane was a knotted process that some never mastered. Your walking into an airport and buying a ticket for the hoodlum wasn't an option. By bureaucratic edict, all trips had to be booked through Omega World Travel, the government-contracted travel agency headquartered in suburban DC. A fresh DO quickly learned to call airlines directly and double-check every leg Omega World booked. The travel agency was so infamous for hanging officers out to dry that it became part of your deportation vernacular. If, for example, you and your partner escorted a Somali prisoner into Khartoum, Sudan, only to discover—while your vocal prisoner screamed for his Sunni Muslim brothers in the airport to rescue him from the infidel kidnappers—that there was no Khartoum–Mogadishu connection and in fact, the carrier printed on your Omega World Travel–cut tickets had gone out of business more than a year ago, you and your partner, for that perilous duration, were said to be in Omega World.

Many were the officers thrown to the dogs, and it was a sharp cut to the nerves when a foreign airport snapped into hostile territory in a blink. When you lacked onward connections, with malevolent civilian bystanders and bone-corrupt security goons circling in for the strike, your mind grabbed for that special gear you'd need to continue the mission and emerge with your skin. It was the textbook case for *Thinking Your Way Out*.

Incidentally, shooting your way out was not an option available to you abroad, nor was even cowing a mob with a flash of holstered firepower. In the irony-riddled Deportation Officer existence, one of the classic touches was that agents flew armed only on departure verification escorts within the United States—by definition, those trips with aliens who had *not* demonstrated violent or crazy behavior. When you had to go international with the established maniacs and berserkers, you left your .40-cal at home. Like virtually all American enforcers, DOs were prohibited from carrying guns into foreign countries, so when it came to bringing certifiably dangerous aliens all the way home, you relied on your hand-to-hand skills to carry the day. DOs had no firepower in Omega World.

In light of those obsolete schedules seemingly favored by Omega World

Travel agents, I found the best bet was to research the route yourself and then to tell Omega exactly what you wanted it to book, right down to the flight numbers. Picking an escort-friendly airline was part of the challenge. At the time Continental imposed a limit of one alien per flight under the best conditions. Lufthansa prohibited all escorts, except for deportees who were proved to have entered America on Lufthansa flights in the first place. And on every airplane, all the time, the captain had the last word. All it took to derail a deportation at any segment along the way was for the man with four bars on his shoulder to say no. You got to know which airlines' pilots were likely to send you walking back up the jet bridge and which were generally happy to have you aboard.

Once the trip was booked, you had to send country-clearance request wires to receiving governments up to two weeks in advance. The governments reviewed the comprehensive itineraries, officer identities, and arrival details, then, with any luck, sent approval back through the U.S. State Department.

This morning I had the approval in a hard-sided folder in my bag, along with signed travel orders, my passport and the deportee's, and the ticketless itinerary for the escort trip Tyrone and I were about to take. All the details were smooth. I hadn't had a failed deport in my career, and I rolled off the curb in front of my Ida Street home confident this one would fall in line.

There was no traffic in the early hour, and in minutes I was watching Tyrone step out of his handsome house on North Robertson. Although virtually every other immigration agent on the ninth floor, from Deportation to Investigations, lived in the suburban mansion estates to the north, east, and west, it was New Orleans city proper, significantly, that was home to each of the detained docket DOs (me in Mid-City, Fenwick in Gentilly, John in the Irish Channel, and Tyrone, whose Treme house was one of two he owned in town). From Tyrone's, it was a five-minute cruise to Orleans Parish Prison.

We pulled up to Templeman III in the OPP compound. I flicked on the blue flasher and buzzed the gate. Tyrone and I both extended our credentials to the camera. The heavy gray gate rolled open, and we cruised in.

I drove straight to the back in the fire lane between the prison building and the outside wall, and I followed the alley counterclockwise around two corners until I was at the rear of the prison. I parked and got out with Tyrone. On one side of the fire lane was the chain-link fence that hugged the jail, and on the other side was the high wall topped with razor wire. We went toward the chain link.

Down the corridor inside, we presented the guards with the full-rollout form for Dragan Madunic. Both parties signed for the transfer. Tyrone and I had rolled Madunic out of Tangi yesterday so he could cash his check, and we'd put him in here overnight for pickup convenience.

Despite their peer's short tenure, the aliens in the two-story dorm howled and rang their bars in a sendoff ceremony for their latest departure when we pulled him out of his cell. Tyrone and I escorted the broad-shouldered Croat to the contained basketball court between the dorms to let him change while we dictated the ground rules for our upcoming trip. He peeled off his blue OPP sweats and tossed them against the brick wall behind the basketball hoop. His muscular torso featured scars and extensive prison ink.

After he had switched into his traveling clothes, I searched him thoroughly, running my fingers through his brown hair, then peering into his mouth and working my way down meticulously to the leather shoes on his feet. Tyrone searched him again for good measure and clicked a pair of handcuffs around his wrists.

"So, we're going then?" Madunic asked.

"We're going," I said. The Croat slid his hard-soled shoes across the buffed prison floor in the direction Tyrone led him.

We took our charge outside to the car. I glanced up the alley of concrete and gleaming wire. None of OPP's detention facilities featured so much as a square of grass for our aliens to walk on. That was one of its charms.

I pushed Madunic's head down under the door frame.

"You ready to go home?" Tyrone asked him.

The Croat didn't answer the question, only asked, "Can I visit my family here?"

"They can visit you there," I said.

Tyrone dropped into the driver seat. "You need to ask a U.S. embassy for a waiver if you want to come back to America. You're an aggravated felon, so you'll need a waiver for the rest of your life."

The Croat leaned back and forth across the seat as we drove to the airport, looking through one window, then the other, absorbing every view.

We were there in twenty minutes. Tyrone swiped his airport badge at the electronic gate and pulled forward. We performed the familiar ritual of slapping the magnetic agency seals onto the exterior door panels for the cruise in. Planes took off around us. Tyrone hit the brakes to allow one jumbo to taxi across our bow to the runway. Madunic stared outside silently, cocooned in the jet engine vibrations as we crawled the tarmac.

Tyrone parked the car in the Immigration slot. This was one way to bring deportees to their gates, directly from the flight line through the back door. Our airport badges cracked nearly every lock on the property.

"Mr. Madunic," I said, pulling open the car door, "do you think we need to keep those handcuffs on you?"

"Can you take them off?" he asked.

"It's up to us," said Tyrone.

"If we believe an alien will behave himself and not force us to use pain compliance techniques to keep him in line, then we sometimes let him go without handcuffs," I said.

"I won't cause any problems," said Madunic, extending his wrists for liberation. "I'm not stupid."

I twisted my key in the handcuffs and pulled the Croat out of the car. Before I closed the door, I tucked the handcuffs under the seat. Both Tyrone and I had string cuffs if we needed to restrain this guy. There were a lot of drawbacks to having the prisoner cuffed on escorts. Handcuffs drew attention, they were valuable enough that corrupt officials in foreign countries frequently confiscated them, and worst of all, handcuffs scared pilots into refusing escorts. I didn't like cuffs at all on trips, unless the deportee was a full-on brawling psychopath, in which case I voted to have him shackled from head to toe, preferably with a contract doctor on hand to stick him with a sedative needle every two hours. In the rest of the cases it was better to stay vigilant and watch the package than it was to worry about how everyone else was going to react to the silver steel handcuffs.

"Here's your wallet, Mr. Madunic," Tyrone said, handing the Croat a worn leather accessory with a button. "We have your cash from your jail check too. I'll give you your money on the last flight." Foreign escorts were an area of the job for which Tyrone needed no training. He'd been a DEO since before I'd joined the force, and he'd flown more missions than I.

"Thank you." The Croat accepted his wallet. He watched people as he stepped through the concourse between me and Tyrone. The time waiting at the gate went by quickly, and soon we were walking down the jet bridge, the first passengers to board US Airways Flight 188 to Charlotte.

The gate agent had already briefed the cabin crew, but I sought out the captain and extended my hand. "Hi, Captain. I'm Ames Holbrook; I'm a Deportation Officer. My partner and I would like to carry a prisoner on your airplane if it's all right with you."

The captain pumped my hand, then Tyrone's with fresh introductions. "You have him under control?"

"We've got him, Captain," Tyrone said with a sure nod.

I said, "We can tie him up if you'd rather."

"That's your area of expertise," the captain replied. "You-all have a good flight."

We marched Madunic to the back row of the empty airplane. We put him against the window. I slid in next to him with Tyrone on the aisle.

Madunic kept his face glued to the window. Madunic wasn't an import from another part of the country. He was one of our locals, and when he looked out the window all the way through takeoff at the boundless green of the trees and liquid brown of the bayou, he was taking in the Deep South, where he'd lived and where he'd done his crimes. He didn't stop looking till we were above the clouds and there was nothing else to see.

I studied the prisoner. The first step was always to gauge the alien on an emotional level: What did his mental state appear to be? Was he getting restless? Was he amassing internal energy? Looking for an opportunity?

I didn't see any signs. Then again sometimes you just didn't. This was a serious criminal who'd been convicted of multiple crimes during his stay in America but who was otherwise a question mark. He'd come from a German-speaking family in Croatia and did not speak Croatian. His consulate had initially refused to issue his TD, forcing me to go to work on his family, one member of whom had in the end mailed me Dragan's passport. Nothing about this case had been easy, and no one expected it to be easy now. It was why Craig hadn't hesitated to assign both Tyrone and me to the mission, even though it meant our urgent docket would stand still for three days. There were too many surprises in this guy's file to play it any other way.

The flight attendant came and took Tyrone's drink order first.

"I'll have a water, please," I said when she looked at me.

"A can of ginger ale," Madunic requested.

Tyrone looked at the attendant and said, "You can give me that can. I'll pour it for him."

She gave all the drinks to Tyrone and smiled nervously. "Let me know if you need anything else."

After some time the flight attendant came around to collect the cups, and some time after that we were on the ground in Charlotte.

Tyrone kept a close eye on the Croat as we wove through the busy concourse. We had him penned in on the move. Charlotte wasn't our airport. Tyrone and I no longer had the advantage of familiarity with the territory. In the lead, I kept checking over my shoulder. This would be the worst time for our charge to go rabbit, and it was also the most likely. Madunic had figured out by now that the next connection would take him overseas.

But we got him onboard US Airways Flight 94 without incident.

By the time we touched down in London's Gatwick Airport, we were still good, except for the fatigue. Madunic did not feel fatigue. He'd slept for the entire flight. This is why some deportees wait till deep in the journey to make their escape. The players' energy reserves move in diametric directions. The deportee eats and sleeps, amassing energy, while the officers maintain continuous alertness, tipping their batteries in a constant drain. Tyrone and I had been up for twenty hours, with another six to go before we set the Croat on his native soil. We were used to the hours. Today's imperfect routing notwithstanding (DOs sometimes had to fly on a particular date, whether or not air schedules were optimal), this wasn't even one of the longer escorts. Knowledge of that was comforting but changed nothing.

You have to stay on. The criminal is waiting for a single instant. All the other instants don't matter if your prisoner catches you off guard in one.

Tyrone and I smothered Madunic as we walked. We were in the sterile area, so Madunic would have to get past guards in order to escape into England, but even an unsuccessful escape here would be damaging. If he managed to get away from us, and security grabbed him in Gatwick, there were two certain results. First, British authorities would quickly return him to America. Second, those same authorities might well use the incident to prohibit Gatwick's use as a transit point for criminal repatriations. It had happened before. No airport could be taken for granted as an eternal throughway, no matter how strategic. Germany this year had been making noise to stop our outbound criminals from transiting through Frankfurt, an invaluable connection airport for every DO. If Madunic slipped away here, and authorities looked into the broad-shouldered Croat's criminal history, there would be an outcry.

Tyrone checked us in at the transfer desk. The agent gave us a pass to the business lounge. Although we never booked anything but coach coming out of America (for going back on long flights the rules prescribed business class), we sometimes got special treatment for our official passports. We also had a lot of miles. The three of us settled into the business lounge, and I grabbed Madunic some sandwiches and a ginger ale. I liked the business lounge for the containment it provided. Just to reach the concourse, Madunic would have had to clear a railing and a door, and I was confident we'd take him before he made the latter.

He didn't try. Fifteen minutes before boarding, we headed to our flight. I watched Madunic's face as the Croatia Airlines signs came into view. I saw no change in his expression. Perhaps he wasn't a runner.

Tyrone cleared us with the airline staff while I stood behind Madunic.

"Let's go," Tyrone said. "They're ready for us."

Tyrone led the way with Madunic on his heels and me trailing. We boarded Flight 499 for Dubrovnik and moved down the empty aisle to our customary seats in the back. There we waited for the rest of the passengers to fill in.

The jet engines spooled up outside the window as the Croatia Airlines craft readied to take off. I watched the Croat intently. The prisoner hadn't tried to run in the terminal, but that didn't mean he wouldn't attack. There were certain intervals when 90 percent of the fighters fought. Much as the process of taking their fingerprints set a lot of criminals off, so the elevating *whoooo* of airplane turbines historically had an unsettling effect on deportees. These seconds before the last takeoff were a traditional alien explosion time.

The plane rolled down the runway and blasted into the air. Madunic's face was glued to the window the whole time. When we'd finally attained cruising altitude, Tyrone stood up and moved to the empty row across the aisle, allowing me to slide over one space to my own aisle seat. A brunette flight attendant put her hand on Tyrone's shoulder. She whispered, "Are you armed?"

"No. But we've had a lot of practice handling people," Tyrone said. "We'll help you with any problem passengers too."

"Thank you," she said.

I kept my eye on Madunic until he fell asleep, and then I still watched him until he woke up. The pilot announced we were halfway to Dubrovnik.

This was far from Omega World, I thought. It was shaping up to be the best kind of deportation there was, an uneventful one. A removal mission was never over until the deportee was past his own country's immigration gates, but now the plane was committed. Even if the alien did snap, we'd just have to hold him down for an hour and a half. For his part, Madunic showed no sign of snapping.

"Hey," Tyrone said, "I've got your money." He pulled a sealed pouch containing over a hundred dollars in American bills out of his bag and handed the bundle to the Croat. "Count it."

"Thank you." Madunic riffled through it quickly. He stuffed the bills into his worn leather wallet, which he buttoned closed.

The flight attendant passed, leaving the aisle clear. Tyrone reached across with a document envelope. "Do you want to take care of these?"

"Yeah." I grabbed the envelope and shook out a small fingerprint pad. I told the Croat, "Let me have your hand." I pressed Madunic's right index into the waxy ink, lifted it, and pressed the finger into two successive pieces of paper, transferring the print. The first page was the warrant of deportation. The other was a warning to the alien of just how long he had to stay out of America, depending upon which section of immigration law applied to him. For Madunic, that was 237(a)(2)(A)(iii), the aggravated felon section. He was never allowed to come back. I gave him a copy of the warning, and he read it with no reaction. There was nothing there that Tyrone and I hadn't already told him. The part about applying for special reentry permission at any U.S. consulate was spelled out at the bottom.

"That's the new ink. You can get rid of it like this." I rubbed my own finger and thumb together.

"Thank you." Madunic rubbed the dry ink away until there was no trace of it on his skin. He folded his warning in half twice and stuffed it in a pocket of his trousers.

I slid my completed documents back into the envelope and handed them back across the aisle to Tyrone. Tyrone and I still had to sign both forms, but we'd do that when the mission was complete.

I studied Dragan Madunic. Now that we were on the final leg into Croatia, I was looking for the typical signs of anxiety in the deportee, and I found only resignation.

Soon we were low enough that through Madunic's window I could see the limestone cliffs rising from the blue Adriatic Sea. And then we touched down. We were here. After every other passenger had gone, Tyrone and I accompanied Madunic off the plane.

As soon as we stepped into the concourse, security personnel met us abruptly. We introduced ourselves, and I told them who the prisoner was. It seemed obvious, but it didn't hurt to emphasize the mission. I hoped they would take Madunic off our hands immediately. They showed no such inclination. They pointed ahead and assumed a rapid clip into the main airport building. Tyrone and I followed with our prisoner between us. We got to the immigration gates, which we bypassed as the security personnel led us around. We were now outside the airport with the sky above our heads. The open sky was normally the signal that my mission was complete. Other countries' officials had played host to me after I'd left the airport before. Some had enlisted me to come with them to transport the prisoner, who was universally understood to be *their prisoner* after I'd left the airport. But I wasn't getting that message today. No one had checked anybody's documents. No one had said thank you for the package. None of the normal procedures had happened. I had reached the point where I'd thought I was going to allow myself to be tired, and suddenly nothing was making sense. Maybe I was tired. Maybe it was just the way I was seeing things. But I looked to Tyrone and saw the same nonplussed expression on his face I imagined he saw on mine.

We were led into a police car. Tyrone and I and Dragan Madunic and the driver made four. The mustached driver was border police.

"What are we doing?" I asked him.

"Some charges we have to talk about regarding Mr. Dragan's citizenship."

Charges regarding citizenship? I didn't see how one related to the other.

The mustached border policeman drove us to his small police station on the edge of the walled city overlooking the water. It would have been a beautiful view if I hadn't been so anxious. Anyway, I told the driver it was: "Dubrovnik is beautiful."

"Yes," he said. "We go inside." Inside the station he introduced us to his captain, a uniformed female with red hair compressed in a bun and blue eyes. There was no one else in sight.

The station captain jumped in right away. In rapid Croatian she engaged Madunic.

"Oh, I don't speak Croatian," Madunic said.

"Why not?"

"I lived in America a long time."

"He knows some Croatian, but he grew up here speaking German," I said.

"German?" The captain rolled her blue eyes as if I were spinning wild tales on the spot. "Do you have some proof of his citizenship?"

Tyrone opened the document envelope. "Here's his passport."

She looked at it and then dismissed it. She looked at Madunic. "So it doesn't seem you were born here. It seems you were born in America, were you not?"

Madunic stammered.

"He was born in Croatia," I said. "If he'd been born in America, we couldn't deport him because he'd be American."

The captain said something to her mustached subordinate in Croatian. They spoke Croatian for a while. I felt another tremor of fatigue. My hotel bed was so close. I imagined the starched pillow. And then I imagined myself being pulled away.

The captain made a loud declaration in her language and gestured toward the table with the fax machine.

The mustached officer approached me with a sheet of paper. "This is the problem."

"I didn't know there was a problem," I said. Tyrone was keeping silent. He was smart to do that. The rule in a standoff is the first person to speak loses, but I was too tired and anxious to shut myself up.

"Oh, yes. There is problem," the captain said.

The man showed me the paper. It was the country-clearance wire I'd sent for our trip. The whole wire process was automated now. You punched in the information, and the computer generated this bold form to be faxed to all the involved agencies and countries.

The border policeman pointed to the field of convictions, which started with burglary and ended with the most recent conviction at the top. It was a comprehensive list. Ever since the Romania scare, I'd eschewed the downplaying convictions ploy unless it was absolutely necessary. In this case I hadn't thought it was; his family had already given me the passport. The border policeman read the top conviction: "Aggravated rape."

"This is a very serious charge," said the captain.

"We agree," I said. "That's why we're here."

"So he's a rapist." She looked at Dragan Madunic, and he stared back at

158

her. I didn't know if hers was a statement or a question, so I waited for her to speak again. "And he doesn't understand the language."

"I understand German," Madunic said.

"Stop with the German," I hissed. "You speak some Croatian."

The captain asked Madunic, "Do you have people meeting you here?"

Our prisoner pulled out a scrap of paper with a phone number. "When I call this, they'll pick me up."

She snatched the phone number. "This is not a Croatian number."

"It's a cell phone. They're my relatives from Germany coming to drive me to my house."

"Everything Germany." The captain sighed and shot her blue eyes at me. "Why don't you take him to Germany?"

My mind was slow in finding gears. In a moment I replied: "He's Croat."

"Oh, that's what you say. But you can't just bring any criminal here and tell us he is Croat and that's the end of it."

"*I'm* not telling you he's Croat. His passport tells you."

"Yes, but he speaks no Croatian. He comes from America. Everything else is German."

"We went through all that with the Croatia consulate in the States," I said. "And they approved this trip."

"But we are here," the captain said with a firm finger pointed to the ground. "And when the consulate makes the mistake, we must not make the same mistake."

"It wasn't a mistake," I said, and while I spoke, I reached for the document envelope Tyrone held. "The consulate saw the passport he came to America on. That proved he was Croat. So did his birth certificate. His house registration to the home he was born in and his family still owns. We still have it all ri—"

"You bring us a rapist!" the captain suddenly exclaimed. Her hair was red, but it was her blue eyes that flamed.

I rubbed my head, dazed. Nothing made sense, and then everything made sense all at once. "Is this about his citizenship or his conviction?" I asked.

The captain's blue eyes trained on me. They were icy now. "There are still planes leaving today. We can get the three of you back to your United States."

She switched to Croatian and spoke with her subordinate again. I understood not a word, but I understood everything. For me and Tyrone, the transport of a hardened felon from the Louisiana swamp all the way to the limestone mountains of former Yugoslavia had been the easy part. The Croatian border police were now looking for an official reason to refuse entry to their legal son and send him right back to America. A mission can die at any time.

I remembered the Muslim terror suspect I'd had to retrieve after authorities at Charles de Gaulle Airport in Paris refused to admit him. This in spite of the man's possession of a valid French passport, which his consulate had issued rightfully to our office following its thorough confirmation of his French citizenship and identity. He hadn't been my case, nor had I been his escorting officer. I'd only been assigned to clean it up. But today the man languished in Tyrone's and my docket, and unless we got another country besides his homeland of France to take him back, we'd see an HQ release letter with his name soon enough. In desperation I had considered escorting him covertly to another problem country, like Guyana, as a French tourist, thereby consummating the deportation and punishing a rogue government at the same time. But then I realized that French authorities had confiscated the valid French passport that the other French authorities had issued. My tourist to Guyana plan worked only if I could go back in time to when we still had his French passport and if I could carry my knowledge with me to the past.

While Tyrone and I waited, with our prisoner still between us, the Croatian police went back and forth over the fate of Dragan Madunic. Our standoff was yet another manifestation of the same old problem: The deportee's citizenship was not in dispute, yet his home government considered it its prerogative not to take him, since my government did not begrudge it that prerogative. The redheaded captain kept glancing at the fax machine while she spoke. At first I thought she was expecting a transmission, but then I realized that must have been the machine she'd gotten the country-clearance wire on, so every time she mentioned the wire or the rape she unconsciously looked at the machine. I figured more out while they spoke: of the two, the captain was the more adamant about refusing Madunic. The mustached subordinate was tentative, as if concerned there might be repercussions. Even though the captain was in charge, she was listening to the subordinate and his reservations. She did not want to make the decisive call until he would fully support her. Slowly it looked as if she were swinging him.

My head hurt. The frustration dug into me. I thought about taking this dangerous Croat back straight, for another thirty hours of propped-up alertness while Dragan Madunic rested up and then looked at us DOs for one moment of weakness. It didn't stop. I should never have been grateful for such an uneventful escort. It would have been better if Madunic had punched me in the head in Charlotte and run for it. At least we would have caught him and flattened him and checked him and destroyed his will to resist, and we would've come in here with a different vibe and not looked so tempting for these border police to run a game on. As it was, we came in here shining like perfect symbols of our spineless American government, which was fat and lazy and overdue for some kind of payback that Tyrone and I, as agents of that government's weakness, would be required to swallow and take back home.

"I don't know what the discussion's about." I interrupted. "But this man is Croat, and we've brought him back to his home country. So is there anything else you want from us?"

They stopped speaking. Slowly the mustached border policeman stood up. "Let's talk," he said.

He took a walk with me for the length of the mountainside station. The floor was tiled white and black. In a corner out of earshot of our respective associates, the mustached officer stopped and looked me in the eye. He posed his next statement to exist wholly within the fraternity of police. We lived oceans apart, but we could speak as joined men, each of whom knew fundamentally the load his equal carried. This was a dialogue between protectors of our respective people.

"Tell me about Dragan Madunic."

"He was born in this country to Croat parents," I said. "Last year he was ordered removed from the United States by an immigration judge, on the basis of his criminal history. My partner and I now present him here in accordance with United States law as well as a treaty between my country and yours wherein each party agreed to accept the repatriation of its citizens expelled by the other."

"Yes, yes." My fellow officer nodded knowingly. "Tell me about the crime. Aggravated rape."

"Oh. Not as bad as it sounds."

"No?" He leaned in.

"Mr. Madunic went to a club. In America the legal drinking age is twenty-one. Some of the teenagers get fake IDs to show that they're twenty-one so they can drink at the bars. Mr. Madunic was at one of these bars, and he met a girl. He assumed the girl was twenty-one, and he took her home and they had sex."

"She was willing?"

"Oh, yes. And it was only one time. But her parents found out. They didn't approve of him, and they called the police. It turned out that the girl hadn't turned eighteen yet. In America that's the age of consent for sex. If the man is over eighteen and the woman is under eighteen, even though they're close, that's called statutory rape."

The policeman drew air through his teeth. "And he's deported for this?"

"Yes. He had a prior record too, so there was no mercy from the court. He ended up with an aggravated rape conviction. From that point there's no discretion in our law. He must be deported."

The border policeman shook his head. He walked me back to the middle of the station, where the captain stood by the fax machine and Tyrone watched our prisoner. Conversation sprang out between the border police in their language again. This time the subordinate was swinging his boss.

The redheaded captain scooped the documents she had dismissed earlier. She picked up Madunic's passport and other papers and lined up their edges with her manicured nails. "Good-bye," she said to me and Tyrone. She directed her subordinate, and he stamped our passports as if we were at the border. She looked at the Croat, who was now her responsibility. "You stay here," she told him.

When I walked out with Tyrone into the sunshine, the world seemed to open up. The white sky and blue sea and the tan rock crossing from one into the other struck so vivid it dizzied me. I walked along the road edge, gazing.

I hated lying to a brother protector. Making up stories, while standing eye to eye with a man who carried a badge like mine and the burden that went with it, was not easy on the soul. But in the fashion of my own country's leaders, my Balkan counterpart had forced me to make a choice I shouldn't have had to make. I could have protected either my people or his people, and when it came to unleashing a Croat predator on one population or the other, I'd choose to follow American law, if not American leadership, to spare my people every time, even if I had to lie across the board to do it.

At least the underage part was true. At the time he raped her, Dragan Madunic's last victim had been fourteen years old.

Tyrone and I enjoyed ourselves in Dubrovnik, treading the polished walking street through the old walled town and exploring cliff elevations. At one picturesque vantage of the city and sea, I commissioned a tourist photographer to snap a postcard of us. I didn't own a camera, but I was in a mood to send a picture off to somebody through the Croatian postal service, something like a message pushed in a bottle and hurled into the Adriatic below.

We had an even better time in Zagreb, where Tyrone and I were grounded for twenty-four hours after our first Croatia Airlines return flight got us in too late to catch our second, and Croatia Airlines put us in a fleabag that we barely saw. We caught the electric train to Zagreb's supreme central square and hopped bars until late that night, when we met a man who said he was the Heineken representative for Zagreb and who backed up his claim by running a Heineken tab and giving us boxes of Heineken glasses from his green company car when the bar finally closed us out.

Tyrone and I didn't dwell on the day of work we missed that put us further behind. In fact we didn't discuss work at all. Flying home on the final leg into New Orleans, I marveled at this. Phil had talked shop after hours infrequently, and now Tyrone didn't seem to ever. Deportation was a war that tended to eat into its soldiers, and I was counting myself lucky to have gotten a new partner who appreciated that time off the front lines needed to be exempt from associations of the fight.

But in my paranoia I considered another explanation: Perhaps Tyrone was keeping his own professional distance on purpose.

Some people resist socializing with coworkers because they want to avoid upsetting the professional rapport. Here it struck me as the opposite. Tyrone and I were friends, but he did not let that spill over onto the job. Tyrone had never even asked me what I'd said to the mustached border policeman. He'd simply completed the mission paperwork with me, tucked it away, and charged headlong into our Croatia recreation. Most of me loved it. That was the kind of partner I wanted and the kind of partner I wanted to be. Only a little bit of me wondered. Did Tyrone know how I played this deportation game when he wasn't around?

Well, what did it matter anyway? Every day I operated with the sense that time was running out. Something was bound to break, and not far in the future. If Tyrone was going to be the one to bust me, better him than someone I didn't respect. Tyrone was a partner and a friend. To this day I sometimes feel guilty for having come up short as Tyrone's training officer. Other times I think failing to teach him was the only good thing I did in all of this.

THIRTEEN

Videl Santos and Exactly What We Knew Would Happen

"Hi, Ames. This is Katie Dennison from Cathol—"

"Of course, Katie. Good to hear from you." I didn't want her to think she had to identify herself. Katie was a friend to my unit. Her employer, Catholic Charities, provided free legal counsel to aliens in Immigration proceedings, meaning that on many days we saw them on the opposite side of the table from us. However, Catholic Charities also helped our locally released aliens get settled on the outside, allowing at least the possibility that our criminal aliens could go straight. "How are you?"

"I'm okay, Ames. I'd like to meet with you when you have time. I'm with Videl Santos . . . the Angolan."

I racked my brain. Many Angolans came to mind, Videl Santos not among them. "Do I know Videl?"

"Maybe not. He's not a criminal. He petitioned for asylum. I think he'll get it. But I'm with him in the hospital now. Last night he had his eye gouged out."

"Oh, no."

"It's really hard," Katie said. I felt the strain in her voice.

"I'm sorry."

"Videl needs to meet with you."

I didn't know why the meeting was necessary: Videl wasn't in my docket, and as a nonfelon he did not appear to be destined for it. But I also did not question the meeting. Katie had never wasted my time before. She had never asked for anything from me or anyone else in my unit. She'd given us nothing but help, every time we'd requested it. Even on our smallest requests Katie had delivered. When we rolled aliens out of detention facilities to return them to their homelands, prisons took back their jumpsuits, and our procedure was to suit the aliens up in the outfits they'd been wearing when we'd first taken control of them. But this was not always practical. Sometimes jails lost the aliens' roll-in clothing. Sometimes the attire was inappropriate for the climate. Say, a Swede had been wearing shorts and a wifebeater at apprehension and we were bringing him home in January. Or it was a biker in a gang jacket you wouldn't put back on him on principle. Occasionally the clothing was splattered in blood, and even if that blood was six months old, you knew no airline captain would let you board his plane. No matter what our reason, when we gave Katie the call and the description of the deportee's build, she came through with a traveling outfit before we rolled. She wanted only to give help to people who needed it. And that help didn't even come close to the service she provided when we *couldn't* get our aliens home.

Most of the aliens whom New Orleans Deportation released to the streets returned to their families. For a sizable number, however, family reunion wasn't viable. Some aliens had never had families or friends. Some had shamed their families and were no longer welcome at home. And a few had killed their families. Halfway house slots occasionally opened up for the alien orphans, but the majority of them were released to the care of Catholic Charities across the street, a block down Loyola Avenue. The agency placed aliens in local jobs and apartments and enrolled them in English classes, among other benefits. I remembered the day, years ago, when Catholic Charities had come to us, offering to help place our released aliens. Since then everything had changed. Now we approached Catholic Charities. Now we were on the verge of burning them out.

I told Katie, "Sure. Absolutely I can meet with Videl."

"Thank you. Can I bring him by the office this afternoon?"

"Shoot. We're looking for someone right now." I scrutinized a derelict Uptown apartment complex through my windshield while I spoke.

"Oh, is tomorrow better?" she asked. I liked how Katie took our job in stride. Some of the religious groups hated us. Even if Katie was a lot more criminal alien–friendly than the average DO, she didn't begrudge us our mission, nor did she hold our enforcement work against us when we asked for her assistance.

"Tomorrow would—never mind, I think we just found him. See you after lunch." I dropped the phone and threw open my car door.

I did not forget Katie that afternoon. I made it back to the office, and I intentionally stayed close to my desk so I'd be easy to find. It was not a visiting day, so when I heard the knock on the lobby door, I knew it was Katie.

My end-of-the-line desk was the closest to the door to the alien waiting room. This ninth-floor portal was the door aliens on supervised release reported to in accordance with their orders of supervision. Sometimes other agencies, like warrant teams from the Orleans Parish Criminal Sheriff's Office, would contact me because one of our released aliens was wanted for a new crime, and then on Report Tuesday we all would sit around my cubicle with our muscles tense and batons ready, joking and waiting for the offender to appear at that door.

I swung the door in without asking who it was. Katie stood there with a sad smile on her face. "Hi, Ames." The strain was still in her voice. I wasn't sure whether this latest incident had spiked the strain, or the strain had been cumulative, the result of the workload we'd laid on her. I shook Katie's hand. Then I turned to the man beside her.

A large white patch covered Videl Santos's left eye. The patch stuck to his head with the aid of hospital tape running its perimeter, across his forehead, down his temple, diagonal over his cheekbone, and up the bridge of his nose. The white patch showed a stain of blood in the middle. I shook Videl's hand. He still had a hospital bracelet circling his wrist. "Nice to meet you," I told him.

"Thank you," Videl said. That was about all the English he knew. From there he began to speak in Portuguese.

He glanced toward the elevator while he spoke, his single eye freighted with fear. I knew he was looking for his attacker. This unshakable affliction is common in victims of brutal crimes, sometimes for years after. They always believe they could be attacked again. I closed the outside door to the waiting room and locked it, hoping to make Santos feel secure. "It's okay," I said.

Since I did not know Portuguese and Katie was fluent, she translated while Videl Santos spoke. Videl faced me. He released the Portuguese tale of misery, trembling the whole time. His eyepatch on one side resembled a giant white eyeball with a blood-red iris. His other eye welled with tears as he described the attack.

Videl Santos was the kind of alien I never wanted to see on the ninth floor. He was an eighth-floor alien by all rights. He struck me as an honest man with a probably legitimate asylum claim. But aliens make the easiest victims in the world. They are uncertain of their surroundings, unaware of their rights, unfamiliar with crime-reporting procedures, more often than not afraid of police, and so engrossed in finding their way in a strange land that they don't see the crime coming. No one knows this better than other aliens. This is why bad aliens frequently prey on good aliens. If America were perfect, aliens like Videl Santos would process through the eighth floor and never see me, never know who I was. But because America is the beast it is, I am forever connected to such decent aliens by the indecent aliens I manage.

As a Deportation Officer you encounter victims. This is part of the job. Many of the victims are aliens, and when you hear their stories, you feel for them. Their stories affect you deeply because they upset that fairy-tale sense of reason inside you that says you handle all the bad aliens while in another universe the good aliens live the American Dream. The sad, jarring truth is that all universes overlap. The American Dream meets the American Nightmare every hour of every day, and you hear about it. You identify with the victim because like you, he is one of the good people. You stand face-to-face with this weeping man, this Angolan with white gauze where his eye is supposed to be, and you regard the world from his perspective. It is you who has the asylum claim. It is you who goes straight from your dishwashing job to the community center where you sit in an hour-long English class every day, gripping a few words that you thought you heard. It is you who leaves the class repeating those few words and mustering up the courage to try to use them. You imagine you will try to use them when you encounter some new people in this land that is so confusing but that you like anyway because it is giving you a chance. Ideally, you would test these words on your friends and family, but you have no friends and family here yet. You know you will one day. You will make a life here and you will fall in love and you will get married and have children and when your children are very young you will hear them use the same words you are now mustering up the courage to try out. This idea inspires you, so you decide to speak the new words when you get home. Your temporary home is a one-room apartment you share with two other aliens who have also been placed here by Catholic Charities. The two other aliens are released criminals, but Catholic Charities does not have the luxury of making distinctions when they find lodging for aliens. You are grateful to have a bed and a roof. You push the door open and see your roommates sitting on the beds and drinking beer in big steins and watching a soccer game on TV. You close the door behind and wonder if they will laugh at you when you speak. They have been in this country much longer than you, and though they are far from fluent, they have regularly mocked your struggle with English. But you are in a hopeful state of mind, so you decide that you will try. You take two steps toward them and take a deep breath. "Hello. It's a nice day today!" you announce with a smile. You brace yourself for the laughter these two usually rain on you when you speak English. But no one laughs. One of your roommates stands up. He curses you in his language. Tracking his angry stare, you realize that you were blocking his view of the television and that you caused him to miss a play. You start to move out of the way, but the massive beer stein in your roommate's grip is already on a fast swing. It catches you in the eye and shatters. In a sudden explosion, beer and blood soak your face and everything else as your roommate rakes a heavy shard through your eye socket. Everything goes black, and you collapse to the floor. When you regain consciousness, your roommates are gone. You are alone in your one-room apartment in this strange new land, and you are half blind.

Katie is choked up. Standing before her in the ninth-floor alien waiting room, I perceive that in her delivery. She stops translating because Videl Santos has stopped talking because he is choked up too. I am the only one who is not choked up. U.S. Deportation Officer is not a job that makes you cry. It is a job that does the opposite. It is a job that numbs you so you can't cry even if you want to. This is not the effect of the random, wanton human tragedy to which you are ever exposed. If that were the cause, then no law enforcement officer would ever cry, and we know that they do. What really takes its toll on the DO, what numbs you and freezes your tear ducts and cancels out your emotional register, is the senselessness. Those who believe emotions and reason are wholly separate could not be more wrong. Emotion hinges on reason. Tears spring from tragedy as laughter erupts from comedy. If there is no logic, no reason for anything that happens, then there is no comedy and no tragedy and no laughter and no tears.

"Who is he?" I asked Videl Santos. "Who did this to you?"

The response followed from the half-blinded Santos with no need for translation. He answered: "Rodolfo."

And I understood right away why Katie had arranged this meeting with me. I was the one who'd sent Rodolfo into Katie's world. I'd asked her to provide aid and comfort to Rodolfo, the man who left no bridge unburned. I'd asked her to help him even though Rodolfo wasn't worth the effort of any good soul on this earth. I'd contaminated her noble work with my disease.

A violent alien I'd set free on orders from the American government had stolen Videl Santos's American Dream. Maybe if it had made sense, I could have cried.

I looked at Katie, and I was so sorry. I was sorry for Santos too. How could I have been this selfish and reckless that I brought my universe crashing down on them?

I'd been on the ground in Luanda once on a turnaround mission, six hours, which for Angola was long enough to appreciate that the government is ruined and the general citizenry has a rotten hand. Now having heard Videl Santos's straightforward tone and seen his pitiful appearance, and adding that to the more essential fact that he was from Angola, I believed his asylum claim was genuine, and his story of Rodolfo's rampage was certainly true. It was infuriating. Santos had fled for his life to the United States, but what Angola hadn't taken from him in twenty-five years America had robbed him of in fewer than twenty-five days. He could have stayed in Angola and not lost his eye.

The doorknob jiggled, and Santos jerked in fright. I looked at the door and for a second believed it might be Rodolfo on the other side. I opened it to reveal journeyman agent Bobby Smith. Bobby was our top fugitive-tracking DO. He integrated himself into our circle, and I explained the situation. I told Bobby how one of the bad aliens I'd released was responsible. I told Bobby it was Rodolfo.

"Let's go get the motherfucker," Bobby said.

"Let's," I said. I looked at the Angolan and wished I could go back in time.

There was no way to undo the damage I'd done. Videl Santos would not grow a new eye, and the maimed left side of his face would not repair itself in his lifetime. He would never regain his old confidence, he would not be attractive to some women, he would live in fear, and he would be confronted with the fragility of his existence for as long as he lived. And he was just *one* of Rodolfo's victims. Katie had brought Videl Santos here to show me that.

Katie now took Santos out to the elevators through the door Bobby had come in. Santos's eye roamed wildly. He was still afraid.

"Don't worry," Bobby told him. "We'll get him."

"Thank you," I told Katie as she stepped with the Angolan into the elevator car.

Katie made sense. She wanted to help people who could be helped, but her visit here today was a tacit but unmistakable ultimatum that I get Rodolfo off the street and never send his type her way again. Before the elevator doors closed, I thought I read a message in Katie's compassionate eyes: Some people weren't worth helping. She might have meant people like Rodolfo, but more likely she meant people like me.

Why didn't more of us think logically like Katie Dennison? All aliens were not the same. The best aliens deserved a shot. The worst aliens did not deserve to stay here, especially not since their gain would come at the expense of the first group. There was an obvious right and wrong at play; this wasn't a political issue.

Oh. When I thought about the politicians, I boiled. I boiled all the way home, overcome by outrage at the U.S. government and its policies that made the criminal alien problem much worse than it needed to be. I regarded the half-blinded Santos and felt my frustration at the system mount. Through clenched teeth I barked at all the leaders who were murdering our country with great efficiency.

"You jellyfish liberals!" I shouted through the open windows of my Honda. "You say everybody deserves a chance. What about the chances you terminate? You give a bad guy a chance, he destroys a good guy. Don't you get it? You feel righteous about rescuing a criminal, but then you drop him and move on while he carves up ten other people and puts them beyond rescue. God forbid if big, bad America leaves a footprint on the globe, but when foreigners hurt America, you make excuses for them. The American Dream is supposed to be earned, not given away to the least deserving savages on earth. Rodolfo's your poster child! How can you sleep when you save toxic trash like Rodolfo at the same time you steal the dreams of asylum seekers like Santos? Are you getting paid by the devil?"

I leaned on my horn as I opened up on Earhart Expressway. It seemed the only thing I could do.

"You hypocrite conservatives!" I screamed. "Don't think I forgot about you. Whose watch do you think this is happening on? You run the show, and it only gets worse. You rail on about terrorism and drop bombs on the other side of the world but do absolutely nothing while America dies the death of a thousand cuts right here at home. Every day invaders are raping, murdering, child molesting, robbing, carjacking, pistol-whipping, destroying our people, while you overlook it by seven thousand miles and try to scare us into following your line of sight. The foreign army is right here on our soil, and you're letting them sodomize us into the grave! Supreme Ruler, you're as responsible as anyone for this fiasco. I hope no harm comes to you, sir, but if one of these deviant freaks takes you out from a rooftop, history will call it a poetic resolution."

My Ida Street apartment and all its peeling light blue paint came into view, and I tried to shake myself out of the rage that had seized me. If I was out of control, I knew I wasn't the only one. I'd have to lose my mind completely to match my government.

FOURTEEN

Life on Edge and the Personal Reckoning

I grabbed Soraya's hand and pulled her through the charged crowd along Bayou St. John. Music from brass instruments collided with the drums and bounced around in our ears and heads and deeper down to our toes. Almost every day in New Orleans there was some kind of festive gathering, someplace to soak in music and the swarm, to see costumed Indians, to be vibrated off your foundation by high school bands, to overload your senses in a wide-open place with a whole lot of strangers who are friends. Soraya and I hadn't even known of this one until we'd walked our dog out to the Orleans Avenue neutral ground. When we'd heard the music and seen the colors, we'd kept walking, letting ourselves be pulled in like the rest.

It was wrapping up now, but I wanted to enjoy a beer with what was left of the spectacle. I had my dog on my leash on one hand, and he seemed to know instinctively that I intended to visit the E-Z Serve at the gas station across the street. He headed that way, pulling me behind him, and I pulled Soraya behind me. I stopped on the grass when I noticed a man selling Milwaukee's Best for seventy-five cents out of the trunk of his Oldsmobile.

I lifted my wallet from my pocket and riffled through the singles. I was a major supporter of the small businesses in New Orleans. I'd get my beverages from this guy now, just as when my car tires blew out, I had them switched at a used tire place farther down Orleans Avenue for ten dollars, including labor, and I liked to buy beef brisket nearby at a house where a lady served it out of her kitchen.

"Big Red!" Soraya exclaimed.

I followed her wide eyes to the second cooler in the Oldsmobile trunk, and I noticed the regional soda cans poking through the ice. I had been in the mood for a beer, but the novelty call won out, and I traded the Milwaukee's Best to the elderly man for two of his Big Reds.

Big Red was an excessively sweet red cream soda that reddened your tongue and was best served without food for the purest experience. I handed one to Soraya, who handed it back. Her exclamation had been more of surprise than appreciation, I realized. I cut into the fading party and enjoyed back-to-back Big Reds until the event disintegrated completely. Soraya reminded me we had a Saints game to get to, and we started to follow our dog back home.

We walked past our apartment on Ida and crossed Carrollton Avenue kitty-corner to the Laundromat where I'd left some clothes tumbling. At this haphazard intersection there was a Vietnamese nail salon, a Moroccan restaurant, another eatery serving Middle Eastern food, and this Vietnamese laundry, with the accompanying immigrants on hand.

"Hello, Officer Holbrook," a pair of voices said.

"All right," I said, sizing up the two men on the corner. They were standing around a pay phone, smoking in the shade of a great oak tree. These two were not immigrants associated with the businesses I just mentioned, although they weren't from America either. Both these men were alien felons I'd set free.

My head started throbbing. Normally I regarded the immigrants and aliens in my neighborhood as a bonus. We had all kinds. A few blocks down, at the supermarket on Carrollton and Canal, I enjoyed the Honduran crowd and the shelves full of Honduran wares, especially when I had a thirst for an ice-cold bottle of Salva Vida. There were also plenty of crewmen who added their respective color to the tapestry. New Orleans was a big port town teeming with crewmen, some on pass and some not, and they normally didn't get a negative reaction from me.

Seeing these two criminal aliens I'd released, on the other hand, rushed blood through my veins in acid currents. I didn't like that they were within a hundred feet of my home. I didn't like that they had laid eyes on my wife or that they'd matched the platinum bands on our fingers and figured out that I had a wife. I was even distressed that they knew what my dog looked like. My dog, Whiskey, was famous in the neighborhood because he enjoyed spending his days on our porch, actually the flat roof of the flower shop underneath us, running along the railingless edge of the second floor and barking at everyone who used the sidewalk. No one complained about his barking because our neighborhood was noisy already, and it was in the middle of the day besides. Some folks liked Whiskey enough to make it a point to visit him and toss Milk-Bones up to "the roof dog." Whiskey would have been easy to poison if someone had a reason to. But I didn't share that with my wife. I asked her to come inside the Laundromat with me. I bundled up our clothes in one arm and, keeping close to her, departed for home.

"Good-bye, Officer Holbrook."

"Good-bye," I answered, holding eye contact until they dropped theirs. They were being friendly. If I'd had it out for either of them, I could have sacked them up right then for violating their OSes. Not that I would have done it with Soraya there, but I might have brought her home and come back in three minutes and done it. They were in violation of the order of supervision clause that forbade them to associate with criminals—i.e., each other. But that was a drastic restriction, especially in this town, and I wouldn't bust somebody solely on that ground unless he was particularly evil. If I wanted to perform DO work on my day off, there were a lot more important crises to get a grip on. It was true that I was aching to take somebody down, but not just anybody and not just to do it. When it came to my revoking their parole, the two by the pay phone would have to do something markedly awful right now for me to move them higher on my list than Rodolfo.

I looked over my shoulder at the pair as I approached my apartment door. They didn't seem to be paying us any attention. As I remembered, they weren't the worst guys in the world. Both had been convicted of drug trafficking, and while their current activity of hanging around a city pay phone didn't exactly plead a new vocation, as far as I knew, they hadn't spilled innocent blood. I was bothered because they were this close.

It wasn't a surprise. Criminals I released flooded the city. If I'd liberated these invaders with the prayer that they'd go everywhere except to my own front yard, that would have put me in the company of the U.S. representatives and senators and justices and commander in chief who did exactly that—exactly that, that is, except that they in their gated communities and fortified compounds could *realistically* bet they would not personally see the fallout from their malfeasance. And I absolutely was not in their company. Of course these criminals on the loose were going to find my neighborhood. This was a painful sign that the city was full, and it hit me where I lived.

I dropped the laundry on the bed and headed back down our apartment steps with Soraya and our dog.

"How's your Blazer for gas?" I asked.

"I just filled it up," she answered.

"Perfect." Down on Ida Street I opened her Chevy truck's passenger door and let Whiskey jump over to the back before Soraya climbed inside. I hit the lock and closed her in.

I pulled off the curb and made a quick U on North Carrollton to head toward the river.

"We need to get money," Soraya told me.

"Right." As I drove, I imagined I saw Rodolfo everywhere.

There was no particular place I expected to find him. There was no place he couldn't be. Healthy numbers of Vietnamese and Hondurans notwithstanding, New Orleans was home to small populations from a great variety of countries, as opposed to crushing populations from a few countries. Our Little Saigon out east was the only neighborhood that could even be compared (and then remotely) with those homogeneous immigrant quarters in other cities that come to mind, like Chicago's block after block of Indians or Poles. When it came to our alien residents, most groups were strewn throughout the local landscape, blended in the New Orleans whirlpool of rich and poor and everything else.

I wondered in what neighborhood I would find Rodolfo when the time came. What forlorn street corner would be his stalking ground? I tried to console myself with the knowledge that the camouflage that helped Rodolfo disappear would also let me lie low when I came to hunt him. That New Orleans's neighborhoods were well shaken up with regard to skin tone was a gift to enforcers since it allowed a cop of any shade to drop into most zip codes without drawing attention. I was already seeing myself parked in the government car with the engine switch on extended idle, AC icing me through my vest as I scanned the block, some block, for my prey.

"Aren't you going to get money here?" Soraya asked.

I was in the left lane, and the bank was on the right at the coming corner. "Shoot. What do we need money for?"

"Rally's. We're supposed to pick up food."

I put my signal on and gunned it to the right when I saw a gap. I made my corner on Canal Street, pulled into the Hibernia Bank parking lot, and rolled into the rightmost line. The ATMs here were all drive-through. I started with three vehicles in front of me. Several minutes later it was down to the last one, an old massive Cadillac common in these parts. I got my wallet ready.

The Cadillac rolled, and I eased forward to his spot. And someone ran in front of my grille to the ATM. "What's this guy doing?"

"Ames, just forget it," Soraya said. "He was probably waiting."

I threw my door open and jumped onto the asphalt. I got to the guy right in front of the machine while he was still fishing his card out. "Hey, there's a line behind me," I said.

The guy didn't answer at first, and I kept looking at him. He was fit and young, collegiate in appearance. He struck me as a lacrosse player for some reason. "Did you hear me?"

He looked at me with immature eyes. His shirt had the name of the local private university Tulane emblazoned across the chest. "Yeah, I was waiting," he said. He got his ATM card in his fingers and extended it toward the machine.

I smacked his hand so the card spun in the air like a Frisbee. It finally lighted ten feet away on the black paved lot. He looked at me for a split second and then scrambled to pick up his card. He stepped back toward me slowly, shaking his hand out. "Are you crazy?" he asked.

"Just wait your turn."

"I did!" he exclaimed, gesturing to the corner column supporting the drive-through roof. "I was waiting right there." His voice edged higher and more frantic as he spoke. "I got here the same time as the car in front of you, and I waited till he was done."

The redness began to drain out of my view, and I realized I was leaning in on him, all compressed muscle and energy, ready to spring. My own energy disturbed me. I took a big step back.

The kid stared at me with his mouth hanging. With a quavering voice he continued to address me. "What's wrong with you? Where are you from?"

"Get your money out!" I ordered.

That instruction froze him. In his fingers his bank card perched in the open air.

I said: "Put your card in the machine and take out your money."

"Why?" he asked, trembling. "So you can rob me?"

In disbelief I studied him. "What? No . . . that's you." I looked away from the collegian. I cast my eyes to the asphalt, and I walked back to the truck.

Inside the truck Soraya faced the other way. She aimed her eyes out the window on her side. Her sniffle triggered a sharp ache inside me.

U.S. Deportation Officer is not a job that makes you cry. It's a job that on the worst days will cause your spouse to cry. Sometimes it's a nonevent that causes the tears, such as when you come home in the middle of the night and don't join your spouse in bed but instead play video games, or surf porn, or do whatever it is you do to tune out the world until the next morning. Your deportation game has become so ugly and illogical and dangerous that you won't think about it yourself, much less share it with the person you love, so you stare at the screen while darkness dissolves to dawn, while the crying from the next room scratches at you. And sometimes your spouse personally witnesses behavior on your part that is sufficient to cause the tears, such as when you bully a young college student for no good reason at all.

I got my cash and pulled back onto Carrollton toward the river.

"When are you going to leave your job?" Soraya asked.

"I don't know," I told her.

Her sniffling was done now. She looked at me with fierce eyes. "You never used to bully anyone. *Anyone.* I liked that about you. You made me feel safe, but you were never bad to people. You've lost so many of the things that I liked about you."

"It may not be my choice when I leave the job."

"Of course it's your choice," Soraya said. "It's not the army. You don't owe them time. You can quit whenever you want."

"I know that." The next red light caught me. I stopped in the middle lane and looked at my wife. "I mean there's a chance they might make me leave."

"Why?"

"A lot of the stuff I've been doing lately . . . I'm kind of rewriting the rules."

"What does that mean?"

I gripped the wheel and drove on. There was a pretty garden on my right with children playing. For a second I thought I saw Rodolfo, but it was another mirage. "I think there could be trouble when they catch me. And not just trouble for me."

"What do you mean not just for you? What could happen?"

"Sometimes in immigration enforcement there's this backlash. Like, I don't know if I told you abou—"

"You never tell me about anything."

"If there's any inquiry, they tie our hands. Recently these two San Francisco DOs took a deportable Indian on an airplane and then got word, while the plane was taxiing, that his lawyer got a stay of removal. They flew with him anyway, and now they have to go back and get him. So HQ is drafting new policy that'll make it even harder for us to deport people. In another case a detention facility was just accused of civil rights abuses on one alien, so they froze deportations out of that whole facility. We can't transfer aliens, can't touch them, and our clock is still ticking. We'll have to release a jail full of criminal aliens to the streets when time runs out, even when we have their passports."

"Why is this happening now?"

"It's getting worse, but it's been like this in immigration for a long time. We're politically sensitive. Craig told me about this time a few years ago. Special agents in Florida raided a flower business and daisy-chained these Haitians in a line outside. There was a public outcry, and now we still can't do work site enforcement. That's how it works. I'm scared if they catch me, they're going to pull back all my cases. Or all New Orleans District cases. Or *all* the cases in the country."

Slowly my wife shook her head. "Ames, how could you be so stupid?"

"There's no chance for me to deport these felons if I don't do something different. I'm just trying to help people."

"Oh, so that's how you look at it?" Soraya said. "You're the one DO who has the compassion and courage to break the rules?"

"Not compassion and courage. Maybe I'm the first one who's thought of it."

"Everyone's thought of it. There's no way to have your job and not think of it," she snapped. "But it's the ones who don't break the rules and jeopardize the whole program who are special, Ames. And you're just like every other stupid man who hates to lose!"

Her words sank into me like the tip of a whip. I didn't want to agree with her. Ours was an important war, and I had to fight it to the best of my ability if we were going to win. My own wife acted as if I were some kind of rogue DO, but I'd never done anything immoral. I'd never claimed a false expense, taken a payoff, or done any of the other things I thought law enforcement officers did when they went bad. All I wanted to do was make the streets safer for the good people living in my country. Didn't the ends justify my means?

"When are you going to quit?" Soraya asked again.

I swung into the Rally's lot. As I settled into the right-hand order line, my mind flashed to the drive-through experience of ten minutes ago. I hated that my chaotic professional life was spilling over into this life.

"I don't know," I answered. "You don't believe me, but it really is a good career. I'm doing a lot of good. And you have to like the security. You and I travel, and we're going to have a family. It's not as if we can do that if I go back to parking cars at the Marriott."

For a second I thought I saw Rodolfo by the walkup window. It was someone else. I ordered the food at the red speaker and drove forward. I pulled one of the crisp ATM twenties from my billfold.

My wife looked at me, and I saw her eyes lose their anger. They filled once more with sadness. "I loved you more when you were parking cars," she said.

FIFTEEN

Bobby and the Hunt for Rodolfo

Craig caught me through his office portal. "Ames! When are you and Bobby going out?"

"I think a half hour," I told my boss.

"What are you doing right now?"

"Nothing special. And everything. The usual."

"Come in and close the door."

"Yes, sir." I pushed the wooden door shut. Hanging on the inside of Craig's door, as always, was a fresh suit wrapped in laundry plastic, awaiting breakout in the event Craig got called to some important meeting or television appearance. The spare suit made me smile because Craig already wore a perfect suit to work every day. I seated myself in the center guest chair opposite his, and I admired his exemplary white shirt and maroon necktie framed by the custom-cut black dinner suit. Any trade-out would have been a wash, in the spirit of the marshals-Deportation shackles swap I'd witnessed at Louis Armstrong Airport.

"How are you doing, Ames?" Craig asked seriously. "I haven't talked to you since Tyrone left." Tyrone had been waiting for an academy class date since he'd been a DO, and the date had finally come. Now I was without a partner again.

"I'm fine, boss."

Craig's eyes seemed to bore through my own. He was searching for something in my head. "I talked to the warden at Tangipahoa Prison. He says you're over there a lot of nights."

"Some nights, yes, sir," I declared. My volume got away from me. It was an uncontrolled self-protection mechanism, as if to talk loudly meant I had nothing to hide. "I have to match up time zones with a lot of countries, get to people while they're awake."

"How many nights are you over there, Ames?"

"It depends. There's nothing about my schedule that's regular."

"Right. How many nights will you be over there next week?"

My mind raced. I didn't know if Craig was planning to tap my phone or if he had already tapped it or what was going on. There were times I thought I wanted to get caught, just to be finished, but whenever I actually felt the jaws closing on me, I knew I wanted to stay free. Getting busted would be horrible. "If I had to guess, I'd say three nights next week."

"So why don't you just plan your three nights and tell me what they are?"

"Uh . . . I don—"

"My concern—"

"You have a concern?" I asked defensively.

"Yes," Craig answered. "You should earn overtime for those night visits if you plan them ahead."

"Overtime?" I exhaled forcefully.

"I see you filling in sixty-five-, seventy-hour weeks. If you're working ten planned night hours at the jails, that's a couple hundred dollars a week the pay rules say you should be getting in your check."

"Thanks, boss. It really depends on the aliens, though. I'm afraid it's unreliable."

"Unreliable? The warden says you practically live there. He told me he was thinking about letting you sleep with the aliens." Craig smiled. "Schedule it in advance, so I can pay you overtime."

"If it works out that way, I will, Craig." I thought about the quick turn in my mind this conference had taken. Initially I'd been sure Craig was about to bring the hammer down on me, and then learned he only wanted to augment my salary. I was overcome with relief and sadness. This conference was still excruciating. My relationship with Craig was important to me. I admired my upright supervisor, and I was painfully aware that the free rein Craig trusted me with was exactly what I was misusing in pursuit of my personal mission. I was dying to tell Craig, "It's not you! It's the people above you I defy. The ones who create this situation, letting criminals go." But I couldn't. I only listened.

"You already pay taxes, Ames. You don't want to give the government more money that you've earned. Our federal pay guidelines stipulate that you will receive overtime pay for every hour that you work outside your regular workday if you schedule it prior to the pay period. In that sense your nights at Tangipahoa Prison are no different from the time you schedule for overseas escorts. They're overtime hours. Those are the rules."

I laughed ruefully. "I know, boss. I know you wouldn't be telling me if it weren't the right way."

"So bring me your schedule."

"If it's ever firm enough, I will, boss."

Craig shook his head. "Get back to work."

I got up and turned the knob, hiding once again the plastic-cloaked emergency suit behind Craig's door.

I never would claim a jail visit as overtime. I couldn't even think about jacking up my paycheck for the unapproved work I did at Tangi, plenty of it spent putting Asians on the phone with passport riggers back home so I could get them into their countries clean. I was already conflicted enough without adding financial incentive to my Tangi games. I shuddered as I pictured getting busted and the OIG inspectors having a field day when they discovered my illicit behavior was enriching me to the tune of ten thousand dollars annually. Not a chance.

I continued the route I'd been on when Craig had intercepted me, a run to the network printer. I got nervous when I didn't see my sheet right away. It was a letter apprising the Gabonese Embassy that the United States would impose sanctions, including a visa moratorium on all its citizens, if it failed to issue a travel document for a criminal in my custody. I gave the Gabonese thirty days. It was a bluff, all my manufacture, and absolutely not a letter that any other agent in my office needed to see. I lobbed a plea over the cubicle walls: "Who just used the printer?"

"I did," came the voice of a female DO who'd arrived in the past few months.

I rushed toward her and found her standing with a sheaf of paper in her hands. "May I see your bottom page?"

She extended my letter, looking at it as she did so. I snatched it away. "Need this in a hurry, sorry," I said. I ran to my desk to maintain the act. Now that Tyrone was at the academy, I was on my own again, running with all the rope the system gave me. Close calls like this at work were becoming more common.

Close calls, especially in high numbers, are not healthy for anyone operating on the fringe. Enough close calls, and a person starts to feel invincible.

So that day I'm standing at my desk feeling invincible, and Bobby pages me. He says we're going out. I partially strip in my cubicle to strap on my bulletproof vest. I drag my polo shirt over last. I lift my H&K compact pistol out of my holster and squeeze the slide back a millimeter to get a glimpse of the brass in the chamber. That press check is a compulsion of mine I've performed many times a day since the outset of my career, when Bobby reprimanded me for not having a round ready to fire. Our custom law enforcement pistols do not have safeties, so I was afraid the gun might go off by accident. "Don't worry about that!" Bobby screamed in my face as he snatched my pistol. He racked a round before handing it back. "You worry about it not going off when you need it, motherfucker! You have your weapon topped off if you want to ride with me, you got it?" I was not riding with Bobby at the moment of his outburst. We were in fact right here in our ninth-floor office, and I had just met him.

All of us here have our talents. Craig is a leader who manages the threat and puts us where we need to be. John's people skills and Fenwick's facility for organization get the majority of our felons to their homelands before time runs out. I'm a back-door fixer. And Bobby apprehends fugitives. We're all cross-trained, and each of us performs all those DO responsibilities, aside from the back-door fixing, which only I do, but those characterizations are accurate. While the river of wanted men pours into New Orleans year after year, other offices, other agencies, and even other governments enlist Bobby to help find their men. It was Bobby I turned to recently when one of my liberated aliens firebombed his apartment to get back at his landlord. And it was Bobby I turned to for help resolving my latest released alien disappointment we'd seen coming.

When I arrive at his desk, Bobby hands me the fugitive folder we've been working with. It is thicker than when we started but still lean, containing only essentials. Over the past week Bobby and I have been riding together, gathering information. We've been to the hospital, police stations, and shelters throughout the city. Today we will continue.

We head outside into the sunshine and walk to Bobby's g-ride on the curb. I slide into the passenger side and review the file while Bobby drives. The New Orleans police report describing the attack on Videl Santos is good and damning, but it is likely as far as the NOPD will get to take the case. The scared Angolan asylum seeker is too afraid to press charges against his attacker. The good news is that Bobby and I don't need another conviction in order to bring in Rodolfo. We have clear evidence that he's violated his order of supervision in multiple ways, from engaging in criminal activity—to wit: maiming Santos—to missing his report date following that attack. I've documented Rodolfo's violations, and I've composed a legal memorandum revoking his parole. What remains is for us to find the threat and take him down.

The folder contains a head shot of Rodolfo that Bobby's blown up to eight and a half by eleven. Bobby tells me to look at it, though he knows photographs have never been much help to me. I have not managed to develop the talent for matching photos with real faces. I've seen Bobby glimpse a photo for a second and spot our target in a dark building. Conversely, Bobby has seen me take off in a dead sprint on a cross-boulevard chase into a massive housing project, only to discover, when he caught up, me gripping a man who outweighed our target by a hundred pounds and bore little resemblance to the photo. But Bobby continues to take me along. There are a few things I do bring to the table. I am fast. I do not escalate situations. So far I have not shown weakness, and our operations have gone smoothly. In fact, and this is shocking even given the amount of preparation Bobby puts in, I have never been on a hunt with Bobby in which he has not ultimately apprehended his man.

I close the folder on the Rodolfo head shot. In this case the photo is useless to me for a completely different reason: I know exactly what Rodolfo looks like. I see him in my sleep.

We do not know where Rodolfo sleeps, but Bobby has a tip on what may be a girlfriend's house where the fugitive spent one night this week. We knock on the door of the place in a tumbledown quarter close to my home. Being on my own turf should comfort me, but there is still the trouble of the door. While I'm working, the mystery of what is on the other side of any door unsettles me. My most nerve-racking memory from any fugitive operation came on the hunt for a criminally insane Angolan with the street name Magic when I found myself inside a blacked-out apartment staring at the impenetrable door to the street, waiting for Magic to step through. Every minute someone would pound on the door. The host would open it, and the outside sun would blind me as I tried to discern whether the silhouette in the door was Magic. The dark apartment filled with men, and I kept them there so they couldn't run out and tell Magic, and the door kept being banged, then opened to display another hulking silhouette in the rectangular blaze of the door frame. I stood amid the swelling crowd in the darkness, choking at each knock on the black door, waiting for the arrival of Magic, which I knew would crack the room open like a bolt of lightning.

For me, and I think many enforcers, it isn't the things that *happen* that take the biggest toll—those are reaction, a grip in high adrenaline and a violent spin to roll out of, then peace—but the things that *could* happen.

A woman answers. She invites us in, and Bobby talks with her while I search the apartment's back rooms. I find no one. Fortunately the woman is an *ex*-girlfriend with an ax to grind. She gives us a room number at a seedy hotel downtown. We thank her.

The advantage to hunting violent hardheads is that they burn up a lot of goodwill. Thugs who beat their girlfriends and rob their family and friends often leave a trail of victims who'd like to be rid of them. And when serious men in full gear show up not simply to arrest the badass but to remove him over water to a distant place, a spirit of helpfulness and cooperation prevails.

Well, at least I say I'll remove him to a distant place. I have failed before, and for reasons I'll explain later, the circumstances are particularly challenging in his case. Still, I would like the chance to give him special attention. One thing at a time with Rodolfo. First we need to get our hands on him.

We park in front of the YMCA at Lee Circle, almost back where we started. The hotel is familiar to us from other cases. "Should've stopped here in the first place," Bobby says with a smile. We head upstairs and knock on the door. I feel my heart pound through my vest the way it always does when I knock on doors.

The man I see when the door opens is not Rodolfo, but he is familiar. He is yet another criminal I have released. The city is crawling with them. He admits Rodolfo stopped by but says he is not here now. A quick scan of the tiny room confirms this. The man says the best place to find Rodolfo is outside where he waits for day labor opportunities on occasions when he needs to avoid police attention—i.e., make money through other than criminal enterprise. In standard reverse police talk we tell the man that if his tip pans out, we won't bother him anymore.

"I'm telling you the truth," the man insists. "I'm through helping Rodolfo. Fuck Rodolfo."

We get back into our vehicle, and Bobby quarters the area. We're scanning the sidewalks where temporary laborers wait for work. There are plenty out. We didn't start early today the way we do with those 4:00 A.M. B&Bs, when we know where our fugitive lives and we want to catch him sleeping. Today we started at a normal hour, so when I check the g-ride clock and then my watch to be sure, I can hardly believe it's not even nine in the morning. It seems like a full day since Craig called me into his office to discuss my Tangi visits. Bobby keeps driving in exploratory clover loops off the Lee Circle axis. As he drives, he tells a story.

"Dude, I lived with this one guy Dave when I first came out here. Dave was a great friend. We did everything together. Only thing was he didn't have a girlfriend. Since I had Sue, it made it hard. He was always the odd man out. Sue wanted to help him. Women especially, they want it to be a double date. You know how that is."

I'm supposed to be looking for Rodolfo, and I am, but I can't help flashing an occasional glimpse at Bobby while he spins the tale. Bobby isn't a big talker, so when he does start to roll a little, it's compelling. Bobby was a U.S. Marine, a helicopter crew chief back in the Vietnam era. Although I've never heard him say it, I've been told that when Saigon fell he was on the last USMC bird to leave and after that he flew counterinsurgent missions in the Philippines. In his final tour he flew on Marine One for President Jimmy Carter. Bobby has a lot of wisdom in him.

"Dave going out to the bars with me wasn't doing it. He was the nicest guy in the world, but Dave couldn't get a girl to save his life, it looked like. Finally Sue said enough was enough. She made big plans to set Dave up with her best friend. The night comes, and Sue's got it all taken care of. A big dinner, we're drinking, her friend says she thinks Dave's cute. Then those two go out on their date. Next day Sue's friend talks to her, and then Sue comes and yells at me, 'Dave's gay!' I'm thinking Sue's just mad, like anyone who doesn't like her best friend must be gay, you know. But no. Dave told her he was gay. Then Dave told me. He really liked dudes. Sue jumped all over me about how Dave was my best friend and I lived with the guy for two years and I didn't notice he was gay.

"So, yeah, I tried to set my gay friend up with a girl. You think *you're* weird, Ames. I'm weird too. We're all weird, so don't worry about it. You don't gotta live in your own world just 'cause you think you're weird."

Bobby rolls into Lee Circle again and puts the g-ride in park. That's the most disappointing Bobby story I've ever heard. I don't even understand it. I mean, I understand the part about trying to set a gay guy up with a woman, but I don't understand Bobby's relating it to me with the theme about my thinking I'm weird. I've never told anyone I thought I was weird because I don't think I'm weird, but I've just learned it's apparently the consensus among the Deportation crew.

Bobby's story classifying me as an outsider rebounds in my head. It makes me think about my hidden side.

"There's that motherfucker right there!" Bobby exclaims, throwing the car in drive. He stamps the pedal, dashing us off the curb.

Riding in the back of a pickup truck a block ahead, nothing between him and us but our windshield, is Rodolfo. Bobby turns on the blue light and rolls up behind the pickup. "Get ready to run if he jumps out," Bobby says.

I grip the door handle in my fingers. Bobby taps the siren. *Bwoop.*

The pickup driver doesn't pull over. He stops right there in the middle of the street. I'm out, running almost as fast as the cars driving around me.

Bobby's out too. "Rodolfo! Get the fuck down!" Bobby says. "You handle him, Ames." Bobby's going for the driver. The cab holds more danger than the open bed. It's unknown.

I spin Rodolfo and get both his hands behind his back before he can figure out what's going on. I click my handcuffs on his wrists and double-lock them.

"Federal agents!" Bobby shouts at the occupants of the cab. "Nobody move!"

I yank Rodolfo in front of our g-ride and lean him over the hood. I start twisting his clothes in the area around his hands. I'm searching for any weapon. My heart's pounding, but Bobby's already downshifted. I hear him interrogating the people in the cab. "How long's he been working for you?"

"A few weeks," the driver answers in panic. "He showed me his employment card. He said he was legal."

"That was legit," Bobby says. "I just need to know if you owe him money."

"No. Well . . . the next check."

Bobby gives the driver his card. "Make the check out to him like normal and bring it to me. I'm Bobby Smith. We're right there in the post office building, ninth floor." Bobby points toward our bleak structure, towering just off the terminus of this road.

"Yes, sir, I'll do that," replies the driver.

Bobby walks to the bed of the truck to see if Rodolfo unloaded anything there. Then he walks back to the window. He regards the driver and the two equally nervous passengers in the cab. "You were carrying a wanted man in your bed, but you wouldn't know that. So you're free to go pick up another guy and get to work." Bobby pats the metal roof with his mitt in a sendoff signal. The pickup pulls away.

I'm still searching Rodolfo when Bobby comes over. My search has spread from the area within immediate reach of his hands. I have both his shoes off in the street, and now I'm checking his collar around his neck.

Bobby yells, "So you like to knock people's eyes out, asshole?"

Rodolfo doesn't bother to protest. Satisfied that he isn't carrying a weapon or anything he could use to beat his handcuffs, I move Rodolfo to the back of the car. In a scene I've performed several times with Rodolfo, I slide him in behind the cage, protecting his head with my hand while I get him through the door frame.

"Well, this time you're not getting out to hurt nobody else," Bobby tells him.

I shut the car door. We're still parked in the middle of the downtown street, cars pouring around us.

Bobby heads to the driver side and smiles at me over the roof. "He's all yours now. You can write it up."

The main reason Bobby brings me on his fugitive operations, I've long suspected, is to have me do the paperwork. It's worth it. "No problem."

We get in up front, Bobby turns off the blue light, and we pull into regular city traffic.

I turn to regard Rodolfo in his traditional backseat berth.

The biggest problem with Rodolfo is that he's listed as Cuban, and Cuba is a country few up the chain want me to touch. It's safe to say that if I do get Rodolfo to Cuba, powerful U.S. government employees will come at me to examine everything I've ever done.

The second-biggest problem with Rodolfo is that he's *not* Cuban. I'll explain. Indeed, normally a felon's non-Cuban nationality is a positive for the DO looking to deport him. However, when the deportable felon who is not Cuban has lied in immigration court and convinced the IJ that he is

Cuban, and as a consequence, all the legal paperwork in his file identifies him as Cuban, you have serious problems. When it comes to your destination possibilities for the removal, you have one country, Cuba, that would be the natural and legal choice for repatriation, except that it refuses criminal repatriations. And you have 195 other countries, including the actual country of citizenship for your felon, that might consider taking him back, except that all his deportation papers identify him as Cuban, so why in the world are you asking them to accept a criminal your own government states in writing is not their problem?

Rodolfo has shielded himself in a deportation-proof persona. Cuba won't take anybody, and even if it did, I couldn't get it to take Rodolfo because he's "not Cuban." Every other country will cite his Cuban citizenship as grounds for refusing him. It's unassailable. If only it were original. Rodolfo's trick is popular among criminal aliens from all Spanish-speaking countries, and it highlights one of the worst by-products of illegal immigration. Once upon a time Rodolfo entered the United States illegally. Accordingly he had no documentation of his citizenship upon his initial arrest. Rodolfo claims Cuban citizenship, and because Cuba refuses the return of its criminals, Rodolfo is "nonremovable," despite overwhelming anecdotal evidence that he is not Cuban. If a reader is curious about whether I support or condemn President George W. Bush's encouragement of illegal influx across our borders, I state clearly for the record that I condemn it. If a reader wishes to know why I condemn it, let me start by pointing back to Rodolfo's trick. If aliens enter illegally, we don't know where they come from. When a sizable group of these illegal aliens reveal themselves to be dangerous predators, as history demonstrates is inevitable, we will be unable to expel them from the United States because we won't know where to send them. We will have to liberate them on our own streets. For a moment forget about all the challenges I've explained in this story about trying to get criminals back to their rightful homelands. *We can't even get to those challenges* if our felons enter illegally and won't say what country they're really from.

That day in the sedan with Bobby, riding with our prize in the back, I was formulating ideas to get around that. There had to be a way to ship

Rodolfo home even though he'd beaten us till now with the old trick. I was convinced Rodolfo was Mexican. Mexicans in the jails told me he was Mexican. His file contained an original arrest report from the southern border in which he'd informed a border patrolman he was Mexican. And Rodolfo's street name, the tag he wore in the criminal community, was simply El Mexicano.

Mexico wasn't just Rodolfo's homeland. It was also my best bet. I thought I could make it work. I had a very close high school friend down in Brownsville, Texas. He was a DEO in the nearest border town to New Orleans, and he drove busloads of deportees into Mexico all the time. It struck me as a workable plan to drive Rodolfo down there and throw him into one of those busloads. But there would be professional risk involved, and that is a lot to ask of even an old high school friend.

I'd continue to mull it over. In the meantime the important thing was Rodolfo was off the street. This time for good. I smiled in satisfaction that Rodolfo wouldn't be free to ruin the lives of innocent people in my country again.

It was a naive smile, for sure.

SIXTEEN

Hambrick Ramkishun and the Dirty Payback

"I'm asking who you work for, Mr. Holbrook," said the Nigerian consular officer.

"The United States government," I answered, trying to sound sincere. I knew what he wanted, and I really wished he'd lose track.

"Of course," said the consular officer impatiently. He spoke in that no-consonant-missed diction that underlined every word. "But the United States government is a big organization, and you know this. I want you to be more specific. Your letter to me says, 'Problem Government Sanctions Team,' which means my office is being classified as a problem government. But my question is who is classifying us as that?"

"The team itself is. The Problem Government Sanctions Team that I'm part of. Is that not specific enough, sir?"

"That's too specific to help." Anger overran his previously bureaucratic tone. "This whole situation offends me. I resent it."

"It's easy to fix, sir. I just need travel documents for those listed citizens of your country."

"I know what you say you need. But until you demonstrate to the satisfaction of the Nigerian government that these criminals are truly our citizens, the—"

"What about the Nigerian passports they came in on?"

"As I stated to you, Mr. Holbrook, we found those passports were issued to fictitious identities."

"By you, sir. The Nigerian government issued those passports. Even if you were wrong to issue them, the bearers were allowed into America because our inspectors honored documents your government issued."

"It's unfortunate, but we can't accept these criminals based on an honest mistake. It would be tantamount to reenacting the same mistake."

"No, sir. It would be taking responsibility for your mistake, rather than passing it on. In addition, these men may have concocted fake identities, but they really are Nigerians."

"That remains to be proved. Until it is, there will be no travel documents issued."

"Then sanctions will be imposed."

"What kind of sanctions?" he demanded.

"We'll start by refusing to honor Nigerian passports since it seems the Nigerian government takes no accountability for them."

"Do you work for Immigration or the State Department?" the consular officer asked shrewdly. "Because we've heard nothing like this from your State Department that has the actual power to issue visas to our citizens."

"State can issue the visas, sir. But Immigration can cancel them as soon as Nigerians get off the plane. We'll send everybody back. And then we'll move on to business restrictions and asset forfeiture."

"Under whose authority?"

"The authority vested in me by the United States government."

"Are you the president?" he said. "Are you President Bush?"

"No, sir."

"Then you have a boss! And I want to talk to this boss because I don't believe you!" he thundered. "I don't believe you exist."

His reaction surprised me. Quite a few foreign agents failed to buckle to my threats because they saw me as impotent, a ranting mid-level bureaucrat who'd been given authority on paper his government wouldn't let him exercise in a million years. But this Nigerian was calling me an impostor. I couldn't just hang up now. He had my name and my 701 Loyola address, and he sounded furious enough to get to the bottom of this whole thing if he had to.

"Of course I have a boss, sir. Right there in DC. I take my orders directly from the Deportation office on I Street." I scrolled my government cell for the headquarters number, which I fed the Nigerian consul. "You can ask them directly about the sanctions team."

"I will."

"And I expect to hear from you shortly thereafter. As long as we have these Nigerians in our custody, this won't go away."

"Then I'll talk to you soon, Officer Holbrook," he said.

"Great." I hung up.

Now a diplomat was out to nail me. He was another loose asteroid that was liable to bring me down. It depended on how much it meant to him. I wasn't going to help him get me, nor had I. Yesterday I'd called 701 Loyola for the number of a specific Deportation manager in Washington, and a clerk with either lazy or sadistic tendencies had given me headquarters' public number. That was the number I'd just shared. I welcomed the Nigerian into HQ's automated phone system horse latitudes that had driven me mad the day before. That number was a lemon, and even if he got another one out of his Rolodex and managed to talk to a real person, HQ in general was a wild-goose chase. I smiled helplessly as I pictured a maze of bureaucrats passing the buck. It was possible they'd give the Nigerian just enough hope with each transfer that he'd follow the dead trail forever.

I hoped the disorganization at HQ would sidetrack the angry diplomat, but he could always call the New Orleans directors. I knew the chances were high that I'd get caught. My hourglass was light on sand.

The door swung open in my Tangi office. Deputy Bid leaned in. "Was you wantin' to go in now?"

"Yeah, perfect. Are you ready?"

Deputy Bid jerked his head toward the dorms. "Let's go."

199

It was time to visit my detainees. I picked up my jail folder and headed into the tunnel.

Deputy Bid stopped at the first dorm. He talked to me outside the door: "This the one with a lot of them Guyanans. When you sendin' them away?"

"I'm working on it. I got four last week, right?"

"Oh, them outa south wing. Yeah, you did. Not as fast as a couple months ago, though. What's wrong with Guyana?"

On the other side of the glass, the aliens were gathering in anticipation of my entrance. Deputy Bid stood on my side with one shoulder against a metal column. He looked at me expectantly for an answer. "Guyana used to be nearly impossible," I said. "Back before you took over for Cox, Guyana was almost as bad as Vietnam and company. The government took back one percent."

"But that changed, didn't it?"

"It did, because some stellar operative on the State Department's Guyana desk did to Guyana what should have been done to all these countries: stop issuing visas. Guyana's ruling class suddenly couldn't get into America. That killed business, killed entertainment, generally hampered the lives of Guyana's rich, so they body-slammed their government and told them to kiss off their jobs. The government was so scared they called America and started issuing on everybody. We were sending criminal Guyanese back by the planeload."

"I remember that." Deputy Bid nodded. "So what happened?"

"Two months later the Guyana desk at the State Department said, 'Hey, it worked. I guess we can start issuing visas again.' So the—"

"Oh, shit. Same person?"

"No. I'm sure the first person got fired. *Protecting America? You know that's against State Department rules!* All of a sudden State just started issuing visas to the Guyanese again. And right on cue, Guyana repatriations stop all over."

Deputy Bid looked through the glass at the mob of awaiting aliens. "Oh, well," he said, turning back to me with a smile, "at least y'all give me job security."

"Me too," I said. "We can give thanks to the mighty government for *that*."

He radioed the control center to open our door, then asked me a final Guyana question: "How'd you get them four out of South Wing?"

"I made a friend in Guyana," I said.

"Well, you better tell your friend about them boys in here."

The door popped open, and we stepped into the dorm.

The roar of demands engulfed us. "Why are we still here?" was the potent chorus of the day. I sized up my crowd and tried to get a grip on an approach. Fewer than a third of the detainees in here were Guyanese, but their voices made up most of the din.

"All right. Hold it." I raised my orange liaison folder as I spoke. "Let me answer the questions you asked me last time, and then I'll hear you out." The mob quieted. I went through my book one answer at a time and articulated my responses to each concerned party. The satisfied detainees peeled away from the core mob and settled into a looser formation a few feet behind. After I gave my last response, I lowered my folder and took a look at the irritable remainder. I tried to spot the most ill tempered of all, and I pointed to him. "You first," I stated. "Let's hear it."

He paused for a moment and shifted his eyes in suspicion, as if he didn't trust the idea that he was being invited to speak. When he finally broke his silence, he had lost some of his cross edge. "Why we still in here past six months when all the Cubans and Chinese and them go straight out?"

"That's a good question," I said. "My first answer is that headquarters will get to you. They are getting to you. But you took them by surprise. A few months ago your country was taking all of you back. HQ expected you to go, so they didn't have the rubber release stamp out the way they do for the Cubans, Chinese, Vietnamese, and those guys. Now that Guyana's jammed up again, HQ's pulling your rubber stamp out of storage. They'll get to you. I just got a release letter for a Guyanese today." I looked around the crowd until I found a dreadlocked long-faced man of thirty. "Hudson, it was you. You're coming out Wednesday, next week. You want me to call your family, or will you?"

"I will, Officer Holbrook," said a smiling Hudson.

The news that one of them was on his way out had an instant calming effect on the crowd. Some even stepped out of the circle to the looser horseshoe behind.

"Understand, I am still getting some of you home. You can keep writing headquarters with release petitions. I'm writing your embassy just as fast with travel document requests."

"So you're in a race?" asked a fresh-faced car thief up front.

"Every day," I said.

"But with Guyana you lost the race?"

Much of the crowd burst into laughter at that line, which had been posed innocently by the fresh-faced car thief. I smiled but countered: "Last month I got enough TDs that New Orleans chartered its own airplane to fly just Guyanese to Georgetown."

"Really?" asked one.

"Really. And four more of you went home last week out of other dorms."

"Bullshit!" came an exclamation from the rear.

"Excuse me?" I watched the crowd part as I tried to peer through them. Their gap revealed obstreperous Hambrick Ramkishun. He stood with his jumpsuit open down to his waist and tied there with the arms. A grungy wifebeater tank top adorned his upper half. His uniform was out of regulation, a punishable infraction that Deputy Bid would've addressed if not for the current static.

"I'm saying bullshit you didn't send no four motherfuckers to Guyana out of other dorms. That's just a excuse. Y'all be makin' up stories now, keep us in here like rats."

I tried to radiate composure to take the charge out of Ramkishun's tone. I counted off four fingers deliberately as I replied: "Majabal, Coates, Davidson . . . Singh. They were all in Tangi last week. They're all in Guyana now."

"Not on the list: Hambrick Ramkishun," declared the rebellious Guyanese. "Never gonna be on the list: Hambrick Ramkishun."

"I wouldn't say never," I said, still calm on the outside. It would have been unacceptable for anybody to see this miscreant fluster me.

Ramkishun unraveled. He started pacing back and forth, letting his heavy arms fly around him as he beat up the energy. "Never!" he shouted. "Motherfuck, never! *I'm* sayin' it." The Guyanese wasn't making eye contact with anybody, probably didn't see anybody in his rolling rage. The dorm was teed up, on its toes. Everybody could feel the crackle.

"Well, until headquarters writes your release letter, I've got a chance." Some of my emotion came out in my speech. Ramkishun was squeezing it out of me.

"No chance!" he yelled. "No fuckin' chance!"

The crowd left a tunnel between Ramkishun and me, and my vision rushed down it. My sight picture crashed into the Guyanese thug. His hands tugged at his wifebeater. He was one step short of pounding his chest. I drew my emotions back. Hambrick had almost pulled my tripwire, but I focused. I recalled a Phil line, and I delivered it to the rest of the crowd much more calmly than my partner ever had: "This guy has all the answers, so just ask him."

I started to withdraw with Deputy Bid. The aliens protested. They still had questions. Some cursed at Ramkishun while others pleaded me to stay. I shook my head. "I'll see you next time."

Over the crowd's clamor Ramkishun continued his tirade. "Next time you see me, you'll be letting me out. Shit! I'll be living in New Orleans. Do I sound like I'm 'posed to be in motherfuckin' South America? I been here too long, and I ain't goin' nowhere!"

I stopped and took a step toward Ramkishun, then controlled myself again and resumed course to the door. "Obviously I've got work to do."

Ramkishun fired back, intent on humiliating me to the last: "Do it! Give it . . . your best . . . shot! Assho—"

The door closed behind Deputy Bid and me. I took a last look through the glass at the agitated dorm. Several detainees rushed Ramkishun to yell at him. Their DO didn't visit them every day. There were a lot of questions that would have to wait until the next jail liaison, whenever that came. Such was the benefit of Phil's line: When you blame your departure on a particular alien, the other aliens turn the heat on him for chasing you out.

I was still hot. I told Deputy Bid I was heading up front. I knew he had to get back into the dorm to settle things down, call out Ramkishun for his uniform, and more. I'd do the rest of the dorms later. Bid let me go. I left him talking on the radio. Up front I was buzzed into the admin area, and I walked straight into my office and closed the door.

I tore Ramkishun out of the file cabinet. His red folder swelled with jail disciplinary reports on top of his conviction roster for numerous assaults outside. I had two phone numbers written on my personal sheet for this case. One was for the Guyana Embassy. That number had outlived its usefulness. After Guyana's quick second freeze, all the headway I'd made had come through the other number. A Guyanese I'd sent home under special terms had given it to me. It belonged to the government office in Georgetown that made the decision on travel document issuance. Just as with Antigua, the issue authority lay in the homeland.

I picked up the jail phone and dialed all the data from my government phone card. I didn't even carry that card anymore; the twenty-six relevant digits had long ago burned into my mind. I punched in the number from my sheet, beginning with Guyana's 592 country code. It rang.

"Yes. Hello?" The voice was wrong. My guy never answered formally either, but this wasn't he. I looked at my watch. It was later than I normally called.

"Hello." I was tempted to hang up. I didn't want to blow the deal with my associate. But I was still angry over that insolence in the dorm, and I wasn't in the mood to slow down. "Is this where they cut travel documents for people getting kicked out of America?"

"For citizens of Guyana, yes." His words came coolly, all business. "Who is this?"

"Hambrick Ramkishun."

"What do you want?"

"To get the fuck out of this jail."

"I don't know if I can help you."

"You can help me." I contradicted in true Hambrick style. "My brother went to your building and said you got all my shit. Just waitin' for you. I'm sittin' here in New Orleans, and I know how to get back, but I gotta let these stupid motherfuckers deport me first."

"You want to be deported?"

"You heard me. We help each other."

"Wait."

The phone went silent, and I dragged my sweating hand on the cool surface of the desk. I didn't know if this guy was getting his boss or if I'd been hung up on or what. I had no idea what to expect.

Eventually the phone engaged again. The same voice came on. "How do we help each other?"

"Send my Deportation Officer my motherfuckin' passport so he can deport me, then I can turn around and come back."

"That's how I help you. What do you have?"

"Ten thousand. I robbed a bank. I could give you one or two. Write my name, Ramkishun: R-A-M—"

"I have it. I have your package from Holbrook."

"DO Holbrook! He's the punk asshole you send my passport to. In New Orleans."

"I have that." The man paused. He took an audible breath and allowed a dramatic interval of contemplation before he finished. "You know, if you arrive here with no money, it will be bad."

"Listen to this motherfucker talk about my money. Yes, it'll be bad. If I lose ten Gs, that's bad."

"It will be more bad for you than just the money."

"I'm not losing the money, so don't worry about me. Just move."

"I'll see you," said the man.

"Late." I hung up the phone.

The room was quiet, except for a dull noise that seemed to come from the painted cinder block walls. The noise wasn't coming through the walls. It was coming from them, as if the walls of my Tangi office were humming.

I shook it off. I had much to do still. I was ready to take another run at the dorms. I radioed Deputy Bid. He came up, and we started over. Jail liaison was smooth this time. Before I knew it, I was done. I emerged from the detention complex, got in the g-ride, barreled down 55 to my exit, and got out.

Behind me was Tangi. In front of me was 848 Ida. I found it problematic to walk out of the prison gate and directly into my apartment door. Instead I stopped on my way home to recalibrate and air myself out before I faced my wife.

I struck a box match and held it at the end of my cigar. I drew in several times, seeing the flame flare, and then I dropped the match on the metal sedan roof. I watched the smoke of the burned match twist and climb in a wisp into my gray environment.

The night had yet to crystallize. It wasn't that late. But I knew it would be all black before I finished my cigar. I let the cigar fall to my waist, still gripped in my fingers, and I took a deep breath. My cigar air was no more beclouded than the native atmosphere of burning diesel, swamp miasma, and gasoline. Either inhalation caused a reaction in my brain. I took a few steps in the earthen lot and regarded the universe from the forlorn bayou gas station where I'd been stopping ritualistically for months.

Work had become different. There were positives and negatives. Hortense was gone. Craig had been promoted to her spot, the head of Deportation for five states (called the field office director, or FOD, subsequent to the Homeland Security fold-in). In anticipation of Craig's replacement, I'd braced for a shake-up with great dread. It was too easy to predict a micromanager hitting the ground as my immediate boss and auditing my conspicuous docket to see what I was doing. But Craig's replacement had come, and so far there had been no shake-up. I'd forgotten how difficult it would be for the supervisor just to get a handle on his own job, especially since in Craig he had a superior who could not be bluffed. As my new boss found his way in the New Orleans office, I was now freer than ever to make my own agenda. I withdrew further into my fixer role. Night and day at Tangipahoa, I cheated, lied, threatened, and now impersonated to get felons out of America.

I thought of those as the positives. The biggest negative was just how many chances there were to hang myself with all the rope I had. The close calls were closer. This morning there had been that Nigeria clash. Last week it had been Djibouti. Not enough time had even gone by for me to classify those properly as close calls. They were looming direct hits. I was stacking diplomats who didn't like me and who threatened to dig. And that was if HQ or my own managers didn't figure me out first.

The cigar burned through the cigar band. It was too short to hold, and I tossed it away. I sniffed my shirt. The jail smell my wife detested was out, replaced by the scent of swamp, octane, and tobacco. I got in the sedan and played the radio all the way home.

The Hambrick Ramkishun TD was soon on my 701 Loyola desk. I stared at the criminal's photo while I contemplated his case. I understood the document was probably the result of my phone call, and if it was, the receiving official expected a payoff from Ramkishun on sight. I suspected there would be traumatic consequences for Ramkishun if he arrived in Guyana without that payoff.

I was equally convinced harm would come to innocent victims on this side of the water if I waited for my government to order the violent felon set free here.

Well, he had told me to give it my best shot.

I pressed Hambrick Ramkishun's photo on the copy machine glass and held it in place while the bright light painted it. I punched the copy into the A-file and put the actual document in the travel envelope before I walked it down the hall to Departure Verification. He was deported in short order.

Seventeen

HQ and the Double Damnation

My belt buzzed with a text from Bobby, and I read it as I cruised into downtown. It was Bobby's invitation to a B&B. He wanted us to take down a PRC fugitive in a kitchen. I called Bobby. I so wanted to go. Despite the immigration rep, I'd never arrested anyone in a kitchen. There was good reason for that: too many knives. Bobby expressed his misgivings about the blade aspect, but there was no telling when there'd be another chance. The Chinese guy never seemed to leave the kitchen. Bobby figured the guy slept on the kitchen shelves.

The arrest promised to be interesting. Those are the calls you live for as a DO.

I thanked Bobby sincerely. I told him I was driving a vanful of prisoners and I'd have to do something with them, but I wondered if he'd wait for me. He told me no. Not enough time. He'd get somebody else or just make the arrest himself.

I collapsed the phone in disgust. I shot a glance at the cargo behind me. The eight aggravated felons stared back unperturbed. It's bad enough to miss a street operation on any ground. When that ground is that you're too busy liberating dangerous offenders at the time, it's enough to make you consider accelerating off the road, directly against a red-brick warehouse. To those readers who imagined that the lengths to which I struggled to acquire TDs for criminal aliens had canceled out the releases, I apologize for not having been clear. The liberation process was alive and well. There'd never been a break. With the latest eight shackled in my van, I gripped the wheel and focused away from the red-brick warehouse wall. These guys were getting out, and that was that.

When you are actively engaged in releasing violent predators, it's impossible not to contemplate the law enforcement blood on your hands. The civilian victims, past and future, already haunt you. What about your fellow agent who's going out alone to arrest a dangerous and desperate fugitive in a kitchen full of long knives because you weren't available to go with him, because you were too busy setting deportable aliens free?

I knocked on the dashboard, the closest thing I had to a wood surface. Bobby would be fine. Bobby was a journeyman DO who'd taught me how to handle the field situations and when to walk away if the air didn't feel right. Even if Bobby didn't manage to find another partner, I assured myself he had the odds on his side.

If only the odds were on the agent's side all the time. You know every day around the country Deportation Officers are occupied releasing criminal aliens, meaning their fellow agents are going into battle without the manpower they should have, and as a direct result, some of those officers will be harmed or killed. This is a fact. The more agents and field experience that law enforcers assemble for an operation, the better the odds for success and survival. And here you are, an extensively trained federal agent with a loaded automatic pistol, high-capacity magazines, a collapsible baton, pepper spray, and handcuffs on your belt, ultimately reduced to taking your several years of field experience and applying it to your government's great criminal alien liberation campaign instead of standing alongside your fellow agent, who asked you for your help.

Unfortunately that is not the only law enforcement blood that weighs on you. Many of the predators you release will make new victims out of innocent people, just as Rodolfo did. When that happens, your brothers and sisters in law enforcement, be they local and state police or federal agents, will try to sack them up again, in the same way Bobby and I went after Rodolfo. Bobby and I were not harmed in the Rodolfo apprehension, but by fate and circumstance other officers will be harmed or killed by other aliens you release. It's the nature of the beast. You are not releasing balloons.

This is the variety of law enforcement blood you see on your hands when you are freeing the aliens who shouldn't be freed: immediately the blood of that officer in the field who needs you by his side and subsequently the blood of the next officer who tries to arrest one of these hardheads again.

I pulled up to the painted LAW ENFORCEMENT curb in front of the office high-rise and got out. I rolled open the van door and set a stool on the sidewalk and watched the chained felons step down. I guided them around the metal detectors inside. Displaying my badge to the bystanders in the lobby, I boarded an elevator car with my criminal freight and took them up to the ninth floor.

I walked through the routine yet another time: the orders of supervision, the parole cards, the fingerprints, the photos, the computer input, the phone calls, the checks, the employment cards, the speech, and finally the descent to the street.

Another DANGEROUS ALIENS ON THE LOOSE headline. They spread like grenade shrapnel, going every way.

I returned to the ninth floor and picked up their A-files. Walking up the central hallway, I crossed paths with Bobby, who was coming in with the Chinese gangster. Bobby smiled at me. He had gotten his man yet again. That made me happy, but my return smile crumbled before I even passed him. It was a depressing encounter, seeing Bobby holding his catch while I was carrying the files of the criminals I had released. How could it be that we wore the same badge?

Seeing Bobby now sent my mind back to when I'd first joined. I knew I'd done a lot more back then, but when I thought of my first days on the job, all I remembered were the B&Bs. That was when we'd pass around the file and photo of our latest most wanted, gear up, and hit the streets in pursuit. Bag and baggage: Sack up the alien, and let him pack a suitcase for the flight home.

When I looked back on those early days, it felt like remembering my youth. Sunshine, celebrations, and the magic taste of beer. Going into the fire and coming out. Seeing tough guys laugh good, real laughs and laughing along with them.

I remembered the street operations with Pablo Campos and with Bobby and Phil and Tyrone and Choppy and Tammy and the rest. I remembered the camaraderie with the team and the knowledge that everything we were doing was right.

I saw the light from that world shine from Bobby as we passed in the hall. It seemed Bobby had never left that, though I certainly had.

I took my place at my end-of-the-line desk with the A-files. I performed final file input and transfers. Just before I got up, I was struck with the urge to validate my own place. I inspected my database to see how many predatory aliens I'd rerouted out of my country from the brink of release here as a direct dividend of my unapproved methods. I sought a count of all the broken cases I'd managed to fix. It was an estimate out of necessity. There was no stating with certainty which cases I might have won by conventional efforts, but in the end I knew the estimate was close. It was fewer than I'd hoped for. At that point I couldn't resist counting the cases I'd lost. This count was more scientific since every release was a loss. I stopped calculating when I saw my releases outnumbered my saves. For all my lying and cheating, all the threats and deception and living in the intolerable gray, for all my struggle and self-delusion, the bottom line was absolute: I had poured more felons into America than I'd gotten out.

I viewed my personal disintegration against my dismal win-loss record and fell into depression. There had been too many days I'd questioned myself and my character. I'd known I was a lot of things, but not until now a failure. It turned out that as a sworn protector of the people I was doing more harm than good.

"Hey, Ames."

I looked up. The mail handler stood at the edge of my cubicle. I took the offered envelope and watched the mail handler move on. The envelope bore the I Street address of headquarters in DC. I reached into the envelope slice and pulled out the latest sheaf of liberations. I flipped through them. I hadn't imagined it before, but somehow, just at that moment when I was flipping through the pages, I knew I would find it. In the middle of the stack, there was the clean new release letter for Rodolfo.

At once I blamed myself for not having worked harder to get the misfit into his native Mexico. I had, after much deliberation, decided not to involve my high school friend, the fellow agent down on the border I'd considered might drive Rodolfo across. I didn't regret that decision, but I very much regretted not having come up with another solution by now. I had always thought I'd have more time.

The document shredder was ten feet from my desk. I worked my thumb and forefinger around Rodolfo's page and separated it from the others. Making Rodolfo's letter disappear would buy me time, I thought. So far that was a line I had not crossed. Breaking all the rules to win the race with HQ was one thing. But once I lost the race, that was it, right? It wasn't fair to pretend I hadn't lost. Or was it just one more rule to rewrite? Why stop anywhere?

It seemed like forever I'd been asking myself those kinds of questions.

Today I'd learned that for all the cost, I still wasn't succeeding. I couldn't win the race against my own government.

Forever was over.

EIGHTEEN

Craig and the Unavoidable End

"You've really come up fast in four years . . . or not even four years, is it?" Craig spoke to me across the grand expanse of his desk. I liked seeing him in his postpromotion corner office. The natural light filled in through the glass panes running the entire street side. The long wall opposite the windows was decked with flags from various countries his team had visited on deportations. I noted some of my gift banners in the resplendent field.

"No, sir."

"You've accomplished a lot on this job, Ames." He looked away, part pained and part formulating what to say next. "You're just getting started, though. There is so much to this job . . . opportunities and challenges. There's too much you haven't done."

"I know, boss."

"You should talk to Bobby about some of the assignments he's had. When we did the Olympics, Bobby trained in different weapons and evasive driving to be CAPO—consenting alien protection officer. He protected a defecting track star. Has he told you about Guantánamo?"

"He has. Amazing."

"You'll get your chance to see it. I don't know if I can adequately explain the degree and number of experiences that lie ahead of you. You like the street operations, but you've never *led* one. I'd like to see you put your leadership skills to work on a major operation, where you're not just putting your hands on the criminals, but taking charge of the agents and leading them in. Did you know headquarters is in the final stages of assembling fugitive teams?"

"I heard something about it. For problem cities? Teams of three DOs?"

"New Orleans is getting two of those teams."

"That's cool," I replied. Craig was preaching to the choir.

As a kid I'd watched police shows and dreamed of becoming a federal agent. There was, however, no dreaming a law enforcement position like the one I had now. We went after hardheads in the streets, just like the cops on TV, but that was only the beginning. Deportation Officers also wrote legal briefs to stand up in federal court, we kept a lid on these aliens in the jails we visited regularly, we met with high-level diplomats to negotiate repatriation deals, and we wrapped it all up with the escorts. Travel in itself was enriching, but there was no describing the extra dimension a journey took on when you were sitting next to a man who wanted to kill you and who was looking for a chance to escape every hair-raising inch of the way. The deportation business was a thrill. We didn't have a sexy TV series or blockbuster movie yet, but I figured that was only because we were such a well-kept secret.

The DO job hadn't lost its benefits. In my case it would have been fair to say the opposite was true. Because of the increase in TDs coming in, I was traveling more than ever and getting paid well for it. With all the overtime, my two-week paychecks were hitting four thousand dollars, a fortune in New Orleans. And wasn't I living my dream? I still woke up in the morning excited to go to work.

"Give me a chance to change your mind, Ames." Craig fixed me directly with his incisive eyes as he spoke. "This doesn't make any sense."

I smiled sadly. I thought about the early days when Craig had taken us running. It had begun with everybody he could grab, but over the months people had dropped out, and then it had just been me and Craig. He'd picked wild routes: sprints through garages, in the front end of a warehouse and out the back, under the ferry terminal, through fountain mist, along the Mississippi. It had been so much fun. Back then I'd thought he and I would run forever. Then one day he'd told me he couldn't do it anymore. Too many old injuries had overwhelmed him. He'd broken down. It shouldn't have depressed me as much as it did. Craig had a dozen years on me, and many of those had been in the Border Patrol in the wide-open 1980s, jumping off desert cliffs, rolling with the infamous bandit teams, the drop house raids, and shootouts at five yards. But his pulling out of the runs had served to remind me that everyone I worked with was getting nicked up. A twisted ankle here, a back strain there and that was the minimum—if they were lucky enough to elude the Big Stomp. Lucky like me. I still felt like a newborn in my muscles and joints. My body was resilient. My body told me to stay.

All my nicks seemed to come in my brain. It was there that I felt like a battered, wasted man who'd skipped his prime entirely. It seemed as if I'd shambled from youth straight into old age with a headful of bitter wisdom. And the human breakdown in turn reminded me of the system we worked in, the system that was breaking down along with us and our country.

"I appreciate it, Craig."

"All right, we'll talk more later. Get to work."

"Yes, sir." I walked out of his office and closed the door. He had just refused my resignation.

I greatly admired my boss, and I was influenced by his request that I stay. In the end, though, there were too many reasons I could not. For one thing, I was more of a risk than an asset to the field. I found my head being chased by the label that for years I'd been sure I'd outgrown, "troublemaker." Now I wondered if troublemaker were a genetic hitch I could not hope to escape but by death. I remembered Hortense and Tammy, and the doubts those two had had about my fitness for the job. I was forced to consider that maybe they'd been right.

Later Craig told me to put my resignation request in writing if I was serious. He said he wouldn't entertain it otherwise. Maybe he believed I was one of those employees who talked about quitting but never did. I composed the request. I was very careful to specify that I was not dissatisfied with my job. I cited my desire to pursue another project, lest management blame Craig for having failed to retain me. I'd been through that in the army: "Lieutenant Holbrook, three of your best soldiers didn't reenlist. That's a clear reflection of your bad influence."

Craig gave back my resignation letter with a penned rejection underneath: "Officer Holbrook, after much careful consideration, I have decided to reject your effort to separate from this Service. Your contributions to this unit are much too valuable to dismiss. And your quality of work cannot easily be replaced. You may review your request to resign in October 2006. Thank you, C. S. Robinson."

October 2006 was Craig's scheduled retirement. I smiled, but I was sad too. I was sad that the DO Holbrook my principled boss saw was not the DO Holbrook I knew. I was sad that my government had beaten me. I was sad that I did not have the fortitude to fight on alongside all my brothers who did.

The next time I saw Craig he didn't try to change my mind. By then we both knew it was the end of the road.

On my last day as a Deportation Officer I turned in all my issued equipment. A special agent down the hall took my H&K automatic pistol, which I'd reset in its original carrying case, along with the accessories: six high-capacity magazines, cleaning kit, shooting log. Everything else went to my supervisor, who went down my issue card one item at a time and initialed each as I laid it on his desk. I'd barely gotten to know him. He seemed like a nice guy. He let me keep my official passport with its exotic stamps and visas, since it wasn't on my checklist, and he said I might get another job that required it. Everything else he accepted and checked off: airport access badge, assorted keys to cells and doors, calling card, Master-Card, cell phone, pager, credentials, and badge.

Free with two hours left in the workday, I made for the central corridor and hit the fire exit stairs. I hiked to the top of my building and walked out onto the roof a final time. New Orleans was below, all around me. I'd always felt like the city's protector when I'd taken this vantage. I knew I'd miss the DO life. I knew I'd never again be what I was right now. I knew I'd never be as good or as bad, or as courageous or as scared, or as rewarded or as punished by a job.

I turned to the stairwell door and walked toward it. This perch was not mine anymore. Even before I began my descent, I knew that all the future days I found this building in my view, I would look from the ground up to this point and remember what my world was like when I held this ground. Oh, the DO. I believed it would be the greatest job if only those in power would let it be done right.

My old friends from the unit never left my life. More than a year later I enjoyed an occasional visit with John Seright in the bars, or Tyrone in his Treme home, or Phil in a Greek restaurant. It had taken me that long to stop thinking of myself as a Deportation Officer, to be able finally to say "your job" instead of "our job." The shared times were always good, and the friendships just as real. My wife was happy, and my life was enjoyable, and I did not second-guess my decision to leave. Nonetheless, a great sense of loss weighed on me when I saw my former fellow agents. If you accept the common analogy of law enforcement officers to wartime soldiers, as I do, then you see that these federal agents are in a war every day. I was the soldier who rotates home from war, leaving his unit in the combat zone, and I kept with me the parallel sorrow and guilt.

I attended a party with my onetime partner Phil. The occasion this time was that Phil's wife was soon to give birth to their first child. The family of Phil's wife was hosting the fete in their gorgeous suburban home.

Phil and I hung out in the kitchen, drinking and talking. There were others around us, law enforcement included, some completely new to me. A multilingual Spanish woman, the wife of one of Phil's friends, arrived at the party and brought a bottle of wine to the kitchen. Phil chatted with her for a while and then waved me closer to meet her.

"Ames," Phil said, *"te quiero presentar a la Señora Consuela."*

I shook her hand. "Nice to meet you."

"Look, he's even lost his Spanish," commented Phil. For the benefit of the woman and anyone else in the room who didn't know, Phil stated: "Ames used to be one of us. Now he's just some dude."

I couldn't have put it better myself.

I raised my glass in salute to those officers who stay in the fight despite the odds—officers made of better stuff than I.

WORD ON ACCURACY

During my service as a Deportation Officer with the New Orleans office from August 1998 through April 2002, I never once considered writing a nonfiction account of my experiences. At the time I saw myself as a law enforcement officer, certainly not as a journalist. I took no notes. Because I began writing this book several years after the fact, I was compelled to re-create my story from memory. I'd consider it nothing short of a miracle if I've managed to capture every quote in its original form, and the same goes for the time line. I apologize to the readers for any details I've gotten wrong, and I apologize to the good officers I served alongside if I left them out of any scenes they were a part of. It would mean only that I wasn't immune to the notorious tunnel vision condition of the DO job.

However—and in this regard I'm convinced my former fellow agents will back me up—I have taken great care to ensure that even if the sequence and dialogue are not exact, they do not misrepresent. Not a single aspect of either my experience or the DO existence has been altered for effect. The events described herein are genuine. There are no composite or "based on" characters on these pages. All persons mentioned are real. At the insistence of the publisher's legal counsel, I have changed names and in some cases even physical descriptions, but I have maintained the real names of most of the agents I served alongside in New Orleans, with their book-unread, pure faith blessing.

I include this statement, though I anticipate no suspicion about the truth of the details of my story. As any veteran U.S. Deportation Officer can attest, my account is not sensational. Despite the prevalent tension and drama, there is nothing in this book that requires suspension of disbelief— that is, if you can stomach the premise: The United States government takes documented alien predators with binding deportation orders and, rather than return them to their homelands, as is the law, sets them loose in American communities every business day.

Rapists, murderers, extortionists, kidnappers, armed robbers, arsonists, carjackers, identity thieves, bombers, child molesters: I have unleashed them all.

For that may I be judged with no more mercy than is due.

Glossary

.40-Cal—.40-caliber duty pistol carried by immigration officers, a compact Heckler & Koch for plainclothes officers and a full-size Beretta for uniformed agents.

A-File—Alien file. Folder containing the record, including all immigration proceedings and pertinent criminal information, of any alien registered in the United States.

Agg Felon—Aggravated felon. Person convicted of a felony of a particularly serious nature. Aliens who are aggravated felons are subject to special exclusion and removal laws.

A-Number—Alien number. The alien registration number assigned by Homeland Security to every registered alien—immigrant, resident, or apprehended illegal—in the United States. As of 2007, beginning with the letter *A* and followed by eight numbers (A12 345 678).

B&B—Bag and baggage. 1. Arrest of a fugitive alien who already has a final order of removal and is legally ready for deportation. "Bag" signifies the arrest, while "baggage" represents the suitcase the alien is allowed to bring to his homeland. 2. Any alien targeted for such an arrest or any alien so arrested.

BIA—Board of Immigration Appeals. Appellate division within the EOIR, the BIA renders final judgments on immigration cases in which aliens or the service appealed the initial decisions.

CCC—See OPP.

DACS—Deportable Alien Control System. National computer system used by authorized immigration employees to manage aliens through the entire deportation process.

DD—District director. Prior to the DHS fold-in, the top official at the immigration district level.

DEO—Detention enforcement officer. Junior-grade, usually uniformed officers, charged with basic transportation, security, and custody functions pertaining to aliens. In 2004 DEOs were slotted for additional training and position upgrades and have since been known as immigration enforcement agents (IEAs).

Detained Docket—Collectively, the cases of all deportable aliens who are kept in jail, as opposed to those who are at large (on the nondetained docket). Because aggravated felons are detained for a period by law, while administrative cases are not, the detained docket is generally the first home to more dangerous aliens.

DHS—Department of Homeland Security. Cabinet-level department formed from preexistent U.S. agencies in 2003 for the purpose of obviating domestic terror attacks. All Immigration employees were incorporated into this department.

DO—Deportation Officer. Read book for eighty-five-thousand-word definition.

DOJ—Department of Justice. Cabinet-level department that housed Immigration employees until their move to the Department of Homeland Security in 2003.

EAD—Employment Authorization Document. Photo ID card entitling aliens without LAPR status to work legally in the United States.

EOIR—Executive Office for Immigration Review. The branch of the Department of Justice in which the immigration judges interpret and administer federal immigration laws through court and appellate proceedings.

Escort—1. To accompany an alien on his deportation. 2. The trip on which the alien is accompanied. 3. Any alien (usually violent or mentally ill) who requires an officer's presence during his deportation.

EWI—Usually pronounced "ee-wee." 1. Entry without inspection. The process of sneaking across the border into the United States, as opposed to being legally admitted by an Immigration inspector. 2. Any alien who has entered the country this way; an illegal alien.

Exams—Examinations. The immigration section charged with administering alien benefits, including naturalization. While primarily an administrative section, Examinations also oversaw the inspections program comprised of seaport and airport inspectors prior to the implementation of DHS.

Final Order—1. The immigration judge's final order of removal, legally prescribing the deportation of an alien from the United States. 2. Any alien issued such an order.

FLETC—Pronounced "fletsy." Federal Law Enforcement Training Center, Glynco, Georgia, home of the Immigration Officer Academy and the majority of other U.S. agencies' basic police training.

FOD—Field office director. (Created after DHS fold-in.) Ranking manager for deportation in any district.

Gitmo—Guantánamo Bay, forty-five-square-mile U.S. naval station on the southeastern tip of Cuba, fenced off from the rest of the country. Guantánamo has been heavily utilized by the United States for holding and processing aliens, including more than fifty thousand Haitian and Cuban migrants in the 1990s and hundreds of terrorist suspects detained following attacks against America in 2001.

G-Ride—(refer to context) 1. Government-issued vehicle, frequently an officer's take-home car. 2. A stolen car (grand theft auto).

H&K—Short for the Heckler & Koch .40-caliber compact pistol issued to plainclothes immigration officers, including DOs.

HOD—See OPP.

ICE—Immigration and Customs Enforcement. An interior Customs and Immigration hybrid implemented as part of the Department of Homeland Security in March 2003 and the agency into which Deportation Officers and Investigations special agents were incorporated. Originally the agency was abbreviated BICE, but planners adopted the subtle subtraction in response to pressure from FBI leaders who did not want the new, formidable agency referred to as the bureau.

IDENT—The Automated Biometric Fingerprint Identification system, containing an "inkless" fingerprint pad and camera, along with a networked database of fingerprints, photographs, lookouts, and offense histories of criminal aliens, used primarily by arresting field agents.

IEA—Immigration enforcement agent. See DEO. In the New Orleans office, IEAs are used primarily for transportation, while local jails are contracted to provide and staff detention space.

IJ—Immigration judge. The justice who hears the immigration cases of aliens charged with deportable offenses. He is the only sitting judge with the authority to order removal (deportation) from the United States, and his decision is administratively final unless it is appealed to the Board of Immigration Appeals.

Investigations—Immigration enforcement program containing the criminal investigators that operates parallel to Deportation. Although there is some overlap in street work, investigators primarily begin cases, whereas Deportation Officers apprehend fugitives, manage existing cases, and effect the removal of criminal aliens from the country.

LAPR—Pronounced "lapper." Lawfully admitted permanent resident. Citizen of another country who has been given legal permission to reside and work in the United States indefinitely; holder of a green card.

LEO—Usually pronounced "leo." Law enforcement officer.

Louis Armstrong—New Orleans's international airport, named after the native jazz great.

Nondetained Docket—Collectively, the cases of all deportable aliens who are at large, as opposed to those who are kept in jail (on the detained docket).

OIG—Office of the Inspector General. Internal investigative unit charged with prosecuting misconduct by government employees.

OPP—Orleans Parish Prison, one of the United States' largest prison complexes, administered by the criminal sheriff of New Orleans. Prior to evacuations resulting from Hurricane Katrina in 2005, contracted space for federal inmates in three primary facilities: Community Correctional Center (CCC) for low- and medium-risk detainees, Templeman III (TP-3) for high risk, and House of Detention (HOD) for maximum-risk and severe disciplinary cases.

OS—Also OSup, order of supervision. Immigration version of probation. 1. An Immigration contract, signed by the alien, spelling out the service-imposed conditions of his release from custody, including a schedule for reporting to the nearest Immigration office. Often used for criminal aliens who are liberated, pending deportation, until their countries agree to take them back. 2. An alien released under such conditions.

Overstay—An alien who was legally admitted into the United States for a set of time, as for vacation or business, but remained in the country beyond that time.

POCR—Post-order custody review, a headquarters-mandated review, applied only to detained aliens with final orders, and normally incorporating an interview at the local level, the purpose of which is to determine whether continued detention of the alien is warranted. Formerly called FOCR, final order custody review.

Rabbit—A runner. One who is likely to flee from custody at any opportunity.

SDEO—Supervisory detention enforcement officer.

SDO—Supervisory Deportation Officer.

Service—The Immigration and Naturalization Service; INS (b. 1891–d. 2003). Also called Immigration.

Shank—1. A sharp or pointed implement for stabbing, a makeshift knife. 2. To stab someone with such an implement. Prison slang.

Snakehead—A smuggler of aliens, especially on intercontinental routes.

'Stans—In Central Asia, the five former Soviet republics of Turkmenistan, Kazakhstan, Kyrgyzstan, Tajikistan, and Uzbekistan.

TD—Travel document. Passport or other document issued by a country's government allowing travel into that country.

TP-3—See OPP.

WD—Warrant of Deportation. Also called Warrant of Removal or 205 (for the government form number I-205). Official document prescribing an alien's expulsion from the United States and specifying the provision of law under which the alien is ordered removed or excluded. Typically issued by the ranking district official (or representative) and executed by street-level agents.

Zadvydas v. Underdown—Lawsuit brought against New Orleans district director by a criminal alien fighting his detention pending his deportation. Ultimately consolidated with another case and submitted to the U.S. Supreme Court (which remanded it with language favorable to criminal aliens in 2001), the *Zadvydas* case resulted in the release of thousands of criminal aliens in America. There is no anticipated end to the *Zadvydas* release policy, which now limits the time Deportation Officers have to deport aliens. Predatory aliens convicted of the most severe crimes continue to be liberated in American communities at the time of this book's publication.

INDEX

14